HUMAN VALUES AND ABNORMAL BEHAVIOR

Readings in Abnormal Psychology

HUMAN VALUES AND ABNORMAL BEHAVIOR

Walter D. Nunokawa, Portland State College

Scott, Foresman and Company

Chicago, Atlanta, Dallas, Palo Alto, Fair Lawn, N. J.

ACKNOWLEDGMENTS

Only through the kind permission of the authors and their publishers has this book been possible. A special note of thanks is due Mr. John Havey of Scott, Foresman and Company for his many constructive criticisms and helpful suggestions. The critical comments of my colleagues, Drs. Max Reed and Morris Weitman, are also appreciated. My greatest debt is to the many scholars who have been actively involved in the examination of value problems in psychology. Because of their concern, this vital area is beginning to receive the reconsideration it deserves.

CONTENTS

Pressed to present the available information and current problems in abnormal psychology, the teacher often lacks the time, perhaps even the predilection, to take excursions into the broader philosophical issues that underlie the discipline. Specialty training is inclined to ignore the larger whole of human knowledge and experience of which it is a part. It is not at all surprising, therefore, that the outcome in an abnormal psychology course is not infrequently the curious view that all men are mentally ill, with some being more mentally ill than others. It is the contention here that abnormal psychology both depends on and contributes to our attempts to reach a coherent understanding of man and his world. It is hoped that the selections in this book will help place abnormal psychology in a larger historical, cultural, and philosophical context, and thus complement an almost singular concern with research and methodology.

To focus the discussion and provide a framework with which to approach the readings, we shall make a broad and perhaps arbitrary distinction between scientific statements and value (ethical) propositions. Science makes statements about reality; ethics makes statements about desirability. The one deals with what is, the other with what ought to be. Scientific work involves a method by which propositions are objectively tested. Value statements, on the other hand, are not the product of scientific method; their confirmation is ultimately a subjective process. In science, it is possible by means of experiment to reach agreement on what factors are the cause of an observed phenomenon or behavior. In the realm of values, we do not have an analogous operation through which a consensus can be reached about whether the observed behavior or its causes are good or bad.

Value statements derive ultimately from a set of fundamental value postulates, and these postulates are not susceptible to "proof." If, for instance, equal opportunity for all is valued, then it is "true" that standards in education or employment which are based on race, color, creed, or gender are bad. But how can the value—

equal opportunity for all—be demonstrated? Many people act as though it were not part of their value system, and it has been argued, for example, that women should not be given the same opportunities for advanced education as men, because they are less likely to put such training to use. Thus, whatever our personal opinions on the matter, we cannot say that equal opportunity is a self-evident value. It is possible, of course, to postulate a prior value, such as the fullest development of human potentialities, and argue that to realize this value we must commit ourselves to equality of opportunity. But then we must either maintain that this prior value is self-evident or derive it from an even more ultimate value. Eventually such a regress will arrive at a fundamental set of values that cannot be proven. Because value assertions are incapable of verification, "truth" in ethics— and, it might be added, in music, literature, and art—is open to a variety of subjective interpretations.

In the struggle to place psychology on a sound scientific footing, its traditional association with philosophy had to be overcome, and subjective value entanglements had to be avoided. But the empirical foundations are now firmly established. Abnormal psychology is based on science. Our interest in values does not indicate any doubt on this point or any lack of appreciation for the power of scientific methodology. The question is whether values also play a part in abnormal psychology. It is possible to mark out an area of "pure science" within the field, but insofar as diagnosis, treatment, and prevention are social concerns, the selections offered here seem to show clearly that values do play an important part in abnormal psychology.

Value questions are implied in the search for enduring and meaningful criteria of normality and abnormality and in the evaluation of the inevitable social, moral, and scientific consequences of such definitions. To discuss abnormality entails some knowledge of normality, and normality suggests that there are some patterns of behavior that are more desirable than others. But how does the psychologist establish the characteristics of the "good" life? And why should such characteristics be preferable to the attributes of a "bad" life? In the value problem, the psychologist is confronted with unanswered—and perhaps unanswerable—basic and age-old human questions: What is the nature of man? What is good? Where is man going?

The reading in this book, of course, cannot resolve all questions of value. But they can develop an awareness of the importance of these questions and the part such questions play in abnormal psychology. They can expose the close association between taxonomy and values—the fact that diagnosis ultimately relates to social and legal standards of conduct. They can help show the extent to which the different approaches to therapy stem from different goals, and how greatly the choice of goals depends on value judgments.

In a more general way, these readings can teach us to look to science for knowledge that leads to wiser value choices and to avoid disguising value choices as scientific facts. They can give us experience in weighing values and assessing goals. And they can illuminate the relation between science and values. In the words of Robert Hutchins:

"The leading phenomena of our time exhibit a curiously ambiguous character. Technology may blow us up, or it may usher in the paradise of which man has been dreaming ever since Adam and Eve got kicked out of the first one. . . . Unfortunately these ambiguities do not lend themselves to scientific procedure. Our essential problem is what kind of people we want to be and what kind of world we want to have. Such questions cannot be solved by experiment and observation. But if we know what justice is, which is not a scientific matter, science and many other disciplines may help us get it. The problems resulting from these ambiguities are not going to be solved by men of fractional or pseudo-culture. The solution depends on moral and intellectual virtues rather than on specialized knowledge. It is a humbling thought to recall that 25 per cent of the SS guards in Nazi Germany were holders of the doctor's degree."[1]

1. *Science, Scientists, and Politics.* An occasional paper on the role of science and technology in the free society. Santa Barbara, Calif.: Center for the Study of Democratic Institutions of the Fund for the Republic, 1963.

C. Marshall Lowe

VALUE ORIENTATIONS—AN ETHICAL DILEMMA

This article examines in a general way the value conflicts faced by clinical psychologists. Unlike research psychologists, who are concerned with the production of new psychological knowledge, psychology's practitioners are engaged in applying such knowledge for the purpose of influencing behavior toward certain ends. Lowe makes a trenchant analysis of some major value orientations associated with these goals. His discussion has obvious applications to the allied occupations of social work and psychiatry. But it should be realized that the ethical dilemma which Lowe examines must be faced by any person engaged in influencing, altering, and shaping behavior, be he clinical practitioner, parent, minister, teacher, politician, or friend.

The psychologist is being called upon today to play a new role. Society is asking him to leave his laboratory and to move out into the world to be of practical service to mankind. While the psychologist must of necessity play this new role, he does so with certain difficulties, for he must divest himself of the robes of scientific impartiality. The psychologist as a scientist limits himself to what is; his choice of field of inquiry in his quest for truth involves values which are purely personal. But as a practitioner, the psychologist must be concerned with what should be; his personal tastes now affect the lives of others and so become social values.

The point of this article is that the involvement of the psychologist's own values in the applied field creates an ethical dilemma. The dilemma exists because the psychologist as a scientist cannot know to which of mankind's brave new worlds he is to be beholden. The educational psychologist facilitates learning; but learning involves understanding, whose nature is determined only by a philosophy of education. The industrial psychologist is employed by a company which seeks a profit, and only personal choice can help him reconcile loyalty to the employer with a broader loyalty to society as it is represented by the consumer and by the fellow employee.

With the counselor and the clinician, the ethical dilemma becomes more severe, for they serve not an organization but rather a particular individual. The clinician is of service by striving to bring back one who is mentally unhealthy to psychic health, and yet his science can scarcely tell him what mental health and psychological maturity really are. The counselor provides guidance for effective living, and yet it is scarcely as a psychologist that he describes the good life.

In therapy, the psychologist works toward ends which he calls "adjustment," "self-realization," "relearning," etc. These words do not even approximately describe the same thing. Further, it is impossible for research to enter the breech and describe the ends of effective counseling. The therapist remembers the words of Williamson (1958) that "every choice and every action must be based upon explicit or implicit acceptance of a value" (p. 524). He recalls the admonition of Rogers (1947) that a person is always controlled by the one upon whom he is dependent. And if the therapist is experimentally minded, he finds scarcely any comfort in the findings of Rosenthal (1955) that those clients who improve in therapy tend to revise certain of their values so that they more closely resemble those of the therapist.

In the counseling interview, it does not matter whether or not the therapist is consciously aware of a value orientation. If he is aware of his value orientation, he finds it often impossible to be loyal both to his own highest values and those of the client. If he has not systematized his beliefs, the therapist will assume his own values to be self-evident, and in ignorance he will project his own values onto the client.

The dilemma of the practicing psychologist is compounded by the existence of a multiplicity of competing sets of values, for one value orientation tends to exclude all others. As we present the controversy over values, we will assemble them into four main orientations: naturalism, culturalism, humanism, and theism. We shall see that each makes a demand for loyalty, setting at the same time its own criterion or goal. We shall see also that every orientation has critics who oppose its claims.

Naturalism

Naturalism, the first value orientation that we shall consider, has taken several current forms. One of these is logical positivism. Insofar as positivism seeks to throw out of the cultural vocabulary all notions that are not susceptible to empirical validation, it implies a naturalistic world view by assuming that scientific laws can account for all phenomena. Since reality is limited to what is defined operationally, naturalism limits psychology to the study of behavior,

From *American Psychologist*, 1959, Vol. 14, pp. 687-693. Reprinted by permission of the author and the American Psychological Association.

the mind being reduced to the physiological and physical, which can be measured. The result is Behaviorism and a limited scientific vocabulary that prevents the erection of any hierarchy of values that will transcend the physical. Both Behaviorism and classical psychoanalysis in turn imply a physical hedonism by placing emphasis on physical laws which reduce the life of the mind to the needs of the body.

Today the foremost naturalist in psychology is B. F. Skinner, who is an exceedingly bold social thinker. The common theme of his social treatises is that the psychologist possesses the means of social control and must use these means effectively for the welfare of society. The function of the psychologist is then to be a behavioral engineer who manipulates behavior in such a way as to insure cultural survival. It is part of his orientation that Skinner chooses not to state values. When forced by critics to state a moral position, he took the position that the criterion for good was to be the survival value for the culture. The psychologist is permitted to do anything and everything that will allow his fellow men to keep breathing (Skinner, 1956).*

Skinner's values for psychology are picturesquely stated in his utopian novel *Walden Two* (1948). Skinner's conception of paradise is a large rural colony where democracy is replaced by behavioral engineering. If the means are scientific control, the end is physical comfort, which is provided by the short work day which the elimination of cultural anachronisms permits. While a small autocracy controls life in the colony, the only technique available to it is positive reinforcement, lest members avail themselves of their one freedom, which is to leave. If at first glance man is a slave, in Skinner's view he is free from the tyranny of chance and free to take advantage of the best that cultural engineering can provide.

Criticisms of naturalism

Naturalism in its many manifestations has been attacked both on ontological and on epistemological grounds. Axiology, however, is our concern in this paper, and understandably there is criticism of naturalism here too. For the sake of brevity, we will let the criticism focus upon the utopian social world of B. F. Skinner. Thus, Carl Rogers (1956)* has charged that Skinner completely abandoned scientific method in *Walden Two*. In Rogers' view, Skinner confuses what is with what should be. Science can compare two values only in terms of a criterion, or third value, which must lie outside science. When science is itself the criterion, or final value, it is miscontrol. It is "locked in the rigidity of initial choice" and "can never transcend itself to seek new goals." Rogers concludes that "*Walden Two* and *Nineteen Eighty Four* are at a deep philosophical level indistinguishable."

The reaction by humanist philosophy has been even more violent. Joseph Wood Krutch has written *The Measure of Man* (1954) to refute *Walden Two*. Krutch is concerned because there is no clear way of differentiating between the positivistic control of *Walden Two* and the fascist control of a Nazi labor camp. He worries because social control is passing from the hands of philosophers and theologians who are aware of moral issues into the hands of experimentalists who are less aware of the value judgments that they make and whose methods are such as to prevent others from questioning them. In Krutch's view, survival is not the ultimate aim of man. Cockroaches have survived for 250,000,000 years, but Krutch feels that it is not enough merely to exist as an animal.

A final criticism is made of *Walden Two* as a novel. It is claimed that the characters have no real personality, but are only puppets whose strings are pulled by the author for polemic purposes. Physical hedonism and literary art are indeed incompatible, for the novel can speak to the reader only by allowing him to identify with characters who do not eliminate their hardships, but surmount them even in the face of tragedy.

Walden Two has significance not as a novel but as a statement of those values by

*[This article appears in the present volume. Ed.]

which Skinner seeks to give coherence to life. Skinner's credo raises the problem that psychology now comes forth and claims that it can determine the conduct of a public whose highest value seemingly is that it is free to choose for itself.

Culturalism

Just as the naturalists take their cue from the physical world and make the physiological processes of the body the final criterion in psychotherapy, so there is another group of thinkers who are oriented to man's social nature. We term this second value orientation "culturalism" and include in the group those who take their cue from the social world and who see man's problems as arising more from his social needs than from his physical wants.

Culturalism makes loyalty to the culture from which man is derived the supreme value. In psychology, it has an explicit pronouncement in the APA's "Ethical Standards of Psychologists," which states: "The psychologist's ultimate allegiance is to society and his professional behavior should demonstrate an awareness of his social responsibilities" (1953, Paragraph 1.12-1). The APA doubtless sought for a code that would speak to its time; but we should not overlook the fact that at other times such a code might have stated that "ultimate allegiance" is to God, or in another period to the "rights of man."

Applying culturalism to the field of mental health, we find those who see wholeness only in relating to other people. We see this emphasis first in such social psychoanalysts as Adler, Sullivan, and Horney who see the cause of neurosis in isolation from other people and who see the cure in being led back to other people.

We see this emphasis secondly in those psychologists who subordinate the individual to the social through emphasis on "adjustment." Adjustment psychology carries social psychoanalysis one step further: one must not only be able to relate to other people, but must also be able to adapt to what others are doing. Thus Shaffer and Shoben in their *Psychology of Adjustment*

(1956) compare the process of social adjustment in humans with that of biological adjustment in animals. They recommend for man the following procedure:

"In response to your need for approval, you may act so as to gain favor in the future or you may display other abilities that bring you recognition. *These are quite sensible things to do under the circumstances*" [Italics added] (p. 4).

As Shoben writes in the journals to a more sophisticated readership, his position becomes more complex. While he rejects the notion that the "normal" is the average, he (1957) considers pathology as being nonconformity to group norms. And like Skinner he has a utopia:

"What kind of world would be ours if we were less concerned about achievement and fully occupied with understanding each other, participating more wholeheartedly in the corporate venture of building a society . . . and developed a sense of worthwhileness of intimate relationships marked by a high degree of cherishing and the mutual pursuit of essentially private interests?" (Shoben, 1956, pp. 330-331)

Criticism of culturalism

The critical problem of culturalism involves the choice of particular cultural values. Man cannot choose to accept or reject social values; his only option is to select particular social values. Arnold Green (1946) writes:

"the history of psychotherapy can be viewed as an unsuccessful struggle to evaluate the role of social values [for] it is safe to say that all behavior resulting in the need for psychotherapy is social [in the sense that] it involves a conflict between self-and-others and between self-values and other(s) values" (pp. 199-200).

Culturalism must seek to reduce diverse social values to a least common denominator, but the result is dissatisfying to many.

First, voices are raised against subservience to a "democratic" ideology which, as Green (1946) points out, is rapidly changing and which at the present time is rather vague, as Walker and Peiffer (1957) remind us in their criticism of Shoben. To provide orientation by the values of mid-century America is thus to build upon sand while the rain is already falling.

Other voices cry out that what is most common is very far from being the best. The popular press reminds us that to be normal is nothing to brag about, and every social reformer has as his bugaboo the person who is too well adjusted to things as they are. Erich Fromm (1955)* sees adjustment as destroying what is distinctive in human personality and postulates a *folie à millions* where multitudes share the same vices. Another psychoanalyst, Robert Lindner (1952), sees man as exchanging the freedom that is his to work out his own destiny for the doped security of accepting things as they are.

And finally, there are psychologists who raise their voices in concern for the abdication of moral responsibility that culturalism implies. In the view of M. Brewster Smith (1954), psychology has helped to destroy values traditionally related to the Western world and, by then abdicating responsibility for values, has added "to the crescendo urging total conformity, a trend which in the long run may not be at all conservative of our traditional values" (p. 515). C. Gilbert Wrenn (1952) points out that the counselor can never be really loyal to society until he is loyal to something more than society. The psychologist to be ethical must do more than observe a code of ethics: "He must be great within himself because he relates himself to God and the greatness of the Infinite" (p. 176).

The conformitizing of the "other directed" person is being accelerated by the "organization man." The dilemma of culturalism is that it allows itself to be caught in a vicious circle — our society can be like a dog following its own tail. If there is nothing external that it can follow, it is doomed to meander meaninglessly in circles. The hope for the world is in following after the most sublime, and not after the most painfully obvious.

Humanism

While the culturalist looks outside of man to what is in the social world, there is another group of thinkers, whom we term the humanists, who believe that the criteria for ethical values lie within certain native human characteristics. In the broad sense, anyone concerned with the dignity of man is a humanist. However, as we use the term, humanism is belief in the self-sufficiency of man to control his own destiny and to realize his inherent potentialities through rational thought processes. Man's final moral obligation is to strive continually to realize all the unique potentialities which are inherent in human nature, the ultimate value being man. Among humanist psychologists, the aim is the same whether the object of therapy be termed "self-actualization" as by Goldstein, "emergent value-attributes" by Cantril, the positive "emotional tone" by Cole, or the "growth potential" by Rogers; each one equates activism with mental health.

The philosophical underpinnings of humanism in psychotherapy is seen in Erich Fromm. Fromm's slogan is *Man for Himself* (1947), the title of his best known book. He finds that "man cannot live statically because his inner contradictions drive him to seek for an equilibrium, for a new harmony instead of the lost animal harmony of nature" (1955, p. 28). Thus: "The whole life of the individual is nothing but the process of giving birth to himself" (1955, p. 26). The life of man consists in *The Art of Loving* (1956), Fromm's most recent book. To love others, one must first love himself and have faith in himself, for man must respect his own self before he can have respect for someone else.

The humanist methodology in therapy is seen in Carl Rogers, who has published his credo in the *Humanist* (1957b):

*[An excerpt from this book appears in the present volume. Ed.]

"The good life, from the point of view of my experience, is the process of movement in a direction which the human organism selects when it is inwardly free to move in any direction" (p. 293).

Rogers' conception of therapy seems to be almost identical with his ideal of the good life, for he believes in a "process conception of psychotherapy" (1958), which seems to be a microcosm of the good life outside. Rogers' humanistic concern determines both what he does and does not do as a counselor: the therapist plays a relatively passive role because man is inherently able to solve his own problems. The task of therapy is to let the rational self shine forth through a constricting fog in all its logic: "The tragedy for most of us is that our defenses keep us from being aware of this rationality" (1957b, p. 299). The client is a human being whose feelings are worthy of complete respect. Thus the counselor empathizes with the client and respects his emotions. Should the counselor be an unbeliever in the worth of the true self and should lack an "unconditional positive regard" for the client, the client's inner personality will not dare emerge and therapeutic change will not occur (1957a). Therapy takes place as the self finds shelter and feasts on its own experience until it becomes the fully developed onion with its concentric layers. Rogers and the client form a "mutual admiration society" whose purpose is clear: the human personality is to be magnified and praised.

Criticism of humanism

Humanistic psychology can first of all be criticized for absolutizing American activism when it is only a cultural phenomenon. Rogers may tell us quite open-mindedly that he has discovered a drive towards self-assertiveness in all his clients, but he does not tell us how many of these clients were unrelated in any way to the middle class, which judges personal worth by the amount of achievement. What Rogers boasts of so proudly as self-actualization may be but the pathology of a culture whose members are frightened at being cut off from past traditions and rush pellmell into the future, as if they were animals in stampede. Today the absolute nature of self-actualization seems threatened on the one hand by the corporation, which, in the organization man, grinds out its own cultural type, and on the other hand by increasing contact with other cultures, which are in many ways superior to our own even if they produce little change over many centuries.

Humanism also lays itself open to the charge that man is not so perfectly rational as he sometimes likes to conceive himself as being. The social criticism of Reinhold Niebuhr (1941) is too complex to be quickly summarized; but, starting from premises similar to Fromm's, he sees man as being anxious. Man resolves this anxiety by deluding himself into thinking that he is really in control of life. He deceives himself into thinking that he is more perfect than he really is, erring because he is unaware of his own ignorance. Having charted the disastrous historical debacles that have been caused by self-inflated prigs, Niebuhr concludes that it is the man who thinks that he is most like God who is the most completely depraved.

Humanists frequently surround themselves with the sanctimonious glow of those who can "intuit" experiences to which the tough minded remain impervious. But being optimistic about human nature does not make a man more saintly, any more than Niebuhr's ability to see the manifestations of human sinfulness wherever he looks makes him less of a believer in God. Humanism represents the Enlightenment. But set against the Enlightenment is the pessimism of Freudian psychoanalysis and Pauline theology, for these two movements span the history of the Western world like the legs of a caliper and provide their own measure for man.

Self-actualization does not seem to be enough. Some men seem so bereft of personality that they have few powers to realize; while others, such as F. Scott Fitzgerald and Francoise Sagan, have drained a rich humanity to the dregs and have felt only *ennui* in the process of living. Man is a creature caught between the need of individuality and the need of belonging, plagued by contradictory loyalties to the self and to others; burdened by the guilt inherent in the realization that he has not fulfilled his potentialities; and inwardly frightened as he seeks to build up walls of meaning out of sand in a delirious attempt to enshrine the human self which he knows the incoming tide of time will surely wash away.

In contradiction to humanism, there are some who believe that man has some other end than merely to feel dignified. They would say that man has the greatest dignity when he feels his own inward wretchedness and that he is the creature of the greatest progress when "his richest gain he counts but loss, and pours contempt on all his pride."

Theism

The final value orientation, theism, believes that man's loyalty is to God and that man is totally dependent upon God. Believers in other value orientations can also be religious in a broad sense of the word. The theist, however, differs from all who believe in the self-sufficiency of man by his belief in a personal God before whom he stands in need of redemption.

While theists have a diversity of beliefs, there is one value that is central: "You shall love the Lord your God with all your heart, and with all your soul, and with all your might." This great commandment involves the theist with the will of God in interpersonal relations, including marriage and family problems; in the choice and resolution of conflicts; in finding a philosophy of life; and in vocational choice.

Theism is distinctive in its belief that man is lost until he has found God. In words which Augustine addresses to God: "Thou hast made us for Thyself, and the heart never rests until it finds its rest in Thee." Man is a creature dependent past, present, and future upon the God who created him. While the humanist believes that man is made in the image of God in a way that enables him to become a little god, the theist believes that man is made in the image of God as one set of gears is made in the image of another set, so that it can receive power in order to pass it on.

The theist believes that the problems that men face are such that they have a solution in religious faith. When despair over the apparent meaninglessness and monotony of life causes a depressed state, the cure is through faith in a God who creates all life for a unique purpose. In the melancholy of change of life and in the despair of old age, he finds in religion that path of transition from physical to spiritual goals. When man is fearful, he finds strength through the spirit of God; and, when he is anxious within, he finds inner reassurance in the love of the Heavenly Father, whose love can bear his inner weaknesses. In loneliness and in isolation from other people, he enters into harmonic relationships with those who seek to radiate a forgiving love that understands all things.

Gordon W. Allport (1950) thus notes that "love is incomparably the greatest psychotherapeutic agent" (p. 80). He notes that religion needs to become a part of psychotherapy, for it "offers an interpretation of life and a rule of life that is based wholly upon love" (p. 82). Allport also notes that religion is needed to give meaning to life, a need also noted by Carl Jung (1933), who, speaking of his patients over 35, claims that

"It is safe to say that everyone of them fell ill because he had lost that which the living religions of every age have given to their followers, and none of them has been really healed who did not regain his spiritual outlook" (p. 264).

Criticism of theism

There are certain objections that are raised against theism. If man is anxious and upset because he has difficulty in believing in anything deeply, then religious faith becomes the problem. While the vast majority of Americans believe in God according to the opinion polls, theism requires a committed faith that rather few people have had in any age.

A second objection takes into account

the wrong use of religion. Finding an awakening of religious interest in the postwar era, a number of America's most prominent churchmen have spoken out against a religious revival, which, lacking any deepseated devotion to God, is centered in a self-serving religious faith that is interested only in comfort by the bland assurance that everything is really all right. Prophetically, at the very start of the postwar era, Arnold Green (1946) saw the dangers in superficial religion, pointing out that "faith cannot be consciously designed to meet a personality need any more than it can be established by fiat or legislative action" (p. 205). He concluded that religion can be therapeutic only when it is not so regarded.

A third objection is that theism keeps man in infantile dependence. Psychoanalysis believes that authoritarian religion is the internalized voice of authority, having the same restrictive effect as had the father. Fromm (1947) thus lists ways in which he feels organized religion has impeded human progress. Somewhat similarly, Rollo May (1953) objects to "the divine right of being taken care of" which blocks growth towards maturity. May further brands as neurotic the use of religion in helping to obviate that loneliness and anxiety which is vital to *Man's Search for Himself*.

There are certain irreconcilable differences between theism and the other value orientations at critical choice-points. For the humanist, man gains his life by holding it close to him, cherishing it, and feeling the self develop within him. The theist on the other hand believes that man finds his life only by losing his life and by emptying the self for others, being filled with a love which is ultimately of God. These are two contrasting ways to mental health, and the psychologist must choose between them.

Conclusion

If the psychologist is by definition to be ethical, he must conform to professional standards of conduct. Having described different value orientations, we can now conclude that there is no single professional standard to which his values can conform. If psychology declares by fiat that one set of values is to become absolute, it ceases to be science and becomes a social movement. If it chooses a syncretistic blend, it has arbitrarily decided in favor of a culturalism that attempts to adapt to as many viewpoints as possible. But when a value is compromised, it has become the means to some other end. Finally, psychology can choose to hide its head in the sand of scientific research. However, the only result of such a move would be a regression to ethical superstitions exceeding even those of the so-called primitives. To do research without intending it to serve a particular value orientation is to build a high speed automobile without any steering wheel.

Williamson has already made a start in untieing the ethical knot by suggesting that value orientations be removed from under the proverbial bushel and, once out in the open, be dealt with as objectively as possible. We would suggest in addition that each area in psychology become more fully aware of the implications of its efforts, much as education does through a philosophy of education. We would further suggest that, as psychologists familiarize themselves with the value orientation under which they operate, that they confess their philosophic biases and then turn those biases to fullest advantage by being of professional assistance to the special interest groups with which their values coincide. In such ways as these the public will receive more of what psychology has to contribute and, dealing with psychology at a more objective level, will be able to put that contribution to better use.

We conclude that differences in value orientations cannot be resolved, each orientation having adherents whose beliefs should be respected. We suggest that each counselor have an understanding of the values both of himself and others and that his values be known by all who are personally affected by his professional behavior.

O. H. Mowrer

WHAT IS NORMAL BEHAVIOR?

This paper and the four that follow are concerned with diagnosis in the most general sense—with distinguishing between what is normal and what is not. In organic illness the normal cell and its functioning serve as the standard for comparison, deviations from which are identified as abnormal. In the biological domain, then, a naturalistic, value-free definition of normality is entirely possible. In the case of functional disorders, we may attempt to distinguish between the normal and the abnormal in a value-free way by means of "statistical" approaches. Thus the average or typical can be taken as the normal. But great men are not typical, and we prefer to consider them extraordinary rather than abnormal. It would seem that a value-free definition of psychological normality eludes us because of our inability to establish an adequate criterion of behavior comparable to the normal cell. In abnormal psychology we are interested in discriminating between what is healthy and desirable and what is not. Diagnosis is a judgment which implies whether or not treatment is necessary. Since treatment is an attempt to change behavior, diagnosis involves a value judgment—as to whether the behavior should be changed; whether it is good for the individual, or for society. The problem, then, is to distinguish between behavior that should be encouraged, admired, and valued and behavior that should be discouraged and changed. It is this problem that Mowrer attempts to resolve.

Chairman: It is almost two years now since our discussion group held its first meetings. At that time, you will recall, we were interested in gaining a better understanding of the Concept of Culture.[1] It is proposed that in the present series of meetings we shall consider the question: What is normal behavior? I am sure we are all aware of the importance of this question, but I imagine we are also all impressed by the many difficulties implicit in it. What we can hope to accomplish by way of answering the question in any definitive sense will be modest at best, but at the same time there is reason to think that our efforts may not be altogether unrewarding. Perhaps the kind of cooperative, interdiscipline approach to which our group is dedicated will enable us to resolve at least certain facets of the problem which have not readily yielded to the more conventional, segmental type of analysis.

From your presence here this evening, I assume that all of you received the written announcement of the meeting and of the proposed topic of discussion. And if our earlier experience is a reliable guide, I can also assume that all of you have done some thinking and reading on the topic from the standpoint of your own particular field of specialization. In keeping with our established practice, I shall not call upon anyone for a formal speech but will simply throw the meeting open for informal, spontaneous discussion.

Statistician: I should like to be the first to point out that my particular specialty is perhaps limited in respect to what it can contribute to the ultimate solution of our problem; but this contribution is so explicit and in certain respects so basic that I venture to open the discussion. I find that in textbooks on abnormal psychology it is a common practice to introduce the concept of normality by first relating it to the statistical facts of "averageness" and "unusualness." Many psychologists, in fact, speak of "abnormal" and "unusual" personal characteristics as if the two terms were equivalent; and I find that a number of psychiatrists likewise place heavy emphasis in this connection upon "deviation from the average." For example, Cobb has said: "One must accept the fact that 'normal' is a range of values about the mean of a distribution curve. The average man and those near him are normal, the most 'perfect' specimen (if one can imagine such a specimen, and perfect for what?) would be far from normal" (1943, p. 129). I believe that I am therefore justified in proposing the purely statistical definition of normality as the starting point for our discussion.

In established statistical parlance, the "norm," in an array of individuals who vary with respect to some measurable characteristic, such as height or intelligence, is usually taken to mean the "central tendency." Thus, in this curve which I have prepared (Figure 1), we see the range and distribution of heights in an unselected population of English men, with a mean of 66.9 inches and with a "normal range" as indicated. Individuals whose height places them either above or below this range may be said to be "abnormal" with respect to height — in the literal sense of ab-normal, i.e., away from the norm.

Where the line of separation between so-called normality and abnormality shall be drawn is, of course, usually quite arbitrary. A common convention is to mark off a point on the distribution which is one *standard deviation* above the mean, and a like distance below, and to designate the intervening area as the *normal range*. In a distribution that conforms to the common "bell-shaped" type of curve, this range will include about 68 per cent of all the cases, with roughly 16 per cent falling above and an equal number falling below this range. However, it is usually understood that the distribution is on a *continuum* and that, for example, a "low normal" score is different only in degree, not in kind, from a nearly equal score that happens to fall in the area

From *An Introduction to Clinical Psychology,* edited by Leon A. Pennington and Irwin A. Berg. Copyright 1954 by The Ronald Press Company. Reprinted by permission of the publishers.

1. A digest of the group's discussion of this topic has been reported by Kluckhohn and Kelly (1945).

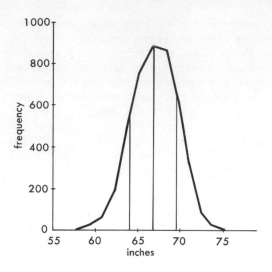

Figure 1. A frequency polygon of heights of 6,194 adult English men (after Vernon, 1940, p. 13). The mean lies at about 66.9 inches, and the vertical lines to the right and to the left of the mean indicate the approximate limits of the "normal range." (By permission of The University of London Press, publishers of P. E. Vernon, The Measurement of Abilities, 1940.)

height, but, for example, intelligence as the basis for such an analysis, we encounter a serious complication. My curve (Figure 2) shows the distribution of intelligence scores earned by 1,600 ninth-grade American school children. Here, again, there is a central tendency, a normal range, and two dwindling extremes. But although it is reasonable to refer to one of these extremes as representing individuals with "abnormally low" intelligence, it seems a strange twist of language to refer to the opposite extreme as representing individuals with "abnormally high" intelligence. It does not, however, seem at all remarkable if we speak of these children as having unusually high intelligence — a fact which focuses attention upon a wide variety of situations in which there is by no means a one-to-one correspondence between the unusual and the so-called abnormal.

Now sociologists and social psychologists have long been aware of this difficulty and have worked out another way of dealing with the problem which ——

Educator: If I may interrupt for just a moment, I should like to register another

just outside the so-called normal range. Rarely does one think of such a line of demarcation as being in any way categorical or absolute, although important practical decisions may depend upon whether a given individual's score falls upon one or the other side of such a line. And in this sense it seems to me that the statistical emphasis has been very helpful; it tends to emphasize the continuity rather than the discreteness of individuals who, on whatever grounds, are classified as normal or abnormal.

Sociologist: I was pretty sure that the statistical point of view would be introduced at an early stage in the discussion so I, too, have brought along a curve. Since it is commonly regarded as undesirable for a person to be extremely tall or extremely short, the foregoing illustration of the concepts of normality and abnormality seems to work well enough. But if we take, not

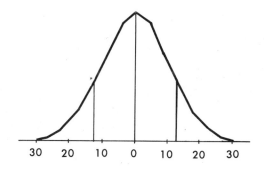

Figure 2. A frequency polygon of intelligence scores of 1,600 ninth-grade students, as determined by nine different tests. The scores are plotted so that the mean score equals zero. The "normal range" is indicated by the two vertical lines to either side of the line indicating the mean. (Adapted from W. F. Dearborn, Intelligence Tests, 1928, p. 22, by permission of Houghton Mifflin Co., publishers.)

objection to the statistical definition of normality. You will notice that our statistician drew his example from data based upon the heights of *English men*. By his criterion, many English women would be "abnormal" with respect to height, although they might not be unusually short *for women*. The same point could be made with respect to the Pygmies of Africa and the Negrillos of Malaysia. And, of course, when we go from adults to children, the case is even more striking: what is normal height for a child ten years old would certainly be abnormal for an adult of either sex.

This point is, of course, fully recognized in our definition of the I.Q. as a function of the individual's age. The problem is here solved by talking, not of "normal intelligence" in any general sense, but in terms of what is normal or usual for a child of a particular age. In other words, we separate children into a number of different groups, or "populations," and then speak of a given individual as normally or not normally intelligent with respect to the age-group into which he falls.

Practically, this type of procedure seems to work out all right in many instances, but I do not regard it as affording a logical solution to our problem. For example, educators have often felt it undesirable to have children with a wide range of intelligence in the same classroom, and have tried to get around the difficulty by means of "homogeneous grouping." By this device the children in a given grade are segregated into two, three, or possibly, more groups, according to their intelligence. Thus, a child with an I.Q. of 80 may be statistically abnormal with respect to the average intelligence of all the children in his grade, but not abnormal with respect to the average of his particular "homogeneous group." However useful this procedure may be pedagogically, it points to a sobering problem logically, namely, that you can make almost anything or body "normal" if you are willing to juggle sufficiently the group, or classification, into which the object or individual falls. In the ultimate case, you can say, in fact, that

everything is "normal" with respect to itself, i.e., if you assume that each individual is *sui generis*.

My point is one which has been well made by John Kendrick Bangs in his poem, "The Little Elf," which ends with the familiar lines:

"I'm quite as big for me," said he,
"As you are big for you."

Physician: I should like to second what has just been said by noting that of all the persons in the world who, for example, have cancer, most of them may be said to be "average cases of cancer," but this fact hardly makes them healthy, which is the sense in which I am inclined to think of normality. Or, to make the same point with another example: we are accustomed to speaking of the inmates of mental hospitals and prisons, respectively, as insane and criminal; and with respect to each of these categories there are many individuals who are quite run-of-the-mill, "average," "usual," but hardly "normal," I should think.

Psychologist: I should like to hear the rest of what our Sociologist was saying, but before he continues I want to raise this question: Does it make any sense, really, to talk about a given person being either normal or abnormal in any comprehensive way? Must we not always speak of a person as normal or abnormal in respect to some specific, measurable characteristic? Incautious writers sometimes refer to the "measurement of personality" as if "personality," or "a person," could be gauged, or rated, in terms of a single variable, on some one master scale. More careful usage demands that we speak instead of "measurements of personality," for personality has *many* dimensions; and there is no one unit of measurement, or scale, that is applicable to all of them. In consequence, it is common practice on the part of many experts in my field to test or rate a given individual with respect to several different characteristics, and then to assemble the result in the form of a "profile," or "psychograph." Here (Figure 3) is an example which I thought the group might find interesting.

This method of defining and dealing with the concept of personality immediately shifts the problem of normality from the purely quantitative to the qualitative plane; for who, on the basis of a psychograph, can say, in any over-all mathematical sense, that one person is normal and another is abnormal? The difficulty is, of course, that one cannot add, mathematically, two units of Energy here to five units of Persistence there, or either of these to one or three units of Intelligence. In practice, a composite graph of this kind is used not so much for determining personal normality or abnormality in any over-all sense as it is for ascertaining whether a given individual seems to "fit" or "match" specifications which have been drawn up for a particular type of employment or for some other purpose.

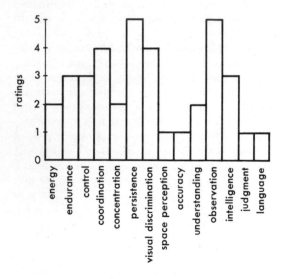

Figure 3. A profile, or psychograph, showing one individual's ratings on a variety of performances. Such a graph has to be evaluated in terms of its total pattern. (Reprinted and adapted from M. S. Viteles, Industrial Psychology, p. 153, with the permission of W. W. Norton and Co., and Jonathan Cape, Ltd.)

Philosopher: In this connection it is interesting to recall Emerson's theory of "compensation," according to which each individual, in his totality, is "equal" to every other individual, since, as Emerson assumed, a deficit in one area tends to be offset by a special advantage or virtue in another. Such thinking seems to be more of a prolegomenon to the theory of democracy than a statement of empirically verified fact. But it is also worth noting that the psychologist, Alfred Adler, has come out with a somewhat similar notion, which I should think might be termed the theory of "reactive compensation." According to this writer, a defect, or "inferiority," in one area initiates compensatory strivings which often succeed not only in counteracting the defect but in producing extraordinary strengths and accomplishments (1930).

Psychologist: One other point I wanted to make is this. Statistically-minded investigators, aware of the difficulties we have just been considering, have sometimes sought to isolate a single measurable attribute as the crucial one in determining personal normality or the lack of it. Various attempts have been made to measure what is commonly termed "nervousness," or more technically "emotional instability," by means of questionnaires. These investigations have recently been reviewed by Maller (1944), and I won't try to describe them here. But perhaps the earliest attempt to get at this variable by means of behavioral observation — and I remember that our question is: *What is normal behavior?* — was reported by Olson in 1929. By means of a careful definition and accurate recording of specified "nervous habits" in children, this writer obtained data indicating "that the amount of nervous habits in a given population takes the form of a continuous distribution. The evidence suggests that the problem of nervous habits is the problem of every child, just as are such matters as weight, height, and educational achievement" (1929, p. 90).

It is interesting to note that Olson found no reliable correlation between a number of pencil-and-paper tests of "personality" and the incidence of "nervous habits" observed in his subjects. As the author points out, "the general intelligence factor makes the interpretation of scores on personality tests of the paper-and-pencil type a difficult matter" (p. 90). The scores on such tests tend to be invalidated "by the tendency to what has been called the 'intellectualization of response' on the part of children when giving a subjective report" (p. 90) i.e., by the tendency to give what they believe to be a "right" answer rather than the "true" one.

Educator: I think I can extend this argument. A few days ago I came across a study, reported by Tiegs and Katz (1941), in which 100 college students were randomly selected from a much larger group and were then observed and rated with respect to fourteen evidences of "nervousness." The results are shown in this graph (Figure 4). The great majority of the students manifested between 7 and 13 of these traits or mannerisms, one manifested only one such trait, and one manifested all 15. It would thus appear that "abnormality," in the sense of "nervousness," is more or less normally distributed, and from a purely statistical

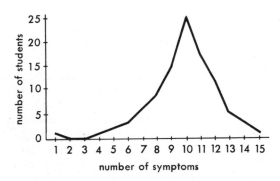

Figure 4. *Incidence of symptoms of "maladjustment" in 100 unselected college students (after Tiegs and Katz, 1941, p. 66). Note that these symptoms tend to be normally distributed. (By permission of The Ronald Press Co., publishers of E. W. Tiegs and B. Katz, Mental Hygiene in Education, 1941.)*

standpoint, the individual who showed only one of these traits would be just as "abnormal" as the one individual who showed all 15 of them.

The authors of this report may be correct in their statement that "identifying and tabulating specific evidences of nervousness produce a more objective basis for determining the probable normality of behavior than does the purely subjective method" (p. 67). Yet one wonders how valid such a procedure is, not only in respect to the statistical point I have just made, but in yet another way. Do we, in point of fact, have any proof at all that children—or, for that matter, adults—who are "fidgety" are necessarily less well organized personally or more likely to succumb to real mental disease than are quieter, less physically active individuals?

(At this point the Biologist, the Psychoanalyst, and the Psychologist all started to speak, but the Chairman interrupted.)

Chairman: Gentlemen, our previous meetings have shown that one of the dangers in this type of discussion is that important lines of thought may become sidetracked and that our deliberations may lack form and continuity. As chairman, I am therefore going to bring the discussion back to what seemed to me to start off on an orderly and promising line of analysis. We began with a statement of, and a number of objections to, the purely statistical concept of normality. Our Sociologist then started to offer some sort of alternative proposal. I wonder if we might now return to what he was going to say.

Sociologist: I am glad to have this opportunity to continue, for I believe that what I was going on to say is important and that it will open up new avenues of thought.

As we have seen, statistical illustrations of the concept of normality are usually drawn from distributions that conform to the well-known bell-shaped curve. But we find that in respect to many characteristics which are most interesting to students of social behavior, human beings form what F. H. Allport and his students refer to as a "J-curve." Let me illustrate this point by means of two diagrams. In the first of these

(Figure 5) is represented the behavior of motorists at a street crossing where there was a stop sign. Here it will be seen that 75.5 per cent of the motorists came to a full stop and an additional 22 per cent proceeded very slowly. Only 2.5 per cent of all the drivers were observed to slow down only slightly or not at all.

From data of this kind one gets a new notion of what is "normal." Here it is apparently not so much a matter of the *average* as of the *ideal*. Here it is less a question of "is" and more a question of "ought." In this type of analysis, the criterion of normality may be subsumed under the concept of *social conformity*.

That the J-curve is often merely a so-called normal curve that has been "pushed out of shape" by the pressure of social rules or laws is indicated by my second diagram (Figure 6). Here one sees the behavior of motorists at an intersection comparable to the first one but where there was no stop sign. Here the distribution of motorists' behavior follows the classical statistical pattern. But it is important to note that comparatively few of our actions may be said to follow the principle of *laissez faire;* most

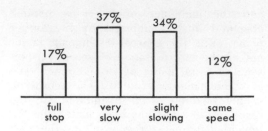

Figure 6. *Behavior of 208 motorists at corners with cross traffic but with no stop signs (after F. H. Allport, p. 228). This distribution gives a roughly bell-shaped curve. (By permission from* Psychology at Work, *edited by Paul S. Achilles, Copyrighted, 1932, by McGraw-Hill Book Co., Inc.)*

of our behavior is constantly impinged upon and shaped by social forces, which may be subtle or blatant but are ubiquitous and powerful. The question of conformity and nonconformity, therefore, seems to me to be much more central to our problem than is the mere matter of averageness, particularly if by average we think of being "in the middle," about equally distant from two extremes. In many situations of the type which I have illustrated, the extreme position of full conformity is the "normal" one.

Philosopher: I am not sure I am keeping up with all the technical implications of what is being said, but I must say that I like the general point of view which has just been suggested. The trouble with scientists, as it seems to me, is that they are always talking about the facts, the bare facts, and have nothing to say about ideals and values. It seems to me that the *best* type of person — who I would say was also the most "normal" type of person — is one who is strongly identified with the total human enterprise, one who is striving to improve the lot of mankind, one who does all he can to contribute to his society and make it "go."

Lest you be inclined to dismiss this point of view as merely a philosopher's whim, let me cite two psychologists in support of my position. Alfred Adler, whom I referred to earlier, has laid great stress upon the individual's relation to mankind as a whole (1938). Adler maintained that the crucial

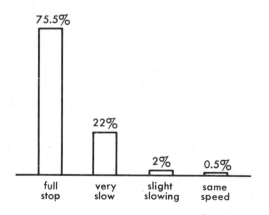

Figure 5. *Behavior of 2,114 motorists at corners with cross traffic and with boulevard stop signs (after F. H. Allport, 1932, p. 228). This heavily skewed distribution forms a J-curve. (By permission from* Psychology at Work, *edited by Paul S. Achilles, Copyrighted, 1932, by McGraw-Hill Book Co., Inc.)*

consideration in determining human normality is whether the individual is an asset or a burden to society and whether he is or is not contributing to the *progressive development of man*. And I also find that Roback (1928), in his volume entitled *Character*, has placed a similar emphasis upon what he calls "absolute normality," i.e., the condition of being ultimately proved "right" by continuing human experience, regardless of how unappreciated or ridiculed one may be at a given time or place.

Anthropologist: I agree that scientists, particularly social scientists, cannot afford to keep on indefinitely insisting that science has nothing to do or say about matters of value, ethics, ideals. For the last three or four hundred years science has been steadily cutting the ground from beneath many of the great myths of our race, and yet when the layman turns to the scientist and asks, "What shall I believe instead?" the scientist shrugs and replies, "That's your affair, not mine." Actually, these matters of ethics and value are of vital, everyday concern to men and women, and we social scientists and psychologists are not going to have a really adequate theory of the self or of society, nor are we going to be of much practical use until we are willing to come to full grips with these so-called "problems of value."

I have some views as to how this can be done, but they would take us too far afield for present purposes. What I particularly want to point out now is how tenuous is the basis just offered as a criterion of normality. What about stupid laws, which it is one's moral duty to oppose and defy? Where would the world be without the radical, the innovator, the reformer? As Shaw has suggested (albeit a little whimsically), even the criminal may have social utility. Social customs and laws have to be changed from time to time; imagine what would happen if we took slavish conformity as our ideal. And to make my point in a different way, suppose you have a person reared in one society who then goes to another society, a society with a very different culture. You can hardly expect such a person suddenly to become a very different sort of individual the moment he crosses the frontier into the new country, and yet if he doesn't, he will, by this definition, suddenly become "abnormal." At any given time there are always thousands of foreigners here in America, and do we look upon them as abnormal just because they have different ideals and standards? And what about the easily conceived case in which a whole culture may be said to be unhealthy, abnormal? Conformity in this case may insure abnormality, not normality.

Philosopher: I am not prepared to defend conformity as the ultimate basis of normality. I think personal *consistency* is a more valid guide than conformity per se—but I do want to say how opposed I am to one thing the preceding speaker has just said. He says we ought to oppose stupid laws by disobeying them. This is a point of view which I think has done a great deal of harm. We have ways to change laws in this country if they don't work, and this is not done by disobeying them. In my judgment the most effective kind of "radical" is a man (or woman) who has made all the renunciations that his society asks him to make, has accepted his full share of personal and social responsibility, and *then* steps forward to make his criticisms. The trouble with most self-styled radicals is that they are immature, irresponsible individuals who don't want to grow up and who cavil against society instead. Lenin obviously had this in mind when he said that the curse of a revolutionary movement is that it always attracts as followers a lot of people who are still adolescent in their mentality and social outlook. And I suspect that something of a similar nature might be said about neurotics, although I am not sufficiently informed technically to be more explicit on this point.

Theologian: I feel a little lost in this discussion, but there is one thing I should like to say. Traditionally, we theologians haven't been much concerned with the concepts of normality and abnormality; we have instead been preoccupied with the problem of good and evil. Yet I feel that the two things are not unrelated. It may be true that some of our most revered and inspired religious leaders have been "abnormal" in terms of modern psychiatric standards; but I can't escape the conviction that there is an important connection between what we theologians mean by goodness and virtue and what you scientists are trying to get at in this discussion of so-called normality. In my long experience with people in my parish, I have repeatedly observed that happy people are, in the main, the good, virtuous people.

It will be clear to you that what I have just said was suggested by the preceding discussion of the problem of conformity. We theologians agree with the sociologists and others about the importance of conformity as a basis for normality and happiness; but the issue is, conformity to what? You scientists say conformity to the standards and ideals of one's social group; we say conformity to the Will of God. And I naturally believe we are in the right.

Anthropologist: Actually, there is less difference between the two points of view than one may at first suppose. The student of comparative sociology soon comes to see that for any given people the Will of God (or gods) is simply the most basic and oldest edicts of culture. But it makes a great deal of difference how one interprets what, in the final analysis, is one and the same thing. Without going into the point at all fully, let me merely remark that it seems to me that some of our most distressing social and personal difficulties today come from the fact that a lot of people still think of moral law, ethics, and values as completely pre-established by divinity. The fact is, as we read it from the records of man's history, that morality and ideals have been slowly and painfully evolved, and many of our present difficulties stem precisely from the fact that morality and ideals have not, in certain respects, yet evolved far enough. I am thinking particularly of our need for a "new morality," leading to the prevention of war, in the international sphere; but other examples could also be given. So long as we think that all wisdom and virtue have already been revealed to man, just so long will we fail to come to realistic grips with some of our most urgent developmental problems.

Lawyer: I should perhaps stay out of this, but I want to remind the theologians how little help formal religion has been to us in our attempts to understand the problem of abnormality. Only a little while ago the theologians were telling us that men and women go mad because they become possessed of devils; and even more recently they were agitating their congregations to persecute as "witches" poor women whom we now know were merely neurotic, eccentric, or perhaps merely more honest than most people. The saints, on the other hand, were supposed to be individuals who had achieved a particularly close communion with God; but if I am any judge of the situation, a lot of them were just as crazy as the people who were said to be witches or possessed of devils.

Psychoanalyst: I don't believe what has just been said is quite fair to the theologians. Granted that there is some justification in the criticism of religion on this score, the fact remains that through the ages it has been the theologians, more than any other group, who have been concerned with the problem of anxiety and neurosis. I think it may interest this group to know that although Freud was not a man who was particularly friendly to formal religion, yet he clearly saw that the medieval religious conception of neurosis was actually not so very different from the conception which he urged. In a paper entitled, "A neurosis of demoniacal possession in the Seventeenth Century," Freud (1934b) makes the following remarks:

"Despite the somatic ideology of the era of 'exact' science, the demonological theory of those dark ages has in the long run justified itself. Cases of demoniacal possession correspond to the neuroses of the present day; in order to understand these latter we have once more had recourse to the conception of psychic forces. What in those days were thought to be evil spirits, to us are base and evil wishes, the derivatives of impulses which have been rejected and repressed. In one respect only do we not subscribe to the explanation of these phenomena current in medieval times; we have abandoned the projection of them into the outer world, attributing their origin instead to the inner life of the patient in whom they manifest themselves" (pp. 436-437).

Chairman: There are several members of our group who have not yet spoken this evening. I wonder if I may call upon some of these gentlemen. I would personally be much interested in hearing, for example, what the biologists have to say about our problems.

Biologist: We biologists seem to have two related yet by no means identical conceptions of normality. King (1945), writing in the *Yale Journal of Biological Medicine*, has recently suggested (though the underlying notion can easily be traced back to the Greeks) that the term "normal" should be used in those instances in which functions are in accordance with the design, or pattern, of the reacting structure and that this usage should be maintained without reference to whether these instances are or are not statistically common. Thus he proposes a "pattern norm" rather than a "pattern mean." Here the emphasis is obviously upon an organism's (or machine's) functioning as it is supposed to, according to its design. Or, to put the matter a little differently, one can say that normality is a question of *efficiency.*

The other notion of normality which one is likely to encounter in biology is that of *survival.* Some biologists say that whatever contributes to survival is normal and that whatever works against it is abnormal. Following Darwin, we often use the term *adaptive* to describe behavior which is conducive to survival; and I notice that psychologists also often use this term, although I cannot be sure whether it is with precisely the same meaning.

Now that I think of it, there is still another notion which one commonly encounters in biological thinking—or perhaps I should say it is merely a way of making at one and the same time both of the points I have just mentioned. I refer here to the concept of normality as equilibrium, or balance. Cannon's (1939) theory of *homeostasis* is a good example of balance at the physiological level. From a more general and somewhat philosophical standpoint, Raup (1925) has

written about much the same idea under the label of *complacency.* I am not able to judge the relevance of these conceptions of normality for our present discussion, but I note that those who are most concerned with the problem of personal, or psychological, normality often use the term "balance," as, for example, when they speak of a person being "well balanced," or "off his balance."

Physician: I think the biologists give us some good leads, and I would like to push the same line of reasoning a little further by pointing out that the problem of personal normality is really a question of health. This point of view is tacitly recognized by the common use of the term "mental diseases." And it seems to me that the concepts of normality that hold in biology and medicine, for the body, are equally valid in the field of psychiatry.

Lawyer: I have no technical training in psychology or psychiatry, but my professional practice brings me into contact with a lot of pretty basic human problems and attitudes; and I want to say that for all the efforts of the medical profession to get personal abnormality looked upon benevolently, as mere illness, I don't think that those efforts have succeeded, or are likely to. Most people are still inclined to look upon madness (save where it has a clearly organic basis, and to some extent even then) as a *moral* failure, not as an accident or misfortune, such as catching mumps, which "might happen to anybody."

Physician: May I remind the preceding speaker that shame is likely to accompany many human afflictions other than those of mental disorder? Take, for example, leprosy or tuberculosis, to say nothing of the venereal diseases.

Biologist: Let me try to restate what I was saying a moment ago. I said that biologists— and probably most physicians also—are inclined to say that an organism or machine is functioning normally if it is doing what it is supposed to do, working in the way it was made to work. In other words, one can say that behavior is normal if it's *natural.* It would seem, therefore, ——

Anthropologist: The simplicity of such a formulation is certainly attractive, but I must point out its unsoundness as far as our present problem is concerned. Kroeber (1917), Murdock (1932), Opler (1944, 1945), and others have shown that one of man's most distinctive characteristics is that he solves problems by means of culture rather than by means of organic specialization. Thus, for example, the only infrahuman organisms that can fly are ones which have, over millions of years, evolved wings; whereas man, through knowledge, skills, and inventiveness, has been able to make a machine in which to fly, without any change in himself save that subtle type of neural change which we call learning.

Now the import of what I have just said is this. It may be possible to use the structure of lower animals as at least a partial basis for determining what kind of behavior, or functioning, is "normal" for them; but this criterion breaks down at the human level. It is true that the nature of man's body puts certain limitations on what he can and cannot do; but a part of man's body, namely his nervous system, is so highly plastic that it gives him a phenomenal range of behavior potentialities. To put the matter somewhat paradoxically, but nonetheless truly, we may say that the human nervous system is specialized in nonspecialization. Save in terms of almost meaninglessly broad limits, it is idle to try to define what is humanly normal on the basis of structure. If "normality" has *any* meaning as applied to behavior at the human level, it is in terms of human culture, not anatomy.

Chairman: That line of argument strikes me as a telling one; and I predict that we will find it useful in our further deliberations. However, I am sure there are probably a number of equally fundamental ideas which have not yet been brought out. Although our psychoanalyst has already spoken briefly, there is undoubtedly much more that he, for example, could tell us about the problem of normality.

Psychoanalyst: Well, I believe there are at least two things which I, as a representative of the analytic group, ought to mention. You will certainly not be surprised if the first thing I suggest is the role of the "unconscious" in the determination of abnor-

mality. As a colleague of mine recently put the matter, if a person's motives are mainly conscious, he is normal; but if they are mainly unconscious, he is abnormal. This, of course, is just another way of saying that, although some degree of repression may be inescapable in civilized existence, the too extensive occurrence of repression is sure to cause trouble sooner or later. By the same token, therapy consists of the release of repressed motives into conscious awareness, and is accompanied by what we call "insight."

My second point is this. One of the most distinctive features of the neurotic individual is what clinicians almost universally term "disproportionality of affect." Our analytic theory of this phenomenon, in its simplest form, is that the individual learns as a child to be afraid of certain things which, in childhood, it is entirely appropriate that he should fear, as, for example, the power and authority of his father. But if an individual continues to have these same fears as an adult when his life circumstances are very different, we then speak of neurosis. In this connection we also use the expression, "over-determination" of behavior, but if I attempted to explain this concept I would not add anything fundamentally new to what I have already said.

Psychologist: As some of you probably know, a lot of psychologists have been interested in trying to "integrate" psychoanalytic concepts with some of our commonly accepted psychological principles. In connection with the last point, for example, many of us would say that it is a question of the individual's having *generalized* certain attitudes and habits from childhood into adult life, without having been able to make the requisite *discrimination*, i.e., without seeing that the situation is now different (Hull, 1943).

Psychiatrist: I don't follow a lot of this new thinking—I am a practical man and have to do things, not just speculate about them. I am inclined to agree with my colleagues, Cobb (1943), Darrah (1939), Hacker (1945), Jones (1942), and others when they maintain that, in theory, there just is no such thing as a normal man. And for similar reasons there is no clear-cut way in which one can differentiate a so-called abnormal man from a so-called normal one. I have been connected with mental hospitals for nearly thirty years, and for every species of craziness you can find in such an institution, I'll find the same one or another in people who are at large. The long and the short of it, as far as I am concerned, is that "abnormal" people are simply people who manage their relationships with other persons in such a way that these other persons are highly motivated to "get them out of the way," whereas "normal" people do a little better.

Neurologist: There is a study,[2] conducted at the Wakefield Mental Hospital, which suggests that the normal brain differs from the abnormal brain in the actual number of functioning cells in the two areas of the cortex, namely, the infragranular layer and the supragranular layers. The more nearly normal the brain, the wider the supragranular layer and the narrower the infragranular layer. I am not sure how good the controls were in this study, and I mention it, not because I think it is definitive, but merely as a means of indicating how nearly inexhaustible are the criteria according to which one can approach this problem of normality. I wonder, in fact, if it isn't desirable to let each professional group approach it from whatever standpoint is best suited to the needs of that group, and if it isn't something of a waste of time to try to agree upon any more general criteria.

Biologist: I don't at all feel that our discussion has been a waste of time this evening, but I am wondering if we will get much further than we already have if we continue to use the same method of approach. As a biologist I tend to be interested in generalizations and principles that are broader than individuals and, at the human level, also broader than particular societies and cultures. Our neurologist has just suggested one way in which we might get a universal basis for talking about abnormality, and I wonder if there aren't other possibilities.

Chairman: One hears a good deal these days about "learning theory." I wonder if that would offer any hope of a solution.

Psychologist: One hesitates to push his own specialty too hard in a group like this, but I think that learning theory does indeed offer some important possibilities in this connection. I can't say that I, personally, have ever attempted to think through the problem of personal normality in terms of the principles of learning; but I believe it would be well worth trying to do so. However, I am afraid the task would be rather complicated.

Anthropologist: I want to enter a vigorous demur concerning this suggestion that we may be able to solve the problem of normality and abnormality in terms of universals. It is perfectly evident to me that normality and abnormality vary enormously from one culture to another, and in the same culture through time; and I, for one, am afraid of any attempt to set up criteria or standards for all mankind. This is a pluralistic world, and different peoples differ. Who is to say that one is right and the other wrong, the one normal and the other abnormal? Remember that the Nazis thought they had a universal set of human standards. And I want to point out that in their zeal as missionaries, members of our own society have done some things which are just about as deplorable. We have gone into simpler societies which were functioning very well and started a campaign to undermine the native culture. All too often we have succeeded, but how often—and here is the tragedy—have we been willing to accept our "converts" into our own society and way of life on an equal footing?

Psychologist: I believe you have missed the point of my last suggestion. In general terms, I agree with all you have just said, and there is nothing in my remarks which is in the least contradictory. I fully agree that, as a result of their particular socialization, human beings often learn quite different things; but, so far as we know, the basic principles governing human learning are the same the world over. We differ, in

2. The details of these studies, conducted in England by Drs. G. A. Watson and J. Shaw Bolton, are discussed in R. J. A. Berry and R. G. Gordon, *The Mental Defective* (New York: Whittlesey House, McGraw-Hill Book Co., Inc., 1931).

other words, in *what* we learn but not in *how* we learn.

Biologist: That sounds right to me. You fellows in the social sciences don't get down to biological bedrock as often as I think you ought to. But I wonder if there isn't another way, in addition to that offered by learning theory, of tackling this problem. I cannot claim to know very much about psychoanalytic theory, but I am favorably impressed by it in terms of the little I do know and am wondering if it does not give us some leads for getting out of our present difficulty.

Chairman: I notice a number of approving nods in response to what the last speaker has just said, and if there is no objection I will take it as the will of the group that at the next meeting, a week from tonight, we shall renew our attack upon the concept of normality but from the more systematic and restricted standpoints of learning theory and psychoanalytic theory.

II

Chairman: From our discussion of last week it became evident how complicated and many-sided is the problem of personal normality. I shall not attempt to summarize the many different points of view which were expressed at that time, except to say that for every way of looking at the problem which was put forward, one or more seemingly valid objections could be advanced. The only prospect of reaching any degree of uniformity in our thinking which emerged was that of identifying certain universal attributes of human beings and trying to resolve our problem in terms of them. It was agreed, you will recall, that at our meeting this evening we should explore first the psychology of learning and then see what psychoanalytic theory might have to offer in this connection. I wonder if we may therefore ask our psychologist to start the discussion.

Psychologist: I find myself somewhat embarrassed on three counts. First of all I must confess, before you point it out to me, that there is by no means universal agreement among psychologists as to what the universal principles of learning are. Nor

have learning theorists been primarily concerned with our problem here tonight. . . . You will therefore have to forgive me if I am slightly arbitrary and simply present what I personally believe to be the best-established concepts and principles in this field. My third reason for being a little uncomfortable about my role this evening is that in order to get across enough information for it to be of any real help to us, I shall have to speak at somewhat greater length than is customary in our group.

To begin with a general statement about the history of learning theory, one can say that there have been three great streams of thought in this connection: associationism, hedonism, and rationalism. These terms will immediately be familiar and meaningful to you, in a general way, so I shall proceed to speak about the contemporary, technical state of each of these three types of theory.

Modern thinking and research concerning associationism tends to be couched in the jargon of "conditioning." This, you will recall, is a method of investigation which the Russian physiologist, I. P. Pavlov (1927), developed for investigating what he called the "physiology of the highest nervous centers." In essence, it involves presenting to the subject (Pavlov worked mainly with dogs) some initially neutral stimulus, such as a buzzer or a light, which is then followed by a stimulus which can be relied upon (either reflexly or through prior learning) to produce some specified response. For example, in much of the work done in Pavlov's laboratory, the signal, or "conditioned stimulus," was presented and then shortly followed by food. The food would prompt the subject (if hungry) to respond by salivating and eating. The result of this procedure was that, after a few paired presentations of signal and food, the subject would begin to salivate to the signal alone.

This kind of learning has sometimes been called "stimulus substitution," and it is easy to see the aptness of this expression. The conditioned stimulus becomes, in a very literal sense, a substitute for the unconditioned stimulus in that it produces much the same reaction as the unconditioned stimulus. Or, to put the matter a little differently, the subject *acts as if* the CS were the UnCS. We say that the CS (buzzer) *has come to mean*, or *stand for*, the UnCS (food).

Although associative learning of this kind has certainly been known for a very long time, it was Pavlov who introduced a method for its precise, quantitative investigation; and so great was the enthusiasm with which this method was received by researchers the world over that, in their enthusiasm, they seem to have overextended the method. They began to experiment, not only with the salivary and other glandular responses, but also with skeletal responses. They found, for example, that if one sounds a buzzer and then shocks a dog on the forepaw in such a way as to elicit a flexion of the leg, after a few paired presentations of this kind the dog will flex the leg to the buzzer alone. Here, ostensibly, was another example of conditioning. But this inference has introduced no end of confusion. We now know that the thing the dog learns first in a situation of this kind is to *be afraid* when the buzzer sounds; this is certainly conditioning. But we also know, or at least strongly suspect, that paw-lifting (and many other things an animal may do in a situation of this kind) occurs, not directly in response to the conditioned stimulus, but rather as a reaction to the fear which the CS produces.

On the basis of a great deal of work which I can't begin to review here, it is becoming increasingly clear that conditioned-response learning, properly speaking, is always restricted to responses of the visceral and vascular tissues, which mediate the various so-called "emotions" and are produced by the autonomic nervous system. Skeletal responses, on the other hand, are learned on another basis.

This now leads us to a discussion of the second great principle of learning. Hedonism, as you all know, is the theory that, as Jeremy Bentham put it, "we are propelled by pleasure and repelled by pain" (1879). Contemporary thinkers who may be said to follow in this stream of thought put the matter a little differently. They say that living organisms experience discomforts, or "drives," are thrown into activity by these drives, and tend to remain active until some response is made which terminates the drive-state, or motivation. We know incontrovertibly that a response which "solves a problem" tends to get reinforced, or learned, in the sense that it will be more likely and quicker to recur when the problem which it has previously solved recurs.

You will, of course, be likely to think of E. L. Thorndike as the person who has worked most extensively with learning of this kind and who has popularized the term, Law of Effect, to characterize it (1931). But there are literally hundreds of other investigators who also know that this type of learning is a genuine phenomenon and who, in a general way at least, subscribe to Thorndike's views.

But here again there have been some oversights which have caused a great deal of confusion. For example, most demonstrations of the Law of Effect have been carried out with subjects (mainly infrahuman animals) which have been motivated by primary drives, e.g., hunger, thirst, pain, or fatigue. What has been commonly overlooked is the fact that the Law of Effect is also valid in the area of emotional problem-solving. We now know that a living organism will learn a given response or type of behavior quite as readily to the drive of fear as to that of hunger. In fact, we may even say that at the human level most of our problem-solving is directed at emotional problems, or secondary drives, rather than at the primary drives, which we manage to keep pretty well satiated most of the time.

There are other sources of misunderstanding which might be discussed, but you will find these rather fully dealt with in the technical literature (Mowrer, 1947) and we need not consider them here.

In short, then, we see that research with animals has shown that there are two great learning processes, conditioning and problem-solving; and there is abundant evidence that these processes occur in human beings no less than in the simpler organisms. But there are many writers, especially those with a more philosophical turn of mind, who have never been content with these two theories as a sufficient basis for explaining human behavior, either at its best or at its worst. These persons have insisted that there is a factor, or faculty, of *rationality* which must be prominently considered, and they have maintained that neither conditioning nor problem-solving, as such, accounts for rationality.

Some of the persons who are the loudest in their protestations on this score are persons who are simply unaware of what the principles of conditioning and problem-solving really imply, and they don't wish to sully—or, as I should prefer to say—discipline their minds by becoming fully informed on these scores. However, I should like at once to say that I admit that there is some justification in these reservations concerning learning theory. Those of us who are technically engaged in the study of learning have not, I think, devoted nearly as much time and thought as we should have to the problems and functioning of the "total personality," if I may use that hackneyed expression. I admit that there is a good deal more to human experience than our theories seem to imply, but I believe that we shall ultimately come to a real understanding of the quintessence of human personality only if we build slowly and securely upon basic principles which can be established by the tested methods of scientific inquiry. If we continue trying to understand man in a global molar manner, I can only foresee confusion being compounded with confusion (Mowrer and Ullman, 1945).

Let me now try to draw together the implications of my remarks for our discussion of the problem of personal normality and abnormality. I should like to suggest, first of all, that the normality-abnormality problem—or, if you prefer, the problem of rationality and irrationality—stems from a deep-seated conflict between the two forms of learning which I have just discussed, namely, problem-solving and conditioning. Note that problem-solving predisposes the individual to behavior which, by definition, solves his problems, makes him comfortable, gives him satisfaction and pleasure, whereas conditioning works in exactly the reverse manner. Through problem-solving behavior, the individual *lessens* his drives, whereas conditioning brings new drives into existence or intensifies old ones. It is through conditioning that fears, resentments, appetites, and other emotions are acquired; and if they are anything, they are "problems," psychologically speaking.

Psychoanalyst: There is something in what you are saying which is reminiscent of the distinction which Freud (1934a) made between the "pleasure principle" and the "reality principle." I wonder if you would agree that there is a similarity.

Psychologist: Yes, indeed. I think my main point is even recognized by the man in the street when he speaks of a neurotic or psychotic as "self-centered" and "unable to face reality." In fact, I was surprised that in the course of our discussion last week no one made any reference to the ability to "face reality" as an important, perhaps the *most* important, attribute of the normal, mature individual. Perhaps the difficulty was that we didn't know quite how to put this notion precisely. Here I think our survey of learning theory may be helpful. The "ability to face reality" is, I believe, the ability or willingness to expose oneself to such conditioning as is essential (a) to the physical survival of the individual and (b) to his social and ethical development. This ability or willingness has to be learned, at least in the case of human beings; and it has to be learned on the basis of the Law of Effect. And here is where the paradox lies and the trouble begins. In order for a human being to be regarded as "normal" in *any* society, he must have learned that the best way to safeguard his comfort and well-being *in the long run* is to "face reality," i.e., to expose himself on occasion to *present* hardship or suffering as the surest way of insuring *future* survival and satisfaction.

To the extent that lower animals may be said to behave in this far-sighted manner, they do so on a predominantly instinctual basis. But man, having been largely freed from the rigidity and fixity of instincts, has to *learn* "wisdom and virtue," either through education or through experience. In either case, it is hard to reach the point of being able to give up a sure and immediate gratification for a remote and perhaps uncertain one.

An earlier speaker referred to abnormality as "moral failure," and pointed to the social opprobrium that abnormality so commonly causes. If he is willing to define the "moral problem" as I have just done, I think I would agree with him entirely; but we ought to be sure we see all the implications which such a view has. It repudiates the concept of normality as mere averageness and makes it a matter of an ideal — full manhood and womanhood are difficult of achievement in any and every society, and the "abnormal" person is the one who hasn't "made the grade."

Philosopher: You would surely be surprised if I, as a philosopher, did not agree with what our psychologist has just said. I am not sure what his fellow psychologists will have to say about his analysis, but it will find good precedent in the thinking of many philosophers. For example, some years ago R. B. Perry published an important book, called *General Theory of Value*, (1926), in which he suggested that an action or object may be valuable or efficient, in any of three frames of reference. An action is valuable if it helps the individual to survive, i.e., if it is *adaptive*. An action is valuable if it helps the individual to experience pleasure, to become more comfortable, i.e., if it is *adjustive*. And, finally, an action is valuable if it helps the individual to reconcile, harmonize, unify the competing, conflicting demands which are made of him, i.e., if it is *integrative*. I was reminded of these three frames of reference, these three value-systems, by the remarks of the preceding speaker concerning what he referred to as *associationism, hedonism,* and *rationalism*. Although the parallelism is not perfect, yet it is noteworthy that in associative learning the emphasis is upon survival, or adaptation; in hedonism it is upon comfort, adjustment; and in integration it is upon the highest kind of mental activity, or rationality.

But what does all this have to do with the problem of normality? The answer, I think, is implicit in what our psychologist has already said. The discussion last week made it evident that the problem of normality cannot be settled statistically but must rather involve the concept of efficiency, a goal, an ideal. But last week we did not come to grips with the question: *Efficiency for what?* What I have just been saying seems to me to provide a possible answer. There are three great frames of reference in which a given action may be said to be efficient or inefficient, or, if you will, normal or abnormal; one can even say, good or evil. In the first of those frames of reference an action is efficient if it promotes the survival of the individual (and, we may add, the perpetuation of his species). In the second, an action is efficient, if it gives pleasure, provides comfort. And in the third frame of reference, an action is efficient if it is ethical, or integrative; and by "integration" I mean the process whereby conflicts, of both a personal and interpersonal nature, are reconciled and the basis laid for individual happiness and social solidarity. One of the principal reasons, I suspect, why our discussion last week appeared to be getting nowhere was that we were not clearly differentiating between these three frames of reference, and it was for this reason that whenever one person proposed a definition of normality, or "efficiency," in terms of one frame of reference, someone else, by jumping to another frame of reference, could always find what seemed like a compelling objection.

Sociologist: It seems to me that there may be a good deal in what you say, but, as philosophers are wont to do, you've put the discussion up on a high plane of abstraction. Can you make what you have just been saying more concrete and specific?

Philosopher: I am not sure that I can, but I will try. Let me first say, however, that I don't feel that I need be apologetic for the philosopher's tendency to translate problems into rather abstract terms: this is the only way in which we sometimes succeed in solving what otherwise seem to be hopeless dilemmas.

But to try, now, to do as our sociologist has just suggested, I shall have to get out of my field of professional competence; but if I err some of you will be able to correct me. From my rather cursory familiarity with psychological and clinical literature, I gather that it is commonly assumed that abnormality, or psychopathology, always involves conflict, but that conflict is not necessarily pathological. In other words, there can be normal conflict as well as abnormal conflict. What is the deciding criterion?

I suppose there can be and sometimes is conflict in human beings between the mechanisms which tend to insure man's physical survival and the mechanisms which dispose him to act in such a way as to make himself comfortable. In a book which I happened to be browsing in recently (Mowrer & Kluckhohn, 1944) I noticed that the point was made that in most instances actions which are adjustive are also adaptive, and that only in relatively rare instances is there any discrepancy. The case of a person who ate food that tasted all right and satisfied hunger but which was poisonous and killed the eater or made him very ill was given as an instance of this. But I doubt that it is conflicts of this kind that lay the basis for what we call abnormality.

I believe, rather, that it is only when we get to adjustment and integration that the plot thickens and the broth begins to boil, if I may mix my metaphors. Man's quest for comfort has taught him that in many situations the best way to be comfortable, *in the long run,* is to forego the possibility of comfort, or pleasure, at the moment. But this has always been a hard thing for man to do. It is, in a word, the moral quest, the ethical struggle — a quest, a struggle which man has never been able either to abandon or to master. And it is in this area that I, like the psychologist, think we shall find the cue to neurosis and to the symptomatic behavior which we term "abnormal."

This thought has been neatly phrased in a manner quite devoid of the philosopher's ponderous touch, in an extraordinary book entitled, *Man: An Autobiography,* which appeared a few months ago (Stewart, 1946). In it the author remarks:

"Some other qualities of the individual I would infer to be very old because I have been trying for centuries to get rid of them, and yet I have them just as much as ever, if not more — pride, vanity, envy, hypocrisy, gluttony, and indifference to the sufferings of others. On the contrary, there are some qualities which I have always been trying to develop and which I never get the hang of: for instance, self-restraint, foresight, and placidity. I am simply not in the class of the beaver or elephant or honeybee. Even the cat fills me with admiration and wonder at her patience before a mouse hole. I am more nearly of the grasshopper's persuasion" (p. 61).

Now I am really little more than a layman when it comes to the technical aspects of psychology and psychiatry, but I have a strong conviction that, philosophically, there is something seriously wrong with the modern conception of neurosis and its treatment. In keeping with the three frames of reference which I described earlier, we seem to find people questing for happiness in three different ways: through long life and good health (adaptation, survival); through the pursuit of pleasure (adjustment, tension-reduction); and by trying to become mature, adequate persons (integration). Human history seems to show that persons who spend much of their time thinking either about health or pleasure usually end up with little of either. Most men — at least most men whom we are likely to look upon as having achieved some semblance of wisdom — seem to have concluded that "pride of Character" is a much sounder guide to happiness and personal normality. This is a point of view which seems to have been largely lost sight of in recent decades. I wonder if our psychoanalyst can carry this line of thought any further?

Biologist: I, too, should like to hear what the analysts have to say in this connection; but may I interrupt with only one question? May I ask our philosopher if we are to conclude that, since the normality-abnormality problem, in his judgment, hinges upon what he has called the "ethical struggle," and since this is a struggle which individuals in every society have to face, we thus approach a universal conception of normality and abnormality and escape from some of the difficulties into which we got last week?

Philosopher: That is certainly in line with my own thinking. And I should like to add that, if my more or less intuitive judgment is any guide in the matter, the solution to the problem of neurosis lies in the direction of conquest of the moral problem, not in the abandonment of it, as I believe is at least implicit in the minds of some of our modern psychotherapists.

Chairman: These last remarks seem to me to make it more incumbent than ever upon our analyst to speak. You will recall, moreover, that last week we planned, in any event, to spend a portion of this evening discussing his specialty.

Psychoanalyst: I ought to say, first of all, that Freud often insisted that psychoanalysis was a science and that it did not lead to any particular philosophy of life (Freud, 1933), but at the same time his writings often had an unmistakable philosophical tinge (Freud, 1930); and I confess some sympathy with the point of view which has just been expressed, to the effect that you can't have an adequate theory of personality or an efficient technique of therapy unless you are willing to come to grips with the ethical problem (Mowrer, 1946). I will leave it to you to judge how well psychoanalytic theory meets these needs, and will confine myself, at least for the time being, to a purely expository role.

Last week I gave two criteria which analysts believe to be important in the identification of neurosis. This evening I don't propose to say anything very different, but I should like to put it in a different way.

At an early point in his career, Freud saw that anxiety was the crucial problem in neurosis, and he succeeded in making the whole world realize that it is futile to treat a so-called abnormal person solely on the basis of his symptoms. Consequently Freud thought and wrote a great deal about the problem of anxiety, and I shall try briefly to indicate his major contributions in this connection.

Freud's first theory of anxiety was published in a series of papers (1924a,b,c)

which appeared between 1892 and 1896. The essence of this theory was that when there is sexual frustration and repression in the life of the individual; sexual tension, or "libido," builds up to such an extent that it erupts, as it were, into the consciousness of the individual but is experienced, not as lust or passion, but as anxiety. Freud said, in fact, that it was as if the sexual impulses were thus "transformed" into anxiety. It followed as a corollary of this theory that psychotherapy should attempt to help the individual accept his own sexual impulses as a part of himself and to find satisfactory outlets for them.

Freud's second theory of anxiety, which came to complete expression many years later (Freud 1933, 1936), was in some respects much the same as the first one, although in some ways notably different. Freud started with the assumption that the individual, usually as a small child, has certain impulses, very commonly of either a sexual or hostile character. These cause him to engage in exploratory behavior—I presume a psychologist might call it trial-and-error or problem-solving behavior—as a result of which a form of gratification is found, a "fixation" is established, a "habit" formed. But this habit, or adjustment, is likely to be socially disapproved; and representatives of the child's society, usually in the form of his parents, "crack down" on him, punish him. The result is that the child, again in the words of our psychologist, becomes conditioned, i.e., when the child starts to do the forbidden act, the fear of punishment is aroused. This fear is likely to be stronger than the original impulse, with the result that when the fear is aroused the child is likely to become more intent upon reducing the fear than upon gratifying the original impulse. Obviously, the most direct way to reduce the fear is for the child to inhibit the contemplated action, i.e., resist the "temptation," as we are likely to say.

Thus far we have only a theory which accounts for the inhibition of an overt action, a theory of what Freud was likely to refer to as "supression." In this situation the individual is still aware of the original impulse, but he decides not to act upon it, not to gratify it, at least not in the way which has previously got him into trouble. But suppose, now, that the child tries other ways of satisfying his needs, and that every time he seems to find a solution, that, too, gets him into difficulty with his elders. Eventually he may decide that it is not a question of some ways of solving his problem being wrong and others being all right. It is rather that any gratification whatever of certain impulses is wrong, and from this it is but a short step to the conclusion that the impulse itself is "wrong."

I don't mean to say that the child necessarily reasons it all out in just this way. Perhaps a more accurate way to put it is to say that eventually the child gets to the point that he is afraid, not simply when he contemplates a given action, but whenever he even experiences the underlying impulse or need. At this point, says Freud, something momentous and, in a way, monstrous often happens: as a means of escaping from the fear that the impulse always arouses, the child repudiates the impulse, represses it, denies it access to consciousness. This strategy, which may be carried through with an admixture of conscious and unconscious elements, often provides a temporary, sometimes a surprisingly durable, state of peace within the individual. Freud believed, however, that a repression is always maintained at a certain cost to the individual, and that in times of crises it is likely to give way altogether. Whenever the repression is weakened and there is a danger that it will be abrogated, whenever there is danger of what Freud termed "a return of the repressed," then one experiences *anxiety;* and it is anxiety, according to Freud, which starts human beings to behaving in those self-defeating, vicious circles that we call neurosis or abnormality.

Neurologist: I think I follow what you have said, but I seem to detect in it the same ambiguity that I have always felt inherent in Freud's writings. In his first theory he said that the repression comes first and the fear, anxiety, or neurosis comes afterwards. In his second theory he seems to be saying that the fear has to be there first; then repression occurs, doesn't work very well, and the fear is experienced again. This all seems somewhat out of focus to me, but I can't say exactly why.

Psychoanalyst: I can well see why you should be a bit confused here. Unfortunately, Freud was not always entirely consistent in his use of the terms fear and anxiety, and many of his followers have been even less so. The first theory of anxiety was weak in that it had no dynamic explanation as to why the frustration and repression occur in the first place. The second theory posits fear as the cause of the repression, and up to this point we do not speak of anxiety. It is only after repression has occurred and the wish, or impulse, has been "lost sight of" that there is the possibility of anxiety. Fear always has an object; we are afraid of *something.* Anxiety, by contrast, is always objectless; we are never *anxious of* — we are *just anxious.* And it is one of the major objectives of therapy to convert anxiety into fear. This can be done — in fact many analysts believe that it can *only* be done — by the technique which Freud worked out. The individual finds what it is that he is really afraid of when he is anxious; he has "insight," as we say; and he then either sees that his fear is no longer valid, or he finds ways of achieving his adult purposes by means which do not arouse the same social disapproval to which his more infantile, immature behavior exposed him.

Chairman: I feel that this exposition must bring us very close to an explicit, and perhaps universal, theory of normality and abnormality; but I think it would be useful if the speaker could guide our thinking a little further along these lines.

Psychoanalyst: To be perfectly candid with you, I am not sure whether I can or not. It is certainly true that Freud has given us a lucid and explicit theory of anxiety, and on the basis of it one might say simply that the most normal person is the one who has the least anxiety. But I confess that I feel confused and uncomfortable when this criterion is suggested. Although we analysts have worked much more with so-called neurotics than we have with criminals or psychotic individuals, we can be pretty certain that there are a lot of criminals — "pure criminals" I like to call them (to distinguish them from the "neurotic criminals") — who probably have no more anxiety, perhaps even less, than do so-called normal persons. Does this, then, make the criminal "normal" too? We cannot, of course, be sure, but it also looks as if there were at least some types of psychotic individuals — I am thinking particularly of the simple, or "pure," schizophrenias — who are remarkably free from anxiety. But surely this does not make them "normal." Yet the fact seems to remain that, as Freud said, anxiety is "the fundamental phenomenon and the central problem of neurosis" (1936, p. 111). If anyone can throw light upon this enigma, I hope he will do so.

Layman: In this group I feel it behooves me to keep still most of the time. The only thing this leaves me to do is to listen, and that I try to do well. If I have been as careful a listener to the discussion this time and last as I have tried to be, I have heard some things that the rest of you, with your intense professional specializations and preoccupations, may have missed; and I am going to try to put these things together in such a way as may give us "closure," as I believe the Gestalt psychologists are fond of saying.

Earlier this evening our psychologist pointed out that there is a conflict between the tendencies on the part of living organisms, including man, to make problems for themselves (through conditioning) and to try to rid themselves of problems (through problem-solving). He suggested that normality might consist of a kind of balance, or equilibrium, between these two tendencies, leading to something which we may call rationality.

Our philosopher has eloquently indicated that he sees the problem as a struggle between the quest for pleasure (or problem-solving in the immediate, headlong manner of animals) and the ethical enterprise (which may be thought of as problem-solving *through* time).

Our psychoanalyst has said, by implication at least, much the same thing: neurotic conflict arises because of a clash between the individual's animal needs and propensities and the tabus and prohibitions of organized society. And, again, by implication, he has said that therapy, or normality, is achieved when a person who is overly inhibited becomes less so, strikes a kind of balance or equilibrium between restraint and gratification, such as our psychologist seems to have had in mind.

I should like to point out what I believe to be the basic misconception in psychoanalytic theory and the one which, if corrected, will do more than anything else to bring all of our views into relatively good agreement. It is a cardinal assumption of the analysts that neurotic individuals are persons in whom the socialization process has been carried too far, with the result that the individual makes more renunciations, is less demanding, and is "better" than there is any need for him to be. The analysts say that the "super-ego is too severe," and they make it the aim of therapy to lessen its tyranny.

According to this conception, the normal person may be thought of as occupying a kind of middle ground, with the criminal on his left, as an undersocialized person, and the neurotic on his right, as an oversocialized person. Therapy thus consists of trying to get the neurotic to move over a little in the direction of the criminal but to stop short of going all the way, on the middle ground of normality.

If I have properly caught the overtones of much that other members of our group have been saying, it is this: that the neurotic is not an overly-socialized, "super-normal" individual but is instead one who falls, in terms of his character development, somewhere between the criminal and the normal person. I believe that this is what our philosopher had in mind when he said that man was so far committed to the moral enterprise that his only real prospect for happiness is to pursue it, rather than to turn away from it, in the direction of criminality. And if this general point of view is correct, then psychotherapy would consist, not in trying to make a neurotic normal by urging him in the direction of criminality, but away from it. One might say, I should think, that the neurotic is a person who has "got stuck" in between, one who has the potentiality (much more than the criminal can be said to have) to become normal, but who needs a little extra help to "get over the hump."

I know the hour is late and I can imagine that many of you who are technically better qualified to speak along these lines than I am probably have a number of objections which you would like to make, but there are just two more things I would like to say and then I will stop. They are merely footnotes to what I have already said.

I do a little reading now and then in a great many different fields, and I gather in this way that psychiatrists have a kind of "wastebasket" category into which they lump persons who are neither clearly neurotic nor clearly criminal, yet who are certainly not normal. They call these persons "psychopaths," and it is acknowledged that they have some of the characteristics of both the criminal and of the neurotic; yet this mixture does not produce a normal person, as the psychoanalytic theory of personality types would lead us to expect. Note how readily this paradox disappears if you put the neurotic in between the normal individual and the criminal: since you then have the neurotic and the criminal side by side, so to say, you can naturally and easily put the psychopath in between them!

But what about the psychotic individual? Here I feel very tentative and deferential indeed; but if my fragmentary reading is any guide, I should suppose that the psychotic individual is merely a neurotic who manages his anxieties in a particular way, i.e., by retreat from and denial of reality. Since it is, in many instances, such a stable style of life, one might say that, from one point of view, it is the most "successful" type of neurosis. But this is something I shall certainly have to leave to the ultimate judgment of more competent individuals than myself.

The final thing I want to point out is that if psychiatrists, psychoanalysts, clinical psychologists, and others who purport to do psychotherapy could take the point of view concerning neurosis which I have tried to suggest, I believe it would accomplish two great things: (a) it would do much to remove the intuitive feeling on the part of many laymen that "most psychiatrists are just as crazy as their patients," and (b) it would do much to bring together the so-called modern scientific theories of human personality and the traditional philosophical and religious conceptions of man. Philosophers, theologians, and laymen alike do not, in my judgment, look with distrust upon modern clinicians because they take a naturalistic as opposed to a supernaturalistic view of human nature and its vagaries, but because clinicians tend to take, at best, an unmoral view of man and, in some instances at least, a view which one is perhaps even justified in calling antimoral.

Chairman: I am sure we are all grateful to the last speaker for his synthesis of the various lines of thought and argument which our discussions have developed. Last week, and again this evening, I have taken rather full notes on what has been said, with a view to presenting an over-all summary. But I am afraid that such a summary would be unduly long or, if I made it reasonably concise, would be so abstract as to have little meaning.

I should, however, like to restate what seems to me to be the fundamental notion at which we have arrived. We have reviewed a great many different ways in which the term "normality" is often used—in statistics, sociology, education, medicine, psychology, psychoanalysis, philosophy, theology, and other fields—but we find that no one of these usages gives us just the conception we are seeking. We find, moreover, that almost any specific action or personal characteristic which is regarded as "abnormal" in one society has been or is regarded as "normal" in another society, all of which raises the specter of "cultural relativity." But we seem to have hit upon a way of laying this ghost. We find that, regardless of the way in which the details of approved action and attitude differ from one society to another, there is one thing common to life in all societies. Every human society is organized and conducted on the basis of certain principles—which are best described as social ethics. These principles have been worked out over a long period of time, with many mistakes and much suffering. Each individual born into a human society is under pressure to adopt the approved ways of that society, and each individual experiences in the course of his own development some of the struggles, difficulties, and dilemmas which were involved in the evolution of his society. To the extent that an individual is able in his lifetime to assimilate the historically hard-won wisdom of society and to experience the fruits thereof, he may be said to be normal; to the extent that he fails, he is abnormal.

Since this is a struggle in which individuals in every society must engage, we arrive in this way at a conception of normality which is not culture-bound, and yet which takes due account of the enormous importance of the culture-assimilation process.

This is not to say, however, that slavish conformity is the touchstone of happiness and normality. It seems empirically well established that, by and large, the good men in a society are the conforming, and happy, men. Only by making one's peace with one's society and "playing the game" does one seem to achieve the kind of freedom and fulfillment that attend the good life. But it is perhaps less a matter of conformity, as such, than of *consistency*. In most instances consistency and conformity dictate the same course of action; but if, for whatever reason, nonconformity seems imperative, then openness therein and willingness to take the consequences are requisite. When nonconformity and inconsistency—in the sense of duplicity and evasion—are combined, the soil of social alienation is prepared and the seeds of personal abnormality are sown.

I assume that we hold this view with an appropriate degree of tentativeness; perhaps some of the members of our group may hardly subscribe to it at all. But when we realize that it represents the coalescence of many of the basic tenets of traditional philosophy and religion, and of much that seems soundest in modern social and psychological science, the plausibility of the position is impressive.

Thomas S. Szasz

THE MYTH OF MENTAL ILLNESS

Szasz finds that the term *mental illness* is used in two ways, both misleading. One usage expresses the view that behavior pathology is the result of disease which affects the brain. Brain disease is clearly the cause of some disorders, but to imply that mental illness is in all cases a physical dysfunction is to fuse a descriptive category—"abnormal behavior" —with an explanation. We may suspect that the desire to avoid value problems and find objective grounds for diagnosis makes this course attractive and, indeed, has led to wider public acceptance of "mental illness." However, Szasz argues that the continued application of the biological model—highly appropriate and successful in the medical field—to psychosocial disorders can only result in heightened confusion. In the other usage of the term, diagnosis is made, not on medical grounds, but "by establishing a deviance in behavior from certain psychosocial, ethical, or legal norms." Yet, Szasz points out, those who use the term in this way continue to suggest treatment by medical (and supposedly value-free) means. It is this contradiction that the rest of the paper explores. One has only to think of these societal norms as consensually affirmed values to see this paper as an important facet of the general problem of values on which these readings focus.

My aim in this essay is to raise the question "Is there such a thing as mental illness?" and to argue that there is not. Since the notion of mental illness is extremely widely used nowadays, inquiry into the ways in which this term is employed would seem to be especially indicated. Mental illness, of course, is not literally a "thing"—or physical object—and hence it can "exist" only in the same sort of way in which other theoretical concepts exist. Yet, familiar theories are in the habit of posing, sooner or later—at least to those who come to believe in them—as "objective truths" (or "facts"). During certain historical periods, explanatory conceptions such as deities, witches, and microorganisms appeared not only as theories but as self-evident *causes* of a vast number of events. I submit that today mental illness is widely regarded in a somewhat similar fashion, that is, as the cause of innumerable diverse happenings. As an antidote to the complacent use of the notion of mental illness—whether as a self-evident phenomenon, theory, or cause—let us ask this question: What is meant when it is asserted that someone is mentally ill?

In what follows I shall describe briefly the main uses to which the concept of mental illness has been put. I shall argue that this notion has outlived whatever usefulness it might have had and that it now functions merely as a convenient myth.

Mental illness as a sign of brain disease

The notion of mental illness derives its main support from such phenomena as syphilis of the brain or delirious conditions—intoxications, for instance—in which persons are known to manifest various peculiarities or disorders of thinking and behavior. Correctly speaking, however, these are diseases of the brain, not of the mind. According to one school of thought, *all* so-called mental illness is of this type. The assumption is made that some neurological defect, perhaps a very subtle one, will ultimately be found for all the disorders of thinking and behavior. Many contemporary psychiatrists, physicians, and other scientists hold this view. This position implies that people *cannot* have troubles—expressed in what are *now called* "mental illnesses"—because of differences in personal needs, opinions, social aspirations, values, and so on. *All problems in living* are attributed to physicochemical processes which in due time will be discovered by medical research.

"Mental illnesses" are thus regarded as basically no different than all other diseases (that is, of the body). The only difference, in this view, between mental and bodily diseases is that the former, affecting the brain, manifest themselves by means of mental symptoms; whereas the latter, affecting other organ systems (for example, the skin, liver, etc.), manifest themselves by means of symptoms referable to those parts of the body. This view rests on and expresses what are, in my opinion, two fundamental errors.

In the first place, what central nervous system symptoms would correspond to a skin eruption or a fracture? It would *not* be some emotion or complex bit of behavior. Rather, it would be blindness or a paralysis of some part of the body. The crux of the matter is that a disease of the brain, analogous to a disease of the skin or bone, is a neurological defect, and not a problem in living. For example, a *defect* in a person's visual field may be satisfactorily explained by correlating it with certain definite lesions in the nervous system. On the other hand, a person's *belief*—whether this be a belief in Christianity, in Communism, or in the idea that his internal organs are "rotting" and that his body is, in fact, already "dead"—cannot be explained by a defect or disease of the nervous system. Explanations of this sort of occurrence—assuming that one is interested in the belief itself and does not regard it simply as a "symptom" or expres-

From *American Psychologist*, 1960, Vol. 15, pp. 113-118. Reprinted by permission of the author and the American Psychological Association.

sion of something else that is *more interesting*—must be sought along different lines.

The second error in regarding complex psychosocial behavior, consisting of communications about ourselves and the world about us, as mere symptoms of neurological functioning is *epistemological*. In other words, it is an error pertaining not to any mistakes in observation or reasoning, as such, but rather to the way in which we organize and express our knowledge. In the present case, the error lies in making a symmetrical dualism between mental and physical (or bodily) symptoms, a dualism which is merely a habit of speech and to which no known observations can be found to correspond. Let us see if this is so. In medical practice, when we speak of physical disturbances, we mean either signs (for example, a fever) or symptoms (for example, pain). We speak of mental symptoms, on the other hand, when we refer to a patient's *communications about himself, others, and the world about him.* He might state that he is Napoleon or that he is being persecuted by the Communists. These would be considered mental symptoms *only* if the observer believed that the patient was *not* Napoleon or that he was *not* being persecuted by the Communists. This makes it apparent that the statement that "*X* is a mental symptom" involves rendering a judgment. The judgment entails, moreover, a covert comparison or matching of the patient's ideas, concepts, or beliefs with those of the observer and the society in which they live. The notion of mental symptom is therefore inextricably tied to the *social* (including *ethical*) *context* in which it is made in much the same way as the notion of bodily symptom is tied to an *anatomical* and *genetic context* (Szasz, 1957a, 1957b).

To sum up what has been said thus far: I have tried to show that for those who regard mental symptoms as signs of brain disease, the concept of mental illness is unnecessary and misleading. For what they mean is that people so labeled suffer from diseases of the brain; and, if that is what they mean, it would seem better for the sake of clarity to say that and not something else.

Mental illness as a name for problems in living

The term "mental illness" is widely used to describe something which is very different than a disease of the brain. Many people today take it for granted that living is an arduous process. Its hardship for modern man, moreover, derives not so much from a struggle for biological survival as from the stresses and strains inherent in the social intercourse of complex human personalities. In this context, the notion of mental illness is used to identify or describe some feature of an individual's so-called personality. Mental illness—as a deformity of the personality, so to speak—is then regarded as the *cause* of the human disharmony. It is implicit in this view that social intercourse between people is regarded as something *inherently harmonious*, its disturbance being due solely to the presence of "mental illness" in many people. This is obviously fallacious reasoning, for it makes the abstraction "mental illness" into a *cause*, even though this abstraction was created in the first place to serve only as a shorthand expression for certain types of human behavior. It now becomes necessary to ask: "What kinds of behavior are regarded as indicative of mental illness, and by whom?"

The concept of illness, whether bodily or mental, implies *deviation from some clearly defined norm.* In the case of physical illness, the norm is the structural and functional integrity of the human body. Thus, although the desirability of physical health, as such, is an ethical value, what health *is* can be stated in anatomical and physiological terms. What is the norm deviation from which is regarded as mental illness? This question cannot be easily answered. But whatever this norm might be, we can be certain of only one thing: namely, that it is a norm that must be stated in terms of *psychosocial*, *ethical*, and *legal* concepts. For example, notions such as "excessive repression" or "acting out an unconscious impulse" illustrate the use of psychological concepts for judging (so-called) mental health and illness. The idea that chronic hostility, vengefulness, or divorce are indicative of mental illness would be illustrations of the use of ethical norms (that is, the desirability of love, kindness, and a stable marriage relationship). Finally, the widespread psychiatric opinion that only a mentally ill person would commit homicide illustrates the use of a legal concept as a norm of mental health. The norm from which deviation is measured whenever one speaks of a mental illness is a *psychosocial and ethical one*. Yet, the remedy is sought in terms of *medical* measures which—it is hoped and assumed—are free from wide differences of ethical value. The definition of the disorder and the terms in which its remedy are sought are therefore at serious odds with one another. The practical significance of this covert conflict between the alleged nature of the defect and the remedy can hardly be exaggerated.

Having identified the norms used to measure deviations in cases of mental illness, we will now turn to the question: "Who defines the norms and hence the deviation?" Two basic answers may be offered: (*a*) It may be the person himself (that is, the patient) who decides that he deviates from a norm. For example, an artist may believe that he suffers from a work inhibition; and he may implement this conclusion by seeking help *for* himself from a psychotherapist. (*b*) It may be someone other than the patient who decides that the latter is deviant (for example, relatives, physicians, legal authorities, society generally, etc.). In such a case a psychiatrist may be hired by others to do something *to* the patient in order to correct the deviation.

These considerations underscore the importance of asking the question "Whose agent is the psychiatrist?" and of giving a candid answer to it (Szasz, 1956, 1958). The psychiatrist (psychologist or nonmedical psychotherapist), it now develops, may be the agent of the patient, of the relatives, of the school, of the military services, of a business organization, of a court of law, and so forth. In speaking of the psychiatrist as the agent of these persons or organizations, it is not implied that his values concerning norms, or his ideas and aims concerning the proper nature of remedial action, need

to coincide exactly with those of his employer. For example, a patient in individual psychotherapy may believe that his salvation lies in a new marriage; his psychotherapist need not share this hypothesis. As the patient's agent, however, he must abstain from bringing social or legal force to bear on the patient which would prevent him from putting his beliefs into action. If his *contract* is with the patient, the psychiatrist (psychotherapist) may disagree with him or stop his treatment; but he cannot engage others to obstruct the patient's aspirations. Similarly, if a psychiatrist is engaged by a court to determine the sanity of a criminal, he need not fully share the legal authorities' values and intentions in regard to the criminal and the means available for dealing with him. But the psychiatrist is expressly barred from stating, for example, that it is not the criminal who is "insane" but the men who wrote the law on the basis of which the very actions that are being judged are regarded as "criminal." Such an opinion could be voiced, of course, but not in a courtroom, and not by a psychiatrist who makes it his practice to assist the court in performing its daily work.

To recapitulate: In actual contemporary social usage, the finding of a mental illness is made by establishing a deviance in behavior from certain psychosocial, ethical, or legal norms. The judgment may be made, as in medicine, by the patient, the physician (psychiatrist), or others. Remedial action, finally, tends to be sought in a therapeutic—or covertly medical—framework, thus creating a situation in which *psychosocial*, *ethical*, and/or *legal deviations* are claimed to be correctible by (so-called) *medical action*. Since medical action is designed to correct only medical deviations, it seems logically absurd to expect that it will help solve problems whose very existence had been defined and established on nonmedical grounds. I think that these considerations may be fruitfully applied to the present use of tranquilizers and, more generally, to what might be expected of drugs of whatever type in regard to the amelioration or solution of problems in human living.

The role of ethics in psychiatry

Anything that people *do*—in contrast to things that *happen* to them (Peters, 1958)—takes place in a context of value. In this broad sense, no human activity is devoid of ethical implications. When the values underlying certain activities are widely shared, those who participate in their pursuit may lose sight of them altogether. The discipline of medicine, both as a pure science (for example, research) and as a technology (for example, therapy), contains many ethical considerations and judgments. Unfortunately, these are often denied, minimized, or merely kept out of focus; for the ideal of the medical profession as well as of the people whom it serves seems to be having a system of medicine (allegedly) free of ethical value. This sentimental notion is expressed by such things as the doctor's willingness to treat and help patients irrespective of their religious or political beliefs, whether they are rich or poor, etc. While there may be some grounds for this belief—albeit it is a view that is not impressively true even in these regards—the fact remains that ethical considerations encompass a vast range of human affairs. But making the practice of medicine neutral in regard to some specific issues of value need not, and cannot, mean that it can be kept free from all such values. The practice of medicine is intimately tied to ethics; and the first thing that we must do, it seems to me, is to try to make this clear and explicit. I shall let this matter rest here, for it does not concern us specifically in this essay. Lest there be any vagueness, however, about how or where ethics and medicine meet, let me remind the reader of such issues as birth control, abortion, suicide, and euthanasia as only a few of the major areas of current ethicomedical controversy.

Psychiatry, I submit, is very much more intimately tied to problems of ethics than is medicine. I use the word "psychiatry" here to refer to that contemporary discipline which is concerned with *problems in living* (and not with diseases of the brain, which are problems for neurology). Problems in human relations can be analyzed, interpreted, and given meaning only within given social and ethical contexts. Accordingly, it *does* make a difference—arguments to the contrary notwithstanding—what the psychiatrist's socioethical orientations happen to be; for these will influence his ideas on what is wrong with the patient, what deserves comment or interpretation, in what possible directions change might be desirable, and so forth. Even in medicine proper, these factors play a role, as for instance, in the divergent orientations which physicians, depending on their religious affiliations, have toward such things as birth control and therapeutic abortion. Can anyone really believe that a psychotherapist's ideas concerning religious belief, slavery, or other similar issues play no role in his practical work? If they do make a difference, what are we to infer from it? Does it not seem reasonable that we ought to have different psychiatric therapies—each expressly recognized for the ethical positions which they embody—for, say, Catholics and Jews, religious persons and agnostics, democrats and communists, white supremacists and Negroes, and so on? Indeed, if we look at how psychiatry is actually practiced today (especially in the United States), we find that people do seek psychiatric help in accordance with their social status and ethical beliefs (Hollingshead & Redlich, 1958). This should really not surprise us more than being told that practicing Catholics rarely frequent birth control clinics.

The foregoing position which holds that contemporary psychotherapists deal with problems in living, rather than with mental illnesses and their cures, stands in opposition to a currently prevalent claim, according to which mental illness is just as "real" and "objective" as bodily illness. This is a confusing claim since it is never known exactly what is meant by such words as "real" and "objective." I suspect, however, that what is intended by the proponents of this view is to create the idea in the popular mind that mental illness is some sort of disease entity, like an infection or a malignancy. If this were true, one could *catch* or *get* a "mental illness," one might *have* or *harbor* it, one might *transmit* it to others, and finally one could get *rid* of it. In my opinion, there is not a shred of evidence to support this idea. To the contrary, all the evidence is the other way and supports the view that what people now call mental illnesses are for the most part *communications* expressing unacceptable ideas, often framed, moreover, in an unusual idiom. The scope of this essay allows me to do no more than mention this alternative theoretical approach to this problem (Szasz, 1957c).

This is not the place to consider in detail the similarities and differences between bodily and mental illnesses. It shall suffice for us here to emphasize only one important difference between them: namely, that whereas bodily disease refers to public, physicochemical occurrences, the notion of mental illness is used to codify relatively more private, sociopsychological happenings of which the observer (diagnostician) forms a part. In other words, the psychiatrist does not stand *apart* from what he observes, but is, in Harry Stack Sullivan's apt words, a "participant observer." This means that he is *committed* to some picture of what he considers reality — and to what he thinks society considers reality — and he observes and judges the patient's behavior in the light of these considerations. This touches on our earlier observation that the notion of mental symptom itself implies a comparison between observer and observed, psychiatrist and patient. This is so obvious that I may be charged with belaboring trivialities. Let me therefore say once more that my aim in presenting this argument was expressly to criticize and counter a prevailing contemporary tendency to deny the moral aspects of psychiatry (and psychotherapy) and to substitute for them allegedly value-free medical considerations. Psychotherapy, for example, is being widely practiced as though it entailed nothing other than restoring the patient from a state of mental sickness to one of mental health. While it is generally accepted that mental illness has something to do with man's social (or interpersonal) relations, it is paradoxically maintained that problems of values (that is, of ethics) do not arise in this process.[1] Yet, in one sense, much of psychotherapy may revolve around nothing other than the elucidation and weighing of goals and values — many of which may be mutually contradictory — and the means whereby they might best be harmonized, realized, or relinquished.

The diversity of human values and the methods by means of which they may be realized is so vast, and many of them remain so unacknowledged, that they cannot fail but lead to conflicts in human relations. Indeed, to say that human relations at all levels — from mother to child, through husband and wife, to nation and nation — are fraught with stress, strain, and disharmony is, once again, making the obvious explicit. Yet, what may be obvious may be also poorly understood. This I think is the case here. For it seems to me that — at least in our scientific theories of behavior — we have failed to *accept* the simple fact that human relations are inherently fraught with difficulties and that to make them even relatively harmonious requires much patience and hard work. I submit that the idea of mental illness is now being put to work to obscure certain difficulties which at present may be inherent — not that they need be unmodifiable — in the social intercourse of persons. If this is true, the concept functions as a disguise; for instead of calling attention to conflicting human needs, aspirations, and values, the notion of mental illness provides an amoral and impersonal "thing" (an "illness") as an explanation for *problems in living* (Szasz, 1959). We may recall in this connection that not so long ago it was devils and witches who were held responsible for men's problems in social living. The belief

---

1. Freud went so far as to say that: "I consider ethics to be taken for granted. Actually I have never done a mean thing" (Jones, 1957, p. 247). This surely is a strange thing to say for someone who has studied man as a social being as closely as did Freud. I mention it here to show how the notion of "illness" (in the case of psychoanalysis, "psychopathology," or "mental illness") was used by Freud — and by most of his followers — as a means for classifying certain forms of human behavior as falling within the scope of medicine, and hence (by *fiat*) outside that of ethics!

in mental illness, as something other than man's trouble in getting along with his fellow man, is the proper heir to the belief in demonology and witchcraft. Mental illness exists or is "real" in exactly the same sense in which witches existed or were "real."

Choice, responsibility, and psychiatry

While I have argued that mental illnesses do not exist, I obviously did not imply that the social and psychological occurrences to which this label is currently being attached also do not exist. Like the personal and social troubles which people had in the Middle Ages, they are real enough. It is the labels we give them that concerns us and, having labelled them, what we do about them. While I cannot go into the ramified implications of this problem here, it is worth noting that a demonologic conception of problems in living gave rise to therapy along theological lines. Today, a belief in mental illness implies — nay, requires — therapy along medical or psychotherapeutic lines.

What is implied in the line of thought set forth here is something quite different. I do not intend to offer a new conception of "psychiatric illness" nor a new form of "therapy." My aim is more modest and yet also more ambitious. It is to suggest that the phenomena now called mental illnesses be looked at afresh and more simply, that they be removed from the category of illnesses, and that they be regarded as the expressions of man's struggle with the problem of *how* he should live. The last mentioned problem is obviously a vast one, its enormity reflecting not only man's inability to cope with his environment, but even more his increasing self-reflectiveness.

By problems in living, then, I refer to that truly explosive chain reaction which began with man's fall from divine grace by partaking of the fruit of the tree of knowledge. Man's awareness of himself and of the world about him seems to be a steadily expanding one, bringing in its wake an ever larger *burden of understanding* (an expression borrowed from Susanne Langer, 1953). *This*

burden, then, *is to be expected and must not be misinterpreted.* Our only *rational* means for lightening it is *more understanding*, and appropriate *action* based on such understanding. The main alternative lies in acting as though the burden were not what in fact we perceive it to be and taking refuge in an outmoded theological view of man. In the latter view, man does not fashion his life and much of his world about him, but merely lives out his fate in a world created by superior beings. This may logically lead to pleading nonresponsibility in the face of seemingly unfathomable problems and difficulties. Yet, if man fails to take increasing responsibility for his actions, individually as well as collectively, it seems unlikely that some higher power or being would assume this task and carry this burden for him. Moreover, this seems hardly the proper time in human history for obscuring the issue of man's responsibility for his actions by hiding it behind the skirt of an all-explaining conception of mental illness.

Conclusions

I have tried to show that the notion of mental illness has outlived whatever usefulness it might have had and that it now functions merely as a convenient myth. As such, it is a true heir to religious myths in general, and to the belief in witchcraft in particular; the role of all these belief-systems was to act as *social tranquilizers*, thus encouraging the hope that mastery of certain specific problems may be achieved by means of substitutive (symbolic-magical) operations. The notion of mental illness thus serves mainly to obscure the everyday fact that life for most people is a continuous struggle, not for biological survival, but for a "place in the sun," "peace of mind," or some other human value. For man aware of himself and of the world about him, once the needs for preserving the body (and perhaps the race) are more or less satisfied, the problem arises as to what he should do with himself. Sustained adherence to the myth of mental illness allows people to avoid facing this problem, believing that mental health, conceived as the absence of mental illness, automatically insures the making of right and safe choices in one's conduct of life. But the facts are all the other way. It is the making of good choices in life that others regard, retrospectively, as good mental health!

The myth of mental illness encourages us, moreover, to believe in its logical corollary: that social intercourse would be harmonious; satisfying, and the secure basis of a "good life" were it not for the disrupting influences of mental illness or "psychopathology." The potentiality for universal human happiness, in this form at least, seems to me but another example of the I-wish-it-were-true type of fantasy. I do not believe that human happiness or well-being on a hitherto unimaginably large scale, and not just for a select few, is possible. This goal could be achieved, however, only at the cost of many men, and not just a few being willing and able to tackle their personal, social, and ethical conflicts.

This means having the courage and integrity to forego waging battles on false fronts, finding solutions for substitute problems — for instance, fighting the battle of stomach acid and chronic fatigue instead of facing up to a marital conflict.

Our adversaries are not demons, witches, fate, or mental illness. We have no enemy whom we can fight, exorcise, or dispel by "cure." What we do have are *problems in living* — whether these be biologic, economic, political, or sociopsychological. In this essay I was concerned only with problems belonging in the last mentioned category, and within this group mainly with those pertaining to moral values. The field to which modern psychiatry addresses itself is vast, and I made no effort to encompass it all. My argument was limited to the proposition that mental illness is a myth, whose function it is to disguise and thus render more palatable the bitter pill of moral conflicts in human relations.

M. Brewster Smith

"MENTAL HEALTH" RECONSIDERED: A SPECIAL CASE
OF THE PROBLEM OF VALUES IN PSYCHOLOGY

This article presents an approach to the value problems in the definition of normal and abnormal behavior. Smith proposes, first of all, that the psychologist (and to this we can add more generally the educated person) has the right—indeed it can be considered a responsibility—to make his values known and to persuade others to share them. Second, he suggests two techniques for such persuasion: (a) "try to open . . . new ways of seeing things," and (b) "give . . . evidence that the position . . . on a particular value has consequences for other values to which [one] is also committed." The moral philosopher, with his knowledge of history and culture, is best suited to employ the first strategy, whereas the behavioral scientist is especially qualified to utilize the second method of persuasion. Finally, Smith's resolution of the problem of itemizing the characteristics of the "good" life—of defining positive mental health—is to abandon the pursuit as fruitless. He argues that we should stop trying to conceptualize mental health as a unitary entity and advises instead the scientific study of "specific evaluative dimensions of human functioning." In his practice, the psychologist is urged to state his value orientation explicitly, so as not to disguise it with the cloak of scientific authority.

The signs are increasingly clear that "mental health" and its complement, "mental illness," are terms that embarrass psychologists. Many of us do not like them (cf. APA, 1959). Unable to define or to conceptualize them to our satisfaction, we use the terms in spite of ourselves, since they label the goals, however nebulous, of many of our service activities and the auspices of much of our research support. Even when we try to avoid them, we are swept along in the social movement of which they are shibboleths, and our scruples make little difference. Little wonder, then, that we and our colleagues in the other "mental health professions" seek to clear our consciences by continuing to engage in sporadic attempts to give them more precise and explicit meaning.

Having contributed from time to time to this discussion, I feel entitled to some skepticism about where it has got us. True, we have made some gains in disposing of several unprofitable ways of thinking about mental health that used to be prevalent. We have come to see that statistical notions of "normality" are no real help in giving psychological meaning to mental health and illness: they beg the question or fail to come to grips with it. We have become suspicious of the once regnant concept of adjustment, as it has fallen into disrepute at the hands of social critics and moralists (e.g., Riesman, 1950) who see it as a pseudoscientific rationalization for conformist values, and of psychological theorists (e.g., White, 1959) who are challenging the sufficiency of the equilibrium model in which it is rooted. And from many quarters we encounter the call for a more positive view of mental health than is involved in the mere absence of manifest mental disorder. Since the appearance of Jahoda's useful book (1958) that reviewed the considerable array of proposals toward such a conception of optimal human functioning, the flow of suggestions has not abated. The discussion goes on in articles, conferences, and symposia, with little evidence of consensus in the offing.

The various lists of criteria that have been proposed for positive mental health reshuffle overlapping conceptions of desirable functioning without attaining agreement — or giving much promise that agreement can be reached. The inventories repeat themselves, and indeed it is inevitable that they should, since each successor list is proposed by a wise psychologist who scrutinizes previous proposals and introduces variations and emphases to fit his own values and preferences. Some give greater weight to the cognitive values of accurate perception and self-knowledge (e.g., Jahoda, 1955); some to moral values, to meaningful commitment, to social responsibility (e.g., Allport, 1960; Shoben, 1957); some to working effectiveness (e.g., Ginsburg, 1955); some to the blander social virtues (e.g., aspects of Foote & Cottrell, 1955); some to zest, exuberance, and creativity (e.g., Maslow, 1954). The terms recur, but in different combinations and with connotations that slant in divergent directions. By way of illustration, Table 1 gives the six headings under which Jahoda (1958) organized the proposals for mental health criteria that she encountered in her review of the literature, and Allport's most recent proposal (1960), rearranged to bring out correspondences and discrepancies in the two lists. While it is an advance that psychologists are now looking for multiple criteria of good functioning rather than seeking the single touchstone of a unitary definition of mental health, we may well ask: How are psychologists to decide what items belong in such a list? By what warrant may we assign priorities to alternative criteria? Surely we need something closer to *terra firma* on which to build our research, from which to guide our practice.

There is little to be gained, I think, from adding to these competing lists. Conceptual clarification, on the other hand, may be more profitable, and my attempt in the present essay lies in that direction. Starting from the now prevalent recognition that mental health is an evaluative term, that personal and social values as standards of the preferable are somehow crucially in-

From *American Psychologist*, 1961, Vol. 16, pp. 299-306. Reprinted by permission of the author and the American Psychological Association.

Table 1 *Two illustrative conceptions of positive mental health in terms of multiple criteria*

Jahoda (1958)	Allport (1960)
attitudes toward the self	self-objectification
growth and self-actualization	ego-extension
integration	unifying philosophy of life
autonomy	
perception of reality	realistic coping skills, abilities, and perceptions
environmental mastery	
	warm and deep relation of self to others
	compassionate regard for all living creatures

Note.—Rubrics rearranged to bring out parallels.

volved in any discourse about mental health, I try first to show that this intrusion of values into psychology, lamented by some, applauded by others, is entirely legitimate. But I question, secondly, whether there is any profit in the argument about which evaluative criteria for appraising human personality and behavior are to be included in a concept of mental health. Rather, I suggest that, at least in the present stage of personality theory, "mental health" should not be regarded as a theoretical concept at all, but as a rubric or chapter heading under which fall a variety of evaluative concerns. I try to show that such a view of the term may help to clear the ground for both practical and theoretical purposes.

In an earlier effort (1959) at clarification in this area, I observed that at the crux of the difficulty of assimilating "mental health" to psychology is the fact that "science has not yet learned how to deal surefootedly with values" (p. 673). Any progress toward clarity in psychological thinking about mental health, I am increasingly convinced,

depends on our becoming clearer, as psychologists, about how we are to think about values. Whatever advances we make on the problem of values in this setting should also stand us in good stead in other contexts where issues of value confront psychology. The value problem is worth a close and sustained look.

Why the search for a value-laden conception of positive mental health?

While evaluative criteria and judgments are involved in the notion of mental disorder, our consensus about what is *un*desirable is close enough for practical purposes that the role of values tends to remain implicit. It is when we want to talk about positive criteria of psychological functioning that we encounter the value problem head on. A good starting point for the present discussion, then, is to ask why we ever got ourselves into this difficult, intellectually treacherous business of positive mental health. Are not the problems of mental disorder enough? Why should the mental health movement be impelled, as it has been since the days of Clifford Beers (cf. Joint Commission on Mental Illness and Health, 1961), to extend itself to concern with the "mental hygiene" of promoting positive mental health—in the absence of firm knowledge or clear guidelines?

The answer to such a question cannot be simple. But I think a generally critical onlooker from England, R. S. Peters (1960), has hit the essential point when he addressed the BBC audience thus:

"We have a highly specialized society and we are often warned that we are developing not merely two nations but a league of nations without a common culture and shared ideals. This should not surprise us; for where are such unifying ideals to be fostered? The study of literature, history, and the classics has had to be cut down to make room for the vast expansion in scientific education without which our society cannot survive, and the Church is rapidly losing the authority it once had as a source of unifying ideals. We tend to treat the doctor who looks after our bodies and the psychiatrist who advises us about our minds with more respect than we treat the priest who advises us about our souls — if we still think we have one. For they are scientists; and it is scientists who are now coming to be thought of as the repositories of wisdom about the mysteries of life.

"This general trend explains why the educationist sometimes inclines his ear towards a new expert, the psychologist, when he is at a loss to find new unifying educational ideals to replace the old religious ones. There is thus much talk in educational circles of "the mental health of the child," "wholeness," "integration," "adjustment," and all that sort of thing. We no longer talk of turning out Christian gentlemen; we talk of letting people develop mental health or mature personalities. Indeed in America Freud's priestly role is much more explicitly acknowledged. . . . Nevertheless the general trend is [also] with us, as is shown in the frequent references to psychological notions such as "mental health" in discussion about educational ideals" (p. 46).

Discount the bias of perspective arising from Peters' assured stance in the tradition of British class education, and hold in abeyance reaction to his critical undertones: his point remains that a good many thoughtful people have turned, appropriately or otherwise, to notions of mental health in order to fill a void left by the attrition of traditionally or religiously sanctioned values. There is consumer demand for psychologists to enter the discussion of goals and aspirations for human behavior; but we had better be clear about our warrant for doing so.

The demand for a psychologically informed phrasing of objectives — for conceptions of positive mental health — comes most compellingly from those concerned with the rearing and education of children. The psychologist or psychiatrist who mainly deals with hospitalized psychotics has enough to do in trying to treat severe mental disorder and get his patients to function at some minimally adequate level; since consensus on these objectives is immediately given, the value problem hardly rises to the surface. But responsibility for the raising of children calls for positive criteria against which the success of one's efforts on their behalf can be measured. Perhaps a counselor may appropriately leave it to his adult client to set the goals for his therapy; the case can hardly be extended to the child as ward of teacher and parent — who in turn look to the psychologist for guidance.

Of course there are intellectual positions from which the responsibility appears to be minimized. If you take a Rousseau-like view that regards optimal development as the unfolding of a benign inner potential, you can at least pretend to leave goal setting entirely to the child's own nature. This doctrine of benign potentiality, which is still very much alive in educational and psychological theory (witness Maslow, 1954), strikes me as involving psychological half-truths and philosophical error. It is we ourselves, in terms of our tacit values, who single out, as optimal, one of an infinite set of possible environments for the developing child, and distinguish the way he develops in such an auspicious setting as the actualization of a naturally given potential. We ignore the infinite variety of other developmental trends that he simultaneously has the potential to actualize, many of which we would not think highly of — and ignore the silent and therefore not fully responsible intrusion of our own values involved in distinguishing one class of possible trends as self-actualizing.

Another way of minimizing responsibility for educational goal setting in terms of mental health is to accept as ultimate the values of the culture, to define the function of education as cultural transmission and, in effect, leave matters of value-choice to parents and school board. The trouble is that this option is no longer really available, even if we prefer it. The state of affairs evoked by Peters is with us: there is no longer such a solid traditional consensus for us to fall back on. Parents and school boards too are confused and involved in the fray. Under these circumstances education can hardly avoid a complex role that combines and balances cultural transmission, on the one hand, and social criticism and reconstruction on the other. This characteristic American philosophy of education has thus become virtually a policy of necessity. It calls for clear-headedness about goals, and has tended to draw on psychology for their formulation.

Insofar as we take the requirements of education seriously, then, we cannot help trying to grapple with conceptions of optimal human functioning. We also need them in planning and assessing programs of counseling and of environmental change. In the face of a waning consensus on traditional values, we join our lay clientele in hoping that psychology can help in this endeavor. But hope does not guarantee success. The strength of our needs may head us the more rigidly down blind alleys, unless we have our wits about us.

The value problem

The skeptical reader imbued with the distinction between scientific objectivity, on the one hand, and the humanistic cultivation of values on the other will have balked at an earlier point, and stayed with the question: By what warrant do psychologists assume the right to posit any set of human values, as we do when we propose criteria of positive mental health? The psychologist has no more right to do so, he will say, than anyone else. Let him stick to his last, and recognize the limits of his competence. My serious rejoinder, which requires somewhat of a detour to develop, reverses this conventional view: the psychologist has *as much* right to posit values as anyone else, in some important respects more. It is time to dispel the shopworn bromide that the humanist (or moralist or philosopher) has a corner on pronouncements about values, while the psychologist (or sociologist or scientist generally) must restrict himself to facts. Things are just not that simple.

For most of us, the two sources to which everyone once looked for what were then regarded as "absolute" values—Tradition and Theology—speak only equivocally if at all. We are still suffering from the crisis

of personal and social readjustment occasioned by this loss. As we regain our bearings, our nostalgia for the old illusion of Absoluteness, of givenness in the eternal scheme of things, begins to fade. But in spite of the pessimism of those who hunger after Absoluteness, we still have values, in the sense of personal standards of desirability and obligation. We see them, now, as committing choices that people make (often unwittingly) in the interplay of cultural tradition and individual experience. We see them as "relative," yes, but relative not only to culture (an exclusive focus on *cultural* relativism was the mistake of the last generation of anthropologists). They are relative also to human nature—in the diverse varieties of this nature that have emerged in human history with a degree of continuity and cumulativeness—and relative to the opportunities and limitations of human situations. Thus the warrior virtues held validity for the traditional Sioux; for the reservation Sioux they no longer make any sense (MacGregor, 1946). And one can fairly doubt whether the petty competitive values of the Alorese studied by Cora DuBois (1944) ever made much sense: she showed them to be part and parcel of a wretched and demeaning way of life that I doubt whether any Alorese would choose were some magic to give him a wider range of opportunity.

If values are social products, they rest, ultimately, on a personal commitment. Everybody, scientist or humanist or man in the street, has the right to posit values. And, since people in society are interdependent, everyone has a right to try to persuade others to his ways of valuing: *de gustibus non disputandum est* may apply to tastes and preferences, but it has never prevented controversy about values, as the course of human history well reveals. We *all* have the right to dispute values, and most of us do it. The humanist and the humane scientist nevertheless have potentially different specialized roles in the argument.

Their roles arise from the peculiar nature of argument about values that follows from the basis of values in an optional personal commitment. If you want to persuade someone to value something as you do, you can follow one of at least two strategies (assuming that physical or social coercion is ruled out, which historically has unfortunately not been the case): You can, first, try to open his eyes to new ways of seeing things—increase the range of possibilities of which he is aware, create the conditions for differentiations and restructurings in his experience from which it is possible (not necessary) that, seeing things like yourself, he may come to value them likewise. Or, second, you can give him evidence that the position he takes on a particular value has consequences for other values to which he is also committed. For the fact that values rest on a personal option does not make them arbitrary in the sense of being detached from cause or consequence. If you show a person that his chosen value of racial purity conflicts with the values of the American Creed that he also embraces, he *may* reconsider it (Myrdal, 1944). Or if you show him that his prejudiced value rests causally on evasive covert tactics of defense against inner weakness, you again have a chance to win out (Adorno, Frenkel-Brunswik, Levinson, & Sanford, 1950). The *ad hominem* argument, in ill favor as it is, is fair play in this peculiar and important realm, so long as it is not taken as conclusive. Since values rest on personal option, *no* argument is conclusive, though many can be persuasive, and appropriately so.

I am thus suggesting that the humanist and the moral philosopher are especially equipped to employ the first of these strategies: drawing on the fund of human history and culture, with its stock of transmitted discriminations, they can sensitize us to differentiations and potentialities of human experience which, unaided, we could never attain individually. Our value choices are enriched and modified by this exposure. The second strategy, that of displaying the causal network in which value choice is embedded, is one for which the humane or behavioral scientist is uniquely qualified.

The old myth had it that man lost his precultural innocence when, biting the fruit of the Tree of Knowledge, he became aware of Good and Evil. In becoming modern, Man has taken a second portentous bite of the same fruit. There are alternative versions of Good and Evil, he discovers to his discomfiture, and it is up to him to choose the commitments he is to live by. From this emerging view that can no longer turn to authoritative interpretations of tradition or divine revelation to resolve questions of value, it makes no sense at all for us to encyst ourselves behind a pass-the-buck notion that we can leave value judgments to some other discipline that specializes in them. There is no discipline that has this mythical competence: the humanist and the theologian speak with no greater authority than we. We are all in it together.

The list problem

I think I have shown the legitimacy, the clear warrant, for psychologists to concern themselves with values, as we do when we involve ourselves with mental health. But my argument gives no help at all on the other problem: what value dimensions are to get on our lists of mental health criteria, and why? If anything, it makes things more difficult. For if values are matters of a committing personal option, how are psychologists—let alone people at large—to come to agree on any particular list any more closely than the limited extent to which they already do? Even with a richer exposure to the humanistic tradition than is customary for psychologists, even with a far more adequate fund of causal knowledge than is presently available, psychological "experts" are not going to agree on the proper goals for human nature, and these are what we are talking about.

The actual situation is well typified by the experience of the Cornell Conference (National Assembly on Mental Health Education, 1960). To quote the conference report:

"Everyone at Cornell seemed to agree that the good life for all was to be desired. They split, however, on what that good life was—as they had split on the definition of mental health, and they split on who, if anyone, should have the right to try to 'impose' it on others" (p. 20).

The definition of mental health, of course, *involves* a conception of the good life, which nobody *can* impose on anyone else (barring "brainwashing" and physical coercion), though, at least among colleagues and equals, it is fair enough for each of us to try to persuade the rest.

But the time has come to cut the Gordian knot, to restructure the problem along more profitable lines. The place to cut, I think, is the notion that the lists we have been considering itemize criteria of some entity called "positive mental health," and are equivalent to a definition of it. Even though we may have forsaken the view of mental health as a unitary phenomenon, and may have no intention of adding up a single score across our multiple criteria, we remain beguiled by the assumption that an articulate theoretical concept or construct of mental health lurks somewhere ready to be discovered. It is the pursuit of this will-of-the-wisp that has made the procession of lists of mental health criteria so fruitless.

As we actually study effective functioning —or commit ourselves to social or educational programs that seek in various ways to promote it—our focus then becomes, not "mental health" variously indexed, but any or all of a number of much more specific evaluative dimensions of human functioning: any that we are ready to commit ourselves to take seriously as relevant and valued potential psychological outcomes of the programs that we are working with, any that we can begin to pin down in operational terms, as many of them as seem important to us and as we can feasibly cope with. Here I find myself in essential agreement with the position recently taken by Levine and Kantor (1960).

From the standpoint of research, the problem of attaining consensus on criteria is thus scaled down to the workaday dimensions we are used to: the practical difficulty of trying to convince at least some of our colleagues to study some of the same things we are studying by similar methods, so that our results can dovetail or add up. There is no reason at all why study of the causes, consequences, and interrelations of stand-ing on various mental health dimensions has to await consensus on a common list that may never be attained—and by my personal value commitments would not even be desirable!

In the long run, it is possible that our understanding of interrelated system properties of personality may advance to a point that warrants a more theoretical conception of mental health—one related, say, to empirically based estimates of such properties as self-maintenance, growth, and resilience (cf. Smith, 1959). We are certainly still far from being able to envision such a conception except in the most schematic terms. But if it is to be attained at all, the road to it should lie through nonevaluative research on personality development and functioning, on the one hand, and, on the other, through the strategy I have just been advocating: modestly exploring the empirical correlates of valued attributes of personality.

But what of the public demands for mental health "expertese" with which we started? What implications does our analysis have for the role of the psychologist in school, clinic, or consulting room? The very fact that no simple rule book of prescribed conduct seems to follow from it gives me greater confidence in the appropriateness of the approach we have taken.

Knowing that he lacks a scientifically sanctioned single set of mental health criteria, the psychologist in his consulting or service or educational relationships will hesitate to prescribe the nature of the good life to others in the name of psychology. Since values rest on a personal option, he will find it easiest to keep a clear scientific and professional conscience when he can use his knowledge and skill to help others identify, clarify, and realize their value commitments—provided that he can reconcile them with the values that he himself is committed to. Yet his own psychologically informed personal commitments about the nature of good human functioning cannot exist in a vacuum. They may lead him to avoid or to terminate service relationships that appear to violate them, to seek relationships that promote them. When his role as teacher or therapist vests him with more direct and personal responsibility for goal setting, he will not hesitate to act in terms of his convictions about what is desirable in the relationship and of the best knowledge and wisdom he can muster. But he will seek to move such relationships in the direction of increasing the responsibility of the other party for choosing his own goals. To his colleagues in and out of psychology and to various publics, he may often appear as an advocate of particular values. But his advocacy will consist in displaying the nature of his personal commitment and of using his psychological knowledge and insight to explore the linkage between holding or attaining a value and its conditions and consequences. In a word, explicitness about values goes with responsible scientific and professional behavior, and when we are explicit about such values as truthfulness, competence, care, responsibility, creativity, we add nothing consequential by labeling them as dimensions or criteria of positive mental health.

Mental health as a rubric

If "mental health" is to lose its presumptive conceptual standing, what does its status become? I see it rather as a rubric, a chapter title, a label for the common concern of various disciplines involved in evaluating human functioning from the perspective of the psychology of personality. Its usefulness in this respect does not depend on its dubious status as a theoretical concept. As chapter title, "mental health" is analogous to "mechanics" in classical physics: a rubric under which we treat a number of theoretical constructs (e.g., mass, force, velocity) and the laws relating them. You do not argue very violently about where chapter boundaries should be drawn.

There remain many meaningful problems concerning the contents and organization of such a chapter, even about its name. Personally, I agree with Levine and Kantor (1960) and with Szasz (1960)* that the term "mental health" is unfortunate for our present purposes, biasing the issues as it does toward a model of physical health and illness that seems quite inappropriate to the analysis of effective and disordered conduct. But with the focus shifted to specific evaluative dimensions, I do not find myself caring very much about this argument, any more than I worry about the chapter titles in a book of applied science. This is an editorial problem, not a substantive one.

As for the contents of the mental health chapter, a variety of pragmatic considerations come to mind to assist in culling, augmenting, and refining the items in the available lists. Candidates for treatment as dimensions of mental health or of goodness of psychological functioning might be expected to meet most of the following criteria, none of which seems to require elaborate justification:

1. They should be serious contenders in the arena of human values (though an impossible consensus is of course not required). The posited value should be explicit.

2. They should be capable of measurement or of inference from identifiable aspects of behavior.

3. They should articulate with personality theory (a weak requirement, since the proviso must be added immediately that personality theories will probably need to be extended and modified to make contact with value dimensions chosen on other grounds).

4. They should be relevant to the social context for which the chapter is being written. In the context of education, for instance, this is to ask: What kinds of psychological assets would we like to see the schools develop in our children? Quite different considerations would come to the fore in the context of a correctional agency. Considerations such as these make it unlikely that the entire range of moral, esthetic, and cognitive values will vie for inclusion in the mental health chapter. But no harm is done if a venturesome soul decides to study the natural history of some

*[This article appears in the present volume. Ed.]

utterly "unpsychological" value under mental health auspices.

A more fundamental choice concerns short vs. long versions of the chapter: in other words, minimal vs. extended conceptions of mental health. I can illustrate this choice best if I introduce at the same time a possible principle for organizing the chapter. Jahoda (1958) observed that "one has the option of defining mental health in at least two ways: as a relatively constant and enduring function of the personality. . . . or as a momentary function of personality and situation" (pp. 7-8). Klein (1960) makes a similar point in his distinction between soundness or general stability, and well-being. We want, that is, to distinguish, on the one hand, the person's present state and behavior as an interactive resultant of his personality and features of the momentary situation that he confronts, and, on the other, the corresponding dispositions of his present personality, with situational effects discounted. Add a time dimension—here in terms of an assessment of mental health in childhood with prognosis to adulthood, since a primary ingredient of our interest in the mental health of children is the foundation it is assumed to provide for adult functioning—and minimal vs. extended views of mental health may be illustrated as in Table 2.

Table 2 *Illustration of narrow and broad conceptions of mental health*

Scope	Mental Health of Child		Adult Prognosis
	Present Behavior	Present Disposition	
Minimal Conception	Freedom from incapacitating symptoms	Good resistance to stress	Absence of mental disorder in adulthood
Extended Conception	Momentary well-being (in specified respects)	Capacities for competent happy, zestful, etc. child life	Capacities for competent, happy, zestful, etc. adult life

To me, this way of mapping the contents of the chapter seems clarifying. As I look at the top row, the narrow conception of the scope of mental health seems thoroughly viable. I am led to think that Jahoda (1958) may have dismissed this version too quickly, that the psychiatrist Walter Barton in his postscript to her volume was certainly right about its relevance and adequacy for the context of institutional psychiatry. But as I compare the top and bottom lines, I agree with her that the narrow version of the chapter is not in itself adequate to the evaluative concerns of education—to pick one relevant context with which psychologists are involved. And it is of course the bottom line, the extended version, that potentially expands greatly as various dimensions of good functioning are specified. Comparison of the two lines reminds me to agree with Clausen (1956) that we know very little about their relationship to one another: no longer regarding mental health as a theoretical concept, we have no particular reason to expect resistance to mental disorder to correlate with various aspects of positive functioning, but the problem calls for research. And finally, the presence of the right-hand column calls to mind how little we know about the continuities of behavior seen in evaluative terms.

So long as we grope futilely toward a *concept* of "mental health," minimal or maximal, the advantages of specificity and researchability appear to be on the side of the minimal conception. Viewing these versions as different locations of chapter boundary lines, however, we can be as specific as we want about our positively valued criteria. It may well turn out to be the case, then, that the extended version includes the valued dimensions of behavior and personality that are most responsive to our interventions. "Mental health promotion" in this sense may not be as impractical as some of us have come to assume.

Conclusion

Where has this analysis of "mental health" as a problem of values led us? It may free us, I hope, from some of the embarrassment that has motivated psychologists' attempts to treat it as a theoretical concept — attempts that have not been additive and have not made the term theoretically respectable. If we understand "mental health" not as an unsatisfactory and vague theoretical concept but as a reasonably adequate rubric or label for an evaluative psychological perspective on personality — even though the term is not of our own choosing — we can get about our business without wasting our efforts on the search for consensus on a unique set of mental health criteria when consensus is not to be had.

Under this rubric, our business, be it research or service, is properly concerned with specific valued dimensions or attributes of behavior and personality. In our focus on these dimensions we are not at all handicapped by the lack of a satisfactory conceptual definition of mental health.

Nor need we be embarrassed by the intrusion of values in our focus on various specified aspects of desirable or undesirable psychological functioning. What is to be avoided is the *surreptitious* advocacy of values disguised under presumptive scientific auspices. The list of psychological desiderata that psychologists have continued to propose, each reflecting the value commitments of its proponent, have this drawback insofar as they are offered as "criteria of positive mental health." But there is nothing surreptitious, nothing illegitimate, in using evaluative dimensions such as those that appear on these lists to appraise behavior and personality, so long as the value position one takes is explicit. And there is much to be gained from psychological study of the empirical antecedents, consequences, and interrelations of realizing different values in the sphere of personality.

In the study of optimal human functioning, I have argued, behavioral and social scientists can put their special qualifications to work toward the clarification of values among which people must choose and of the causal relations that are relevant to value choice. From it we should not only increase our knowledge about ways and means of attaining the values we agree on; we should also bring to light factual relationships that have a bearing on our choice of what values to pursue, individually and socially. To the extent that the behavioral sciences develop in this direction, they contribute to providing a badly needed bridge between what C. P. Snow (1959) has called "the two cultures" of the scientists and the humanistic intellectuals.

Ruth Benedict

ANTHROPOLOGY AND THE ABNORMAL

Societies specify certain behavior patterns
as acceptable and even commendable and con-
demn others as undesirable and "sick."
Immersed in our own culture, we usually find
that our personal values are compatible with
the values of our society. This makes it easy to
view adjustment to society as desirable. But
the implications of this view are seen more
clearly when we separate our personal values
from cultural ones by looking at other societies.
Consider, for example, whether adjustment to
society would necessarily have been indicative
of mental health in Nazi Germany. But consider also how dependent we are on our culture
and how much strain and doubt result from
conflict with it. A behavior pattern that is
condemned by society is likely to lead to stress
and breakdown. In other cultures, behavior
that is praised in our society may be censured
as unhealthy, while behavior we find symptomatic of psychological disturbance is accepted
or even highly valued. It is with this larger
cultural perspective on the problem of evaluating behavior that Benedict's paper is concerned.

Modern social anthropology has become more and more a study of the varieties and common elements of cultural environment and the consequences of these in human behavior. For such a study of diverse social orders primitive peoples fortunately provide a laboratory not yet entirely vitiated by the spread of a standardized world-wide civilization. Dyaks and Hopis, Fijians and Yakuts are significant for psychological and sociological study because only among these simpler peoples has there been sufficient isolation to give opportunity for the development of localized social forms. In the higher cultures the standardization of custom and belief over a couple of continents has given a false sense of the inevitability of the particular forms that have gained currency, and we need to turn to a wider survey in order to check the conclusions we hastily base upon this near-universality of familiar customs. Most of the simpler cultures did not gain the wide currency of the one which, out of our experience, we identify with human nature, but this was for various historical reasons, and certainly not for any that gives us as its carriers a monopoly of social good or of social sanity. Modern civilization, from this point of view, becomes not a necessary pinnacle of human achievement but one entry in a long series of possible adjustments.

These adjustments, whether they are in mannerisms like the ways of showing anger, or joy, or grief in any society, or in major human drives like those of sex, prove to be far more variable than experience in any one culture would suggest. In certain fields, such as that of religion or of formal marriage arrangements, these wide limits of variability are well known and can be fairly described. In others it is not yet possible to give a generalized account, but that does not absolve us of the task of indicating the significance of the work that has been done and of the problems that have arisen.

One of these problems relates to the customary modern normal-abnormal categories and our conclusions regarding them. In how far are such categories culturally determined, or in how far can we with assurance regard them as absolute? In how far can we regard inability to function socially as diagnostic of abnormality, or in how far is it necessary to regard this as a function of the culture?

As a matter of fact, one of the most striking facts that emerge from a study of widely varying cultures is the ease with which our abnormals function in other cultures. It does not matter what kind of "abnormality" we choose for illustration, those which indicate extreme instability, or those which are more in the nature of character traits like sadism or delusions of grandeur or of persecution, there are well-described cultures in which these abnormals function at ease and with honor, and apparently without danger or difficulty to the society.

The most notorious of these is trance and catalepsy. Even a very mild mystic is aberrant in our culture. But most peoples have regarded even extreme psychic manifestations not only as normal and desirable, but even as characteristic of highly valued and gifted individuals. This was true even in our own cultural background in that period when Catholicism made the ecstatic experience the mark of sainthood. It is hard for us, born and brought up in a culture that makes no use of the experience, to realize how important a rôle it may play and how many individuals are capable of it, once it has been given an honorable place in any society.

Some of the Indian tribes of California accorded prestige principally to those who passed through certain trance experiences. Not all of these tribes believed that it was exclusively women who were so blessed, but among the Shasta (Dixon, 1907) this was the convention. Their shamans were women, and they were accorded the greatest prestige in the community. They were chosen because of their constitutional liability to trance and allied manifestations. One day the woman who was so destined, while she was about her usual work, would fall suddenly to the ground. She had heard a voice speaking to her in tones of the greatest

From *Journal of General Psychology*, 1934, Vol. 10, pp. 59-80. Reprinted by permission of The Journal Press.

intensity. Turning, she had seen a man with drawn bow and arrow. He commanded her to sing on pain of being shot through the heart by his arrow, but under the stress of the experience she fell senseless. Her family gathered. She was lying rigid, hardly breathing. They knew that for some time she had had dreams of a special character which indicated a shamanistic calling, dreams of escaping grizzly bears, falling off cliffs or trees, or of being surrounded by swarms of yellow jackets. The community knew therefore what to expect. After a few hours the woman began to moan gently and to roll about upon the ground, trembling violently. She was supposed to be repeating the song which she had been told to sing and which during the trance had been taught her by the spirit. As she revived her moaning became more and more clearly the spirit's song until at last she called out the name of the spirit itself, and immediately blood oozed from her mouth.

When the woman had come to herself after the first encounter with her spirit she danced that night her first initiatory shamanistic dance, holding herself by a rope that was swung from the ceiling. For three nights she danced, and on the third night she had to receive in her body her power from her spirit. She was dancing, and as she felt the approach of the moment she called out, "He will shoot me, he will shoot me." Her friends stood close, for when she reeled in a kind of cataleptic seizure, they had to seize her before she fell or she would die. From this time on she had in her body a visible materialization of her spirit's power, an icicle-like object which in her dances thereafter she would exhibit, producing it from one part of her body and returning it to another part. From this time on she continued to validate her supernatural power by further cataleptic demonstrations, and she was called upon in great emergencies of life and death, for curing and for divination and for counsel. She became in other words by this procedure a woman of great power and importance.[1]

It is clear that, so far from regarding cataleptic seizures as blots upon the family escutcheon and as evidences of dreaded disease, cultural approval had seized upon them and made of them the pathway to authority over one's fellows. They were the outstanding characteristic of the most respected social type, the type which functioned with most honor and reward in the community. It was precisely the cataleptic individuals who in this culture were singled out for authority and leadership.

The availability of "abnormal" types in the social structure, provided they are types that are culturally selected by that group, is illustrated from every part of the world. The shamans of Siberia dominate their communities. According to the ideas of these peoples, they are individuals who by submission to the will of the spirits have been cured of a grievous illness—the onset of the seizures—and have acquired by this means great supernatural power and incomparable vigor and health. Some, during the period of the call, are violently insane for several years, others irresponsible to the point where they have to be watched constantly lest they wander off in the snow and freeze to death, others ill and emaciated to the point of death, sometimes with bloody sweat. It is the shamanistic practice which constitutes their cure, and the extreme physical exertion of a Siberian seance leaves them, they claim, rested and able to enter immediately upon a similar performance. Cataleptic seizures are regarded as an essential part of any shamanistic performance (Czaplicka, 1914).

A good description of the neurotic condition of the shaman and the attention given him by his society is an old one by Canon Callaway (1884, pp. 259 ff.) recorded in the words of an old Zulu of South Africa:

"The condition of a man who is about to become a diviner is this; at first he is

1. In all cultures behavior which is socially rewarded attracts persons who are attracted by the possibility of leadership, and such individuals may simulate the required behavior. This is as true when society rewards prodigality as when it rewards catalepsy. For the present argument the amount of shamming is not considered though it is of obvious importance. It is a matter which cultures standardize quite as much as they standardize the type of rewarded behavior.

apparently robust, but in the process of time he begins to be delicate, not having any real disease, but being delicate. He habitually avoids certain kinds of food, choosing what he likes, and he does not eat much of that; he is continually complaining of pains in different parts of his body. And he tells them that he has dreamt that he was carried away by a river. He dreams of many things, and his body is muddied (as a river) and he becomes a house of dreams. He dreams constantly of many things, and on awaking tells his friends, 'My body is muddied today; I dreamt many men were killing me, and I escaped I know not how. On waking one part of my body felt different from other parts; it was no longer alike all over.' At last that man is very ill, and they go to the diviners to enquire.

"The diviners do not at once see that he is about to have a soft head (that is, the sensitivity associated with shamanism). It is difficult for them to see the truth; they continually talk nonsense and make false statements, until all the man's cattle are devoured at their command, they saying that the spirit of his people demands cattle, that it may eat food. At length all the man's property is expended, he still being ill; and they no longer know what to do, for he has no more cattle, and his friends help him in such things as he needs.

"At length a diviner comes and says that all the others are wrong. He says, 'He is possessed by the spirits. There is nothing else. They move in him, being divided into two parties; some say, "No, we do not wish our child injured. We do not wish it." It is for that reason he does not get well. If you bar the way against the spirits, you will be killing him. For he will not be a diviner; neither will he ever be a man again.'

"So the man may be ill two years without getting better; perhaps even longer than that. He is confined to his house. This continues till his hair falls off. And his body is dry and scurfy; he does not like to anoint himself. He shows that he is about to be a diviner by yawning again and again, and by sneezing continually. It is apparent also from his being very fond of snuff; not allowing any long time to pass without taking some. And people begin to see that he has had what is good given to him.

"After that he is ill; he has convulsions, and when water has been poured on him they then cease for a time. He habitually sheds tears, at first slight, then at last he weeps aloud and when the people are asleep he is heard making a noise and wakes the people by his singing; he has composed a song, and the men and women awake and go to sing in concert with him. All the people of the village are troubled by want of sleep; for a man who is becoming a diviner causes great trouble, for he does not sleep, but works constantly with his brain; his sleep is merely by snatches, and he wakes up singing many songs; and people who are near quit their villages by night when they hear him singing aloud and go to sing in concert. Perhaps he sings till morning, no one having slept. And then he leaps about the house like a frog; and the house becomes too small for him, and he goes out leaping and singing, and shaking like a reed in the water, and dripping with perspiration.

"In this state of things they daily expect his death; he is now but skin and bones, and they think that tomorrow's sun will not leave him alive. At this time many cattle are eaten, for the people encourage his becoming a diviner. At length (in a dream) an ancient ancestral spirit is pointed out to him. This spirit says to him, 'Go to So-and-so and he will churn for you an emetic (the medicine the drinking of which is a part of shamanistic initiation) that you may be a diviner altogether.' Then he is quiet a few days, having gone to the diviner to have the medicine churned for him; and he comes back quite another man, being now cleansed and a diviner indeed."

Thereafter for life when he achieves possession, he foretells events, and finds lost articles.

It is clear that culture may value and make socially available even highly unstable human types. If it chooses to treat their peculiarities as the most valued variants of human behavior, the individuals in question will rise to the occasion and perform their social rôles without reference to our usual ideas of the types who can make social adjustments and those who cannot.

Cataleptic and trance phenomena are, of course, only one illustration of the fact that those whom we regard as abnormals may function adequately in other cultures. Many of our culturally discarded traits are selected for elaboration in different societies. Homosexuality is an excellent example, for in this case our attention is not constantly diverted, as in the consideration of trance, to the interruption of routine activity which it implies. Homosexuality poses the problem very simply. A tendency toward this trait in our culture exposes an individual to all the conflicts to which all aberrants are always exposed, and we tend to identify the consequences of this conflict with homosexuality. But these consequences are obviously local and cultural. Homosexuals in many societies are not incompetent, but they may be such if the culture asks adjustments of them that would strain any man's vitality. Wherever homosexuality has been given an honorable place in any society, those to whom it is congenial have filled adequately the honorable rôles society assigns to them. Plato's *Republic* is, of course, the most convincing statement of such a reading of homosexuality. It is presented as one of the major means to the good life, and it was generally so regarded in Greece at that time.

The cultural attitude toward homosexuals has not always been on such a high ethical plane, but it has been very varied. Among many American Indian tribes there exists the institution of the berdache (Grinnell, 1923; Parsons, 1916), as the French called them. These men-women were men who at puberty or thereafter took the dress and the occupations of women. Sometimes they married other men and lived with them. Sometimes they were men with no inversion, persons of weak sexual endowment who chose this rôle to avoid the jeers of the women. The berdaches were never regarded as of first-rate supernatural power, as similar men-women were in Siberia, but

rather as leaders in women's occupations, good healers in certain diseases, or, among certain tribes, as the genial organizers of social affairs. In any case, they were socially placed. They were not left exposed to the conflicts that visit the deviant who is excluded from participation in the recognized patterns of his society.

The most spectacular illustrations of the extent to which normality may be culturally defined are those cultures where an abnormality of our culture is the cornerstone of their social structure. It is not possible to do justice to these possibilities in a short discussion. A recent study of an island of northwest Melanesia by Fortune (1932) describes a society built upon traits which we regard as beyond the border of paranoia. In this tribe the exogamic groups look upon each other as prime manipulators of black magic, so that one marries always into an enemy group which remains for life one's deadly and unappeasable foes. They look upon a good garden crop as a confession of theft, for everyone is engaged in making magic to induce into his garden the productiveness of his neighbors'; therefore no secrecy in the island is so rigidly insisted upon as the secrecy of a man's harvesting of his yams. Their polite phrase at the acceptance of a gift is, "And if you now poison me, how shall I repay you this present?" Their preoccupation with poisoning is constant; no woman ever leaves her cooking pot for a moment untended. Even the great affinal economic exchanges that are characteristic of this Melanesian culture area are quite altered in Dobu since they are incompatible with this fear and distrust that pervades the culture. They go farther and people the whole world outside their own quarters with such malignant spirits that all-night feasts and ceremonials simply do not occur here. They have even rigorous religiously enforced customs that forbid the sharing of seed even in one family group. Anyone else's food is deadly poison to you, so that communality of stores is out of the question. For some months before harvest the whole society is on the verge of starvation, but if one falls to the temptation and eats up one's seed yams, one is an outcast and a beachcomber for life. There is no coming back. It involves, as a matter of course, divorce and the breaking of all social ties.

Now in this society where no one may work with another and no one may share with another, Fortune describes the individual who was regarded by all his fellows as crazy. He was not one of those who periodically ran amok and, beside himself and frothing at the mouth, fell with a knife upon anyone he could reach. Such behavior they did not regard as putting anyone outside the pale. They did not even put the individuals who were known to be liable to these attacks under any kind of control. They merely fled when they saw the attack coming on and kept out of the way. "He would be all right tomorrow." But there was one man of sunny, kindly disposition who liked work and liked to be helpful. The compulsion was too strong for him to repress it in favor of the opposite tendencies of his culture. Men and women never spoke of him without laughing; he was silly and simple and definitely crazy. Nevertheless, to the ethnologist used to a culture that has, in Christianity, made his type the model of all virtue, he seemed a pleasant fellow.

An even more extreme example, because it is of a culture that has built itself upon a more complex abnormality, is that of the North Pacific Coast of North America. The civilization of the Kwakiutl (Boas, 1897, 1921, 1925, 1930; Boas & Hunt, 1905), at the time when it was first recorded in the last decades of the nineteenth century, was one of the most vigorous in North America. It was built up on an ample economic supply of goods, the fish which furnished their food staple being practically inexhaustible and obtainable with comparatively small labor, and the wood which furnished the material for their houses, their furnishings, and their arts being, with however much labor, always procurable. They lived in coastal villages that compared favorably in size with those of any other American Indians and they kept up constant communication by means of seagoing dug-out canoes.

It was one of the most vigorous and zestful of the aboriginal cultures of North America, with complex crafts and ceremonials, and elaborate and striking arts. It certainly had none of the earmarks of a sick civilization. The tribes of the Northwest Coast had wealth, and exactly in our terms. That is, they had not only a surplus of economic goods, but they made a game of the manipulation of wealth. It was by no means a mere direct transcription of economic needs and the filling of those needs. It involved the idea of capital, of interest, and of conspicuous waste. It was a game with all the binding rules of a game, and a person entered it as a child. His father distributed wealth for him, according to his ability, at a small feast or potlatch, and each gift the receiver was obliged to accept and to return after a short interval with interest that ran to about 100 per cent a year. By the time the child was grown, therefore, he was well launched, a larger potlatch had been given for him on various occasions of exploit or initiation, and he had wealth either out at usury or in his own possession. Nothing in the civilization could be enjoyed without validating it by the distribution of this wealth. Everything that was valued, names and songs as well as material objects, were passed down in family lines, but they were always publicly assumed with accompanying sufficient distributions of property. It was the game of validating and exercising all the privileges one could accumulate from one's various forbears, or by gift, or by marriage, that made the chief interest of the culture. Everyone in his degree took part in it, but many, of course, mainly as spectators. In its highest form it was played out between rival chiefs representing not only themselves and their family lines but their communities, and the object of the contest was to glorify oneself and to humiliate one's opponent. On this level of greatness the property involved was no longer represented by blankets, so many thousand of them to a potlatch, but by higher units of value. These higher units were like our bank notes. They were incised copper tablets, each of them named, and having a value that depended upon their illustrious history. This was as high as ten thousand blankets, and to possess one of them, still more to enhance its value at a great potlatch, was one of the greatest glories within the compass of the chiefs of the Northwest Coast.

The details of this manipulation of wealth are in many ways a parody on our own economic arrangements, but it is with the motivations that were recognized in this contest that we are concerned in this discussion. The drives were those which in our own culture we should call megalomaniac. There was an uncensored self-glorification and ridicule of the opponent that it is hard to equal in other cultures outside of the monologues of the abnormal. Any of the songs and speeches of their chiefs at a potlatch illustrate the usual tenor:

"Wa, out of the way. Wa, out of the way. Turn your faces that I may give way to my anger by striking my fellow chiefs."

"Wa, great potlatch, greatest potlatch.[2] The little ones[3] only pretend, the little stubborn ones, they only sell one copper again and again and give it away to the little chiefs of the tribe.
Ah, do not ask in vain for mercy. Ah, do not ask in vain for mercy and raise your hands, you with lolling tongues! I shall break,[4] I shall let disappear the great copper that has the name Kentsegum, the property of the great foolish one, the great extravagant one, the great surpassing one, the one farthest ahead, the great Cannibal dancer among the chiefs."[5]

"I am the great chief who makes people ashamed.
I am the great chief who makes people ashamed.
Our chief brings shame to the faces.
Our chief brings jealousy to the faces.
Our chief makes people cover their faces by what he is continually doing in this world, from the beginning to the end of the year.
Giving again and again oil feasts to the tribes.

"I am the great chief who vanquishes.
I am the great chief who vanquishes.
Only at those who continue running round and round in this world, working hard, loving their tails,[6] I sneer, at the chiefs below the true chief.[7]
Have mercy on them![8] Put oil on their dry heads with brittle hair, those who do not comb their hair!
I sneer at the chiefs below the true, real chief. I am the great chief who makes people ashamed.

"I am the only great tree, I the chief.
I am the only great tree, I the chief.
You are my subordinates, tribes.
You sit in the middle of the rear of the house, tribes.
Bring me your counter of property, tribes, that he may in vain try to count what is going to be given away by the great coppermaker, the chief.
Oh, I laugh at them, I sneer at them who empty boxes[9] in their houses, their potlatch houses, their inviting houses that are full only of hunger. They follow along after me like young sawbill ducks. I am the only great tree, I the chief."

I have quoted a number of these hymns of self-glorification because by an association which psychiatrists will recognize as fundamental these delusions of grandeur were essential in the paranoid view of life which was so strikingly developed in this culture. All of existence was seen in terms of insult. Not only derogatory acts performed by a neighbor or an enemy, but all untoward events, like a cut when one's axe slipped, or a ducking when one's canoe overturned, were insults. All alike threatened first and foremost one's ego security, and the first thought one was allowed was how to get even, how to wipe out the insult. Grief was

2. The feast he is now engaged in giving.
3. His opponents.
4. To break a copper, showing in this way how far one rose above even the most superlatively valuable things, was the final mark of greatness.
5. Himself.
6. As salmon do.
7. Himself.
8. Irony, of course.
9. Of treasure.

little institutionalized, but sulking took its place. Until he had resolved upon a course of action by which to save his face after any misfortune, whether it was the slipping of a wedge in felling a tree, or the death of a favorite child, an Indian of the Northwest Coast retired to his pallet with his face to the wall and neither ate nor spoke. He rose from it to follow out some course which according to the traditional rules should reinstate him in his own eyes and those of the community: to distribute property enough to wipe out the stain or to go head-hunting in order that somebody else should be made to mourn. His activities in neither case were specific responses to the bereavement he had just passed through, but were elaborately directed toward getting even. If he had not the money to distribute and did not succeed in killing someone to humiliate another, he might take his own life. He had staked everything, in his view of life, upon a certain picture of the self, and, when the bubble of his self-esteem was pricked, he had no interest, no occupation to fall back on, and the collapse of his inflated ego left him prostrate.

Every contingency of life was dealt with in these two traditional ways. To them the two were equivalent. Whether one fought with weapons or "fought with property," as they say, the same idea was at the bottom of both. In the olden times, they say, they fought with spears, but now they fight with property. One overcomes one's opponents in equivalent fashion in both, matching forces and seeing that one comes out ahead, and one can thumb one's nose at the vanquished rather more satisfactorily at a potlatch than on a battle field. Every occasion in life was noticed, not in its own terms, as a stage in the sex life of the individual or as a climax of joy or of grief, but as furthering this drama of consolidating one's own prestige and bringing shame to one's guests. Whether it was the occasion of the birth of a child, or a daughter's adolescence, or of the marriage of one's son, they were all equivalent raw material for the culture to use for this one traditionally selected end. They were all to raise one's own personal status and to entrench oneself by the humiliation of one's fellows. A girl's adolescence among the Nootka (Sapir, 1913) was an event for which her father gathered property from the time she was first able to run about. When she was adolescent he would demonstrate his greatness by an unheard of distribution of these goods, and put down all his rivals. It was not as a fact of the girl's sex life that it figured in their culture, but as the occasion for a major move in the great game of vindicating one's own greatness and humiliating one's associates.

In their behavior at great bereavements this set of the culture comes out most strongly. Among the Kwakiutl it did not matter whether a relative had died in bed of disease, or by the hand of an enemy, in either case death was an affront to be wiped out by the death of another person. The fact that one had been caused to mourn was proof that one had been put upon. A chief's sister and her daughter had gone up to Victoria, and either because they drank bad whiskey or because their boat capsized they never came back. The chief called together his warriors. "Now I ask you, tribes, who shall wail? Shall I do it or shall another?" The spokesman answered, of course, "Not you, Chief. Let some other of the tribes." Immediately they set up the war pole to announce their intention of wiping out the injury, and gathered a war party. They set out, and found seven men and two children asleep and killed them. "Then they felt good when they arrived at Sebaa in the evening."

The point which is of interest to us is that in our society those who on that occasion would feel good when they arrived at Sebaa that evening would be the definitely abnormal. There would be some, even in our society, but it is not a recognized and approved mood under the circumstances. On the Northwest Coast those are favored and fortunate to whom that mood under those circumstances is congenial, and those to whom it is repugnant are unlucky. This latter minority can register in their own culture only by doing violence to their congenial responses and acquiring others that are difficult for them. The person, for instance, who, like a Plains Indian whose wife has been taken from him, is too proud to fight, can deal with the Northwest Coast civilization only by ignoring its strongest bents. If he cannot achieve it, he is the deviant in that culture, their instance of abnormality.

This head-hunting that takes place on the Northwest Coast after a death is no matter of blood revenge or of organized vengeance. There is no effort to tie up the subsequent killing with any responsibility on the part of the victim for the death of the person who is being mourned. A chief whose son has died goes visiting wherever his fancy dictates, and he says to his host, "My prince has died today, and you go with him." Then he kills him. In this, according to their interpretation, he acts nobly because he has not been downed. He has thrust back in return. The whole procedure is meaningless without the fundamental paranoid reading of bereavement. Death, like all the other untoward accidents of existence, confounds man's pride and can only be handled in the category of insults.

Behavior honored upon the Northwest Coast is one which is recognized as abnormal in our civilization, and yet it is sufficiently close to the attitudes of our own culture to be intelligible to us and to have a definite vocabulary with which we may discuss it. The megalomaniac paranoid trend is a definite danger in our society. It is encouraged by some of our major preoccupations, and it confronts us with a choice of two possible attitudes. One is to brand it as abnormal and reprehensible, and is the attitude we have chosen in our civilization. The other is to make it an essential attribute of ideal man, and this is the solution in the culture of the Northwest Coast.

These illustrations, which it has been possible to indicate only in the briefest manner, force upon us the fact that normality is culturally defined. An adult shaped to the drives and standards of either of these cultures, if he were transported into our civilization, would fall into our categories of abnormality. He would be faced with the psychic dilemmas of the socially unavailable. In his own culture, however,

he is the pillar of society, the end result of socially inculcated mores, and the problem of personal instability in his case simply does not arise.

No one civilization can possibly utilize in its mores the whole potential range of human behavior. Just as there are great numbers of possible phonetic articulations, and the possibility of language depends on a selection and standardization of a few of these in order that speech communication may be possible at all, so the possibility of organized behavior of every sort, from the fashions of local dress and houses to the dicta of a people's ethics and religion, depends upon a similar selection among the possible behavior traits. In the field of recognized economic obligations or sex tabus this selection is as nonrational and subconscious a process as it is in the field of phonetics. It is a process which goes on in the group for long periods of time and is historically conditioned by innumerable accidents of isolation or of contact of peoples. In any comprehensive study of psychology, the selection that different cultures have made in the course of history within the great circumference of potential behavior is of great significance.

Every society,[10] beginning with some slight inclination in one direction or another, carries its preference farther and farther, integrating itself more and more completely upon its chosen basis, and discarding those types of behavior that are uncongenial. Most of those organizations of personality that seem to us most incontrovertibly abnormal have been used by different civilizations in the very foundations of their institutional life. Conversely the most valued traits of our normal individuals have been looked on in differently organized cultures as aberrant. Normality, in short, within a very wide range, is culturally defined. It is primarily a term for the socially elaborated segment of human behavior in any culture; and abnormality, a term for the segment that that

10. This phrasing of the process is deliberately animistic. It is used with no reference to a group mind or a super-organic, but in the same sense in which it is customary to say, "Every art has its own canons."

particular civilization does not use. The very eyes with which we see the problem are conditioned by the long traditional habits of our own society.

It is a point that has been made more often in relation to ethics than in relation to psychiatry. We do not any longer make the mistake of deriving the morality of our own locality and decade directly from the inevitable constitution of human nature. We do not elevate it to the dignity of a first principle. We recognize that morality differs in every society, and is a convenient term for socially approved habits. Mankind has always preferred to say, "It is morally good," rather than "It is habitual," and the fact of this preference is matter enough for a critical science of ethics. But historically the two phrases are synonymous.

The concept of the normal is properly a variant of the concept of the good. It is that which society has approved. A normal action is one which falls well within the limits of expected behavior for a particular society. Its variability among different peoples is essentially a function of the variability of the behavior patterns that different societies have created for themselves, and can never be wholly divorced from a consideration of culturally institutionalized types of behavior.

Each culture is a more or less elaborate working-out of the potentialities of the segment it has chosen. In so far as a civilization is well integrated and consistent within itself, it will tend to carry farther and farther, according to its nature, its initial impulse toward a particular type of action, and from the point of view of any other culture those elaborations will include more and more extreme and aberrant traits.

Each of these traits, in proportion as it reinforces the chosen behavior patterns of that culture, is for that culture normal. Those individuals to whom it is congenial either congenitally, or as the result of childhood sets, are accorded prestige in that culture, and are not visited with the social contempt or disapproval which their traits would call down upon them in a society that was differently organized. On the other hand, those individuals whose characteristics are not congenial to the selected type of human behavior in that community are the deviants, no matter how valued their personality traits may be in a contrasted civilization.

The Dobuan who is not easily susceptible to fear of treachery, who enjoys work and likes to be helpful, is their neurotic and regarded as silly. On the Northwest Coast the person who finds it difficult to read life in terms of an insult contest will be the person upon whom fall all the difficulties of the culturally unprovided for. The person who does not find it easy to humiliate a neighbor, nor to see humiliation in his own experience, who is genial and loving, may, of course, find some unstandardized way of achieving satisfactions in his society, but not in the major patterned responses that his culture requires of him. If he is born to play an important rôle in a family with many hereditary privileges, he can succeed only by doing violence to his whole personality. If he does not succeed, he has betrayed his culture; that is, he is abnormal.

I have spoken of individuals as having sets toward certain types of behavior, and of these sets as running sometimes counter to the types of behavior which are institutionalized in the culture to which they belong. From all that we know of contrasting cultures it seems clear that differences of temperament occur in every society. The matter has never been made the subject of investigation, but from the available material it would appear that these temperament types are very likely of universal recurrence. That is, there is an ascertainable range of human behavior that is found wherever a sufficiently large series of individuals is observed. But the proportion in which behavior types stand to one another in different societies is not universal. The vast majority of the individuals in any group are shaped to the fashion of that culture. In other words, most individuals are plastic to the moulding force of the society into which they are born. In a society that values trance, as in India, they will have supernormal experience. In a society that institutionalizes homosexuality, they will be homosexual. In a society that sets the gath-

ering of possessions as the chief human objective, they will amass property. The
deviants, whatever the type of behavior the
culture has institutionalized, will remain
few in number, and there seems no more
difficulty in moulding the vast malleable
majority to the "normality" of what we
consider an aberrant trait, such as delusions
of reference, than to the normality of such
accepted behavior patterns as acquisitive-
ness. The small proportion of the number
of the deviants in any culture is not a
function of the sure instinct with which
that society has built itself upon the fundamental sanities, but of the universal fact
that, happily, the majority of mankind quite
readily take any shape that is presented to
them.

The relativity of normality is not an academic issue. In the first place, it suggests
that the apparent weakness of the aberrant
is most often and in great measure illusory.
It springs not from the fact that he is lacking
in necessary vigor, but that he is an individual upon whom that culture has put more
than the usual strain. His inability to adapt
himself to society is a reflection of the fact
that that adaptation involves a conflict in
him that it does not in the so-called normal.

Therapeutically, it suggests that the inculcation of tolerance and appreciation in any
society towards its less usual types is fundamentally important in successful mental hygiene. The complement of this tolerance, on
the patient's side, is an education in self-
reliance and honesty with himself. If he can
be brought to realize that what has thrust
him into his misery is despair at his lack
of social backing he may be able to achieve
a more independent and less tortured attitude and lay the foundation for an adequately functioning mode of existence.

There is a further corollary. From the
point of view of absolute categories of
abnormal psychology, we must expect in
any culture to find a large proportion of
the most extreme abnormal types among
those who from the local point of view are
farthest from belonging to this category.
The culture, according to its major preoccupations, will increase and intensify
hysterical, epileptic, or paranoid symp-

toms, at the same time relying socially in
a greater and greater degree upon these very
individuals. Western civilization allows and
culturally honors gratifications of the ego
which according to any absolute category
would be regarded as abnormal. The por-
trayal of unbridled and arrogant egoists as
family men, as officers of the law, and in
business has been a favorite topic of novel-
ists, and they are familiar in every community. Such individuals are probably
mentally warped to a greater degree than
many inmates of our institutions who are
nevertheless socially unavailable. They are
extreme types of those personality configurations which our civilization fosters.

This consideration throws into great
prominence the confusion that follows, on
the one hand, the use of social inadequacy
as a criterion of abnormality and, on the
other, of definite fixed symptoms. The confusion is present in practically all discussions of abnormal psychology, and it can be
clarified chiefly by adequate consideration
of the character of the culture, not of the
constitution of the abnormal individual.
Nevertheless, the bearing of social security
upon the total situation of the abnormal cannot be exaggerated, and the study of comparative psychiatry will be fundamentally
concerned with this aspect of the matter.

It is clear that statistical methods of
defining normality, so long as they are based
on studies in a selected civilization, only
involve us, unless they are checked against
the cultural configuration, in deeper and
deeper provincialism. The recent tendency
in abnormal psychology to take the laboratory mode as normal and to define abnormalities as they depart from this average has
value in so far as it indicates that the aberrants in any culture are those individuals
who are liable to serious disturbances because their habits are culturally unsup-
ported. On the other hand, it overlooks the
fact that every culture besides its abnormals of conflict has presumably its abnormals of extreme fulfillment of the cultural
type. From the point of view of a universally
valid abnormal psychology the extreme
types of abnormality would probably be
found in this very group—a group which in

every study based upon one culture goes undescribed except in its end institutionalized forms.

The relativity of normality is important in what may some day come to be a true social engineering. Our picture of our own civilization is no longer in this generation in terms of a changeless and divinely derived set of categorical imperatives. We must face the problems our changed perspective has put upon us. In this matter of mental ailments, we must face the fact that even our normality is man-made, and is of our own seeking. Just as we have been handicapped in dealing with ethical problems so long as we held to an absolute definition of morality, so too in dealing with the problems of abnormality we are handicapped so long as we identify our local normalities with the universal sanities. I have taken illustrations from different cultures, because the conclusions are most inescapable from the contrasts as they are presented in unlike social groups. But the major problem is not a consequence of the variability of the normal from culture to culture, but its variability from era to era. This variability in time we cannot escape if we would, and it is not beyond the bounds of possibility that we may be able to face this inevitable change with full understanding and deal with it rationally (Dewey, 1922). No society has yet achieved self-conscious and critical analysis of its own normalities and attempted rationally to deal with its own social process of creating new normalities within its next generation. But the fact that it is unachieved is not therefore proof of its impossibility. It is a faint indication of how momentous it could be in human society.

There is another major factor in the cultural conditioning of abnormality. From the material that is available at the present time it seems a lesser factor than the one we have discussed. Nevertheless, disregard of its importance has led to many misconceptions. The particular forms of behavior to which unstable individuals of any group are liable are many of them matters of cultural patterning like any other behavior. It is for this obvious reason that the epidemic disorders of one continent or era are often rare or unreported from other parts of the world or other periods of history.

The baldest evidences of cultural patterning in the behavior of unstable individuals is in trance phenomena. The use to which such proclivities are put, the form their manifestations take, the things that are seen and felt in trance, are all culturally controlled. The tranced individual may come back with communications from the dead describing the minutiae of life in the hereafter, or he may visit the world of the unborn, or get information about lost objects in the camp, or experience cosmic unity, or acquire a life-long guardian spirit, or get information about coming events. Even in trance the individual holds strictly to the rules and expectations of his culture, and his experience is as locally patterned as a marriage rite or an economic exchange.

The conformity of trance experience to the expectations of waking life is well recognized. Now that we are no longer confused by the attempt to ascribe supernormal validity to the one or the other, and realize how trance experience bodies forth the preoccupations of the experiencing individual, the cultural patterning in ecstasy has become an accepted tenet.

But the matter does not end here. It is not only what is seen in trance experience that has clear-cut geographical and temporal distribution. It is equally true of forms of behavior which are affected by certain unstable individuals in any group. It is one of the prime difficulties in the use of such unprecise and casual information as we possess about the behavior of the unstable in different cultures, that the material does not correspond to data from our own society. It has even been thought that such definite types of instability as Arctic hysteria (Novakovsky, 1924) and the Malay running-amok were racial diseases. But we know at least, in spite of the lack of good psychiatric accounts, that these phenomena do not coincide with racial distributions. Moreover, the same problem is quite as striking in cases where there is no possibility of a racial correlation. Running amok has been described as alike in symptoms and alike in the treatment accorded it by the rest of the group from such different parts of the world as Melanesia (Fortune, pp. 54-55) and Tierra del Fuego (Coriat, n.d.).

The racial explanation is also ruled out of court in those instances of epidemic mania which are characteristic of our own cultural background. The dancing mania (Hecker, 1885) that filled the streets of Europe with compulsively dancing men, women, and children in mediaeval times is recognized as an extreme instance of suggestibility in our own racial group.

These behaviors are capable of controlled elaboration that is often carried to great lengths. Unstable individuals in one culture achieve characteristic forms that may be excessively rare or absent in another, and this is very marked where social value has been attached to one form or another. Thus when some form of borderline behavior has been associated in any society with the shaman and he is a person of authority and influence, it is this particular indicated seizure to which he will be liable at every demonstration. Among the Shasta of California, as we have seen, and among many other tribes in various parts of the world, some form of cataleptic seizure is the passport to shamanism and must constantly accompany its practice. In other regions it is automatic vision or audition. In other societies behavior is perhaps closest to what we cover by the term hystero-epilepsy. In Siberia all the familiar characteristics of our spiritualistic seances are required for every performance of the shaman. In all these cases the particular experience that is thus socially chosen receives considerable elaboration and is usually patterned in detail according to local standards. That is, each culture, though it chooses quite narrowly in the great field of borderline experiences, without difficulty imposes its selected type upon certain of its individuals. The particular behavior of an unstable individual in these instances is not the single and in-evitable mode in which his abnormality could express itself. He has taken up a traditionally conditioned pattern of behavior in this as in any other field. Conversely, in every society, our own included, there are forms of instability that are out of fashion. They are not at the present time at least being presented for imitation to the enormously suggestible individuals who constitute in any society a considerable group of the abnormals. It seems clear that this is no matter of the nature of sanity, or even of a biological, inherited tendency in a local group, but quite simply an affair of social patterning.

The problem of understanding abnormal human behavior in any absolute sense independent of cultural factors is still far in the future. The categories of borderline behavior which we derive from the study of the neuroses and psychoses of our civilization are categories of prevailing local types of instability. They give much information about the stresses and strains of Western civilization, but no final picture of inevitable human behavior. Any conclusions about such behavior must await the collection by trained observers of psychiatric data from other cultures. Since no adequate work of the kind has been done at the present time, it is impossible to say what core of definition of abnormality may be found valid from the comparative material. It is as it is in ethics: all our local conventions of moral behavior and of immoral are without absolute validity, and yet it is quite possible that a modicum of what is considered right and what wrong could be disentangled that is shared by the whole human race. When data are available in psychiatry, this minimum definition of abnormal human tendencies will be probably quite unlike our culturally conditioned, highly elaborated psychoses such as those that are described, for instance, under the terms of schizophrenia and manic-depressive.

Erich Fromm

ARE WE SANE?

Out of a background of psychoanalytic practice, Erich Fromm has emerged as a social critic and humanist philosopher. Here we present his sobering opinion of the sanity of our "civilized" society. While Benedict helped us examine the relation of culture to psychological disorders in other societies, Fromm prompts us to turn the same critical focus upon ourselves and ask, "Are we sane?" Though the evidence is incomplete, his interpretation is compelling. At the very least, it is clear that the question must continually be asked. Diagnosis need not be limited to individuals; society can be evaluated as well. As Fromm's argument shows, such evaluation involves the same kinds of uncertain and unavoidable value judgments that are implied by diagnosis of the individual.

Nothing is more common than the idea that we, the people living in the Western world of the twentieth century, are eminently sane. Even the fact that a great number of individuals in our midst suffer from more or less severe forms of mental illness produces little doubt with respect to the general standard of our mental health. We are sure that by introducing better methods of mental hygiene we shall improve *still further* the state of our mental health, and as far as individual mental disturbances are concerned, we look at them as strictly individual incidents, perhaps with some amazement that so many of these incidents should occur in a culture which is supposedly so sane.

Can we be so sure that we are not deceiving ourselves? Many an inmate of an insane asylum is convinced that everybody else is crazy, except himself. Many a severe neurotic believes that his compulsive rituals or his hysterical outbursts are normal reactions to somewhat abnormal circumstances. What about ourselves?

Let us, in good psychiatric fashion, look at the facts. In the last one hundred years we, in the Western world, have created a greater material wealth than any other society in the history of the human race. Yet we have managed to kill off millions of our population in an arrangement which we call "war." Aside from smaller wars, we had larger ones in 1870, 1914 and 1939. During these wars, every participant firmly believed that he was fighting in his self-defense, for his honor, or that he was backed up by God. The groups with whom one is at war are, often from one day to the next, looked upon as cruel, irrational fiends, whom one must defeat to save the world from evil. But a few years after the mutual slaughter is over, the enemies of yesterday are our friends, the friends of yesterday our enemies, and again in full seriousness we begin to paint them with appropriate colors of black and white. At this moment, in the year 1955, we are prepared for a mass slaughter which would, if it came to pass, surpass any slaughter the human race has arranged so far. One of the greatest discoveries in the field of natural science is prepared for this purpose. Everybody is looking with a mixture of confidence and apprehension to the "statesmen" of the various peoples, ready to heap all praise on them if they "succeed in avoiding a war," and ignoring the fact that it is only these very statesmen who ever cause a war, usually not even through their bad intentions, but by their unreasonable mismanagement of the affairs entrusted to them.

In these outbursts of destructiveness and paranoid suspicion, however, we are not behaving differently from what the civilized part of mankind has done in the last three thousand years of history. According to Victor Cherbulliez, from 1500 B.C. to 1860 A.D. no less than about eight thousand peace treaties were signed, each one supposed to secure permanent peace, and each one lasting on an average two years![1]

Our direction of economic affairs is scarcely more encouraging. We live in an economic system in which a particularly good crop is often an economic disaster, and we restrict some of our agricultural productivity in order to "stabilize the market," although there are millions of people who do not have the very things we restrict, and who need them badly. Right now our economic system is functioning very well, because, among other reasons, we spend billions of dollars per year to produce armaments. Economists look with some apprehension to the time when we stop producing armaments, and the idea that the state should produce houses and other useful and needed things instead of weapons, easily provokes accusations of endangering freedom and individual initiative.

We have a literacy above 90 per cent of the population. We have radio, television, movies, a newspaper a day for everybody. But instead of giving us the best of past and present literature and music, these media of communication, supplemented by advertising, fill the minds of men with the cheapest trash, lacking in any sense of

1. From H. B. Stevens, *The Recovery of Culture*, Harper and Brothers, New York, 1949, p.221.

reality, with sadistic phantasies which a halfway cultured person would be embarrassed to entertain even once in a while. But while the mind of everybody, young and old, is thus poisoned, we go on blissfully to see to it that no "immorality" occurs on the screen. Any suggestion that the government should finance the production of movies and radio programs which would enlighten and improve the minds of our people would be met again with indignation and accusations in the name of freedom and idealism.

We have reduced the average working hours to about half what they were one hundred years ago. We today have more free time available than our forefathers dared to dream of. But what has happened? We do not know how to use the newly gained free time; we try to kill the time we have saved, and are glad when another day is over.

Why should I continue with a picture which is known to everybody? Certainly, if an individual acted in this fashion, serious doubts would be raised as to his sanity; should he, however, claim that there is nothing wrong, and that he is acting perfectly reasonably, then the diagnosis would not even be doubtful any more.

Yet many psychiatrists and psychologists refuse to entertain the idea that society as a whole may be lacking in sanity. They hold that the problem of mental health in a society is only that of the number of "unadjusted" individuals, and not that of a possible unadjustment of the culture itself. [We deal here] with the latter problem; not with individual pathology, but with the *pathology of normalcy*, particularly with the pathology of contemporary Western society. But before entering into the intricate discussion of the concept of social pathology, let us look at some data, revealing and suggestive in themselves, which make reference to the incidence of *individual* pathology in Western culture.

What is the incidence of mental illness in the various countries of the Western world? It is a most amazing fact that there are no data which answer this question. While there are exact comparative statistical data on material resources, employment,

birth and death rates, there is no adequate information about mental illness. At the most we have some exact data for a number of countries, like the United States and Sweden, but they only refer to admissions of patients to mental institutions, and they are not helpful in making estimates of comparative frequency of mental illness. These figures tell us just as much about improved psychiatric care and institutional facilities as they tell us about increase in incidence of mental illness.[2] The fact that more than half of all hospital beds in the United States are used for mental patients on whom we spend an annual sum of over a billion dollars may not be an indication of any increase in mental illness, but only of an increasing care. Some other figures, however, are more indicative of the occurrence of the more severe mental disturbances. If 17.7 per cent of all rejections of draftees in the last war were for reasons of mental illness, this fact certainly bespeaks a high degree of mental disturbance, even if we have no comparative figures referring to the past, or to other countries.

The only comparative data which can give us a rough indication of mental health, are those for suicide, homicide and alcoholism. No doubt the problem of suicide is a most complex one, and no single factor can be assumed to be *the* cause. But even without entering at this point into a discussion of suicide, I consider it a safe assumption that a high suicide rate in a given population is expressive of a lack of mental stability and mental health. That it is not a consequence of material poverty is clearly evidenced by all figures. The poorest countries have the lowest incidence of suicide, and the increasing material prosperity in Europe was accompanied by an increasing number of suicides.[3] As to alcoholism, there is no doubt that it, too, is a symptom of mental and emotional instability.

The motives for homicide are probably less indicative of pathology than those for

2. cf. H Goldhamer and A. Marshall, *Psychosis and Civilization*, Free Press, Glencoe, 1953.
3. cf. Maurice Halbwachs, *Les Causes du Suicide*, Felix Alcan, Paris, 1930, pp. 109 and 112.

suicide. However, though countries with a high homicide rate show a low suicide rate, their combined rates bring us to an interesting conclusion. If we classify both homicide and suicide as "destructive acts," our tables demonstrate that their combined rate is not constant, but fluctuating between the extremes of 35.76 and 4.24. This contradicts Freud's assumption of the comparative constancy of destructiveness which underlies his theory of the death instinct. It disproves the implication that destructiveness maintains an invariable rate, differing only in directions toward the self or the outside world.

The following tables show the incidence of suicide, homicide and alcoholism for some of the most important European and North American countries.[4]

Table I

	(Per 100,000 of adult population)	
Country	Suicide	Homicide
Denmark	35.09	0.67
Switzerland	33.72	1.42
Finland	20.05	6.45
Sweden	19.74	1.01
United States	15.52	8.50
France	14.83	1.53
Portugal	14.24	2.79
England and Wales ..	13.43	0.63
Australia	13.03	1.57
Canada	11.40	1.67
Scotland	8.06	0.52
Norway	7.84	0.38
Spain	7.71	2.88
Italy	7.67	7.38
Northern Ireland	4.82	0.13
Ireland (Republic) ...	3.70	0.54

4. The information in the first and second tables is derived from 1, World Health Organization (1951), *Annual epidemiological and vital statistics, 1939-46. Part 1. Vital statistics and causes of death,* Geneva, pp. 38-71 (the figures from this source have been converted for greater accuracy from total to adult population), and 2. World Health Organization (1952), *Epidem. vital Statist. Rep. 5,* 377. That of the third table, from the Report on the First Session of the Alcoholism Subcommittee, of the Expert Committee on Mental Health, World Health Organization, Geneva, 1951.

Table 2

Country	Destructive Acts
	Homicide and suicide combined
Denmark	35.76
Switzerland	35.14
Finland	29.80
United States	24.02
Sweden	20.75
Portugal	17.03
France	16.36
Italy	15.05
Australia	14.60
England and Wales	14.06
Canada	13.07
Spain	10.59
Scotland	8.58
Norway	8.22
Northern Ireland	4.95
Ireland (Republic)	4.24

(Both the above tables show the figures for 1946)

Table 3

Country	Estimated Number of Alcoholics With or Without Complications (Per 100,000 of adult population)	
United States	3,952	(1948)
France	2,850	(1945)
Sweden	2,580	(1946)
Switzerland	2,385	(1947)
Denmark	1,950	(1948)
Norway	1,560	(1947)
Finland	1,430	(1947)
Australia	1,340	(1947)
England and Wales	1,100	(1948)
Italy	500	(1942)

A quick glance at these tables shows a remarkable phenomenon: Denmark, Switzerland, Finland, Sweden and the United States are the countries with the highest suicide rate, and the highest combined suicide and homicide rate, while Spain, Italy, Northern Ireland and the Republic of Ireland are those with the lowest suicide and homicide rate. The figures for alcoholism show that the same countries—the United States, Switzerland, Sweden and Denmark—which have the highest suicide rate, have also the highest alcoholism rate, with the main difference that the United States are leading in this group, and that France has the second place, instead of the sixth place it has with regard to suicide.

These figures are startling and challenging indeed. Even if we should doubt whether the high frequency of suicide alone indicates a lack of mental health in a population, the fact that suicide and alcoholism figures largely coincide, seems to make it plain that we deal here with symptoms of mental unbalance.

We find then that the countries in Europe which are among the most democratic, peaceful and prosperous ones, and the United States, the most prosperous country in the world, show the most severe symptoms of mental disturbance. The aim of the whole socio-economic development of the Western world is that of the materially comfortable life, relatively equal distribution of wealth, stable democracy and peace, and the very countries which have come closest to this aim show the most severe signs of mental unbalance! It is true that these figures in themselves do not *prove* anything, but at least they are startling. Even before we enter into a more thorough discussion of the whole problem, these data raise a question as to whether there is not something fundamentally wrong with our way of life and with the aims toward which we are striving.

Could it be that the middle-class life of prosperity, while satisfying our material needs leaves us with a feeling of intense boredom, and that suicide and alcoholism are pathological ways of escape from this boredom? Could it be that these figures are a drastic illustration for the truth of the statement that "man lives not by bread alone," and that they show that modern civilization fails to satisfy profound needs in man? . . .

II

What is so deceptive about the state of mind of the members of a society is the "consensual validation" of their concepts. It is naïvely assumed that the fact that the majority of people share certain ideas or feelings proves the validity of these ideas and feelings. Nothing is further from the truth. Consensual validation as such has no bearing whatsoever on reason or mental health. Just as there is a *"folie à deux"* there is a *"folie à millions."* The fact that millions of people share the same vices does not make these vices virtues, the fact that they share so many errors does not make the errors to be truths, and the fact that millions of people share the same forms of mental pathology does not make these people sane.

There is, however, an important difference between individual and social mental illness, which suggests a differentiation between two concepts: that of *defect*, and that of *neurosis*. If a person fails to attain freedom, spontaneity, a genuine expression of self, he may be considered to have a severe defect, provided we assume that freedom and spontaneity are the objective goals to be attained by every human being. If such a goal is not attained by the majority of members of any given society, we deal with the phenomenon of *socially patterned* defect. The individual shares it with many others; he is not aware of it as a defect, and his security is not threatened by the experience of being different, of being an outcast, as it were. What he may have lost in richness, and in a genuine feeling of happiness, is made up by the security of fitting in with the rest of mankind—*as he knows them.* As a matter of fact, his very defect may have been raised to a virtue by his culture, and thus may give him an enhanced feeling of achievement.

An illustration is the feeling of guilt and anxiety which Calvin's doctrines aroused in men. It may be said that the person who is overwhelmed by a feeling of his own powerlessness and unworthiness, by unceasing doubt as to whether he is saved or condemned to eternal punishment, who is hardly capable of genuine joy, suffers from a severe defect. Yet this very defect was culturally patterned; it was looked upon as particularly valuable, and the individual was thus protected from the neurosis which he would have acquired in a culture where the same defect gave him a feeling of profound inadequacy and isolation.

Spinoza formulated the problem of the socially patterned defect very clearly. He says: "Many people are seized by one and the same affect with great consistency. All his senses are so strongly affected by one object that he believes this object to be present even if it is not. If this happens while the person is awake, the person is believed to be insane.... But if the *greedy* person thinks only of money and possessions, the *ambitious* one only of fame, one does not think of them as being insane, but only as annoying; generally one has contempt for them. But *factually* greediness, ambition, and so forth are forms of insanity, although usually one does not think of them as 'illness.' "[5]

These words were written a few hundred years ago; they still hold true, although the defects have been culturally patterned to *such* an extent now that they are not even generally thought any more to be annoying or contemptible. Today we come across a person who acts and feels like an automaton; who never experiences anything which is really his; who experiences himself entirely as the person he thinks he is supposed to be; whose artificial smile has replaced genuine laughter; whose meaningless chatter has replaced communicative speech; whose dulled despair has taken the place of genuine pain. Two statements can be made about this person. One is that he suffers from a defect of spontaneity and individuality which may seem incurable. At the same time, it may be said that he does not differ essentially from millions of others who are in the same position. For most of them, the culture provides patterns which enable them to *live with a defect without becoming ill*. It is as if each culture provided the remedy against the outbreak of manifest neurotic symptoms which would result from the defect produced by it.

Suppose that in our Western culture movies, radios, television, sports events

and newspapers ceased to function for only four weeks. With these main avenues of escape closed, what would be the consequences for people thrown back upon their own resources? I have no doubt that even in this short time thousands of nervous breakdowns would occur, and many more thousands of people would be thrown into a state of acute anxiety, not different from the picture which is diagnosed clinically as "neurosis."[6] If the opiate against the socially patterned defect were withdrawn, the manifest illness would make its appearance.

For a minority, the pattern provided by the culture does not work. They are often those whose individual defect is more severe than that of the average person, so that the culturally offered remedies are not sufficient to prevent the outbreak of manifest illness. (A case in point is the person whose aim in life is to attain power and fame. While this aim is, in itself, a pathological one, there is nevertheless a difference between the person who uses his powers to attain this aim realistically, and the more severely sick one who has so little emerged from his infantile grandiosity that he does not do anything toward the attainment of his goal but waits for a miracle to happen and, thus feeling more and more powerless, ends up in a feeling of futility and bitterness.) But there are also those whose character structure, and hence whose conflicts, differ from those of the majority, so that the remedies which are effective for most of their fellow men are of no help to them. Among this

5. cf. Spinoza, *Ethics*, IV Prop. 44 Schol.

6. I have made the following experiment with various classes of undergraduate college students: they were told to imagine that they were to stay for three days alone in their rooms, without a radio, or escapist literature, although provided with "good" literature, normal food and all other physical comforts. They were asked to imagine what their reaction to this experience would be. The response of about 90 per cent in each group ranged from a feeling of acute panic, to that of an exceedingly trying experience, which they might overcome by sleeping long, doing all kinds of little chores, eagerly awaiting the end of this period. Only a small minority felt that they would be at ease and enjoy the time when they were with themselves.

group we sometimes find people of greater integrity and sensitivity than the majority, who for this very reason are incapable of accepting the cultural opiate, while at the same time they are not strong and healthy enough to live soundly "against the stream."

The foregoing discussion on the difference between neurosis and the socially patterned defect may give the impression that if society only provides the remedies against the outbreak of manifest symptoms, all goes well, and it can continue to function smoothly, however great the defects created by it. History shows us, however, that this is not the case.

It is true indeed, that man, in contrast to the animal, shows an almost infinite malleability; just as he can eat almost anything, live under practically any kind of climate and adjust himself to it, there is hardly any psychic condition which he cannot endure, and under which he cannot carry on. He can live free, and as a slave. Rich and in luxury, and under conditions of half-starvation. He can live as a warrior, and peaceably; as an exploiter and robber, and as a member of a co-operating and loving fellowship. There is hardly a psychic state in which man cannot live, and hardly anything which cannot be done with him, and for which he cannot be used. All these considerations seem to justify the assumption that there is no such thing as a nature common to all men, and that would mean in fact that there is no such thing as a species "man," except in a physiological and anatomical sense.

Yet, in spite of all this evidence, the history of man shows that we have omitted one fact. Despots and ruling cliques can succeed in dominating and exploiting their fellow man, but they cannot prevent *reactions* to this inhuman treatment. Their subjects become frightened, suspicious, lonely and, if not due to external reasons, their systems collapse at some point because fears, suspicions and loneliness eventually incapacitate the majority to function effectively and intelligently. Whole nations, or social groups within them, can be subjugated and exploited for a long time, but *they react*. They react with apathy or such impairment of intelligence, initiative and skills that they gradually fail to perform the functions which should serve their rulers. Or they react by the accumulation of such hate and destructiveness as to bring about an end to themselves, their rulers and their system. Again their reaction may create such independence and longing for freedom that a better society is built upon their creative impulses. Which reaction occurs, depends on many factors: on economic and political ones, and on the spiritual climate in which people live. But whatever the reactions are, the statement that man can live under almost any condition is only half true; it must be supplemented by the other statement, that if he lives under conditions which are contrary to his nature and to the basic requirements for human growth and sanity, he cannot help reacting; he must either deteriorate and perish, or bring about conditions which are more in accordance with his needs. . . .

Rollo May

HISTORICAL AND PHILOSOPHICAL PRESUPPOSITIONS

FOR UNDERSTANDING THERAPY

We have considered various ways in which questions of value enter the problem of diagnosis; here we turn to the relation between values and therapy. But it should be pointed out that the problems of diagnosis and therapy cannot really be separated. Some view of what constitutes mental health is necessary in either case: as a norm by which behavior is evaluated, in the case of diagnosis; as a goal toward which patient and therapist strive, in the case of therapy. May's discussion begins with an examination of other historical periods. The perspective that results, like the perspective provided by Benedict's examination of other societies, demonstrates the importance of the culture in which the individual functions. In some historical periods, individuals seem to have been relatively free of psychological disorders, and May argues that such individual integration results from a high degree of cultural integration. We might expect that integration at such a comprehensive level would depend heavily on an ethical, or value, consensus. May's finding that "psychotherapy historically has been until the modern period a function of philosophy, ethics, and religion" seems to support this view and foreshadows his discussion of the ethical aspect of therapy.

Every alert practicing therapist must have asked himself countless times the naïve question, Why do people come for psychotherapeutic help? The symptoms which are their *occasions* for coming and the reasons why they *say* they come are simple enough: they are caught in marital conflicts, they cannot love or accept love, they are always quitting jobs, they feel perpetually unhappy, or they experience anxiety attacks and sudden fits of hostility, depression, or despair. But the incidence of this or that symptom changes from decade to decade. Most people came for therapy in Freud's day because of some conflict related to the repression of sexual impulses. While this is no longer the case, no one would hold that the degree or extent of psychological illness is less in our day than in Freud's. So the therapist cannot answer his question by citing symptoms; the naïve question leads to the most profound problems: What is the nature of the human mammal that it should be peculiarly prey to psychological conflict, anxiety, and despair? What goes wrong in a given culture, such as ours, that so many people should need to come to therapists for help? And, assuming the nature of the human being was much the same throughout recorded history, did such psychological problems occur in other historical periods, possibly more in certain periods than in others? And to whom did people go for help before Freud and the development of modern psychotherapy?

Every alert therapist has likewise asked himself countless times why Mr. Jones overcame his psychological problems in therapy and attained a great deal of release of creative potentiality, while Mrs. Smith made only partial gains and we could not help Mr. Brown at all? Many of us have endeavored, over a period of months and years, to determine what factors are at work in our therapy with the subjects who make excellent progress, and what factors are present in the cases which turn out to be psychotherapeutic failures. But to arrive at any communicable understanding of the conditions for therapeutic success or failure, we need first to arrive at some sound presuppositions as to what the nature of therapy is. . . .

A historical and cultural perspective on therapy

A historical perspective should help the therapist to achieve a more dynamic attitude toward the problems of the persons who come to him. With this perspective, he can more easily see, in the form of a trajectory, how certain cultural forces and events have shaped and formed the attitudes and behavior patterns which underlie contemporaneous psychological conflicts. Furthermore, a historical perspective can help the therapist to free himself from the danger of absolutizing a theory or method which is really relative to a given point in history. Freud's universalizing of certain sexual patterns is a clear case in point: the specific sexual problems which Freud in his Victorian culture thought were universal would not have occurred in the same way in ancient Greece or in the Middle Ages, and indeed they do not emerge in exactly the same way in the middle of our twentieth century. Lastly, a historical perspective can help us to see the common sources of human behavior problems as well as common goals through our observing how people in different ages have struggled through their conflicts with authority, anxiety, and responsibility, and how they have sought in their literature, science, philosophy, and religion to bring their wisdom — or lack of it — to bear on their common problems.

But as soon as one endeavors to explore history, one confronts the almost insuperable hurdle of limitations of time and space. In this paper we shall limit ourselves to certain significant aspects of the culture of ancient Greece which bear on psychological illness and therapy and then trace certain motifs in the modern period since the Renaissance.

In classic Greece one discovers immediately a kind of "normal" psychotherapy operating spontaneously through certain commonly accepted symbols and practices in the Greek religion, philosophy, art, and drama. This is to be seen most clearly in the Greek myths. The stories of Oedipus' conflict with his father, of Prometheus' struggle with forbidden creative urges, and of Orestes' slaying of his mother obviously had powerful psychological meaning for the Greek people. Aristotle spoke of the "cathartic," purging effect of these dramas upon the observers. And it is not difficult to imagine how profound and clarifying a psychological effect the presentation of Sophocles' Oedipus trilogy might create in some young man who was struggling with an authoritarian father. Or imagine some person who was burdened with guilt feelings because of hostility toward an exploitative mother observing the drama of Orestes killing the mother who had assassinated his father, then being pursued to the ends of the earth by the fierce Erinyes,[1] and finally achieving peace when he was forgiven by Zeus. How abreactive must have been the emotional impact!

We do not mean to imply that these psychotherapeutic experiences would be consciously articulated by the citizen of Greece in the fifth century B.C. Indeed, it seems that just the opposite was true—that "therapy" in that period was part of the normal, unarticulated functions of the drama, religion, and other forms of communication of the day. These Greek myths—born back in unknown sources in the archaic days of the culture, related by the early poets like Homer, shaped, reshaped, and passed on by later dramatists in the classical period, discussed by the philosophers, presented in religious ceremonies in which the whole citizenry participated, and used as a basis for education of the young—these myths in their very existence must indicate how therapeutic processes and experiences are developed and operate in a society by spontaneous, natural means. The fact, also, that these myths have become classics demonstrates that they speak out of profound human conflicts and struggles which were and are felt by human beings in other periods and other parts of the world as well as by the ancient Greeks. Despite Freud's predilection for interpreting the myths too narrowly, it was part of his genius that he

sensed the deep, classical meaning of the Greek myths and borrowed from them for the central concepts in modern psychoanalysis.

If a citizen of Greece in the fifth century B.C. had a psychosomatic illness and if he were sophisticated and at least of medium wealth, he would go to the town of Epidaurus. Here, centering around the shrine dedicated to Aesculapius, the god of healing, medical and religious practices had developed and dramatic, social, and vocational "therapy" took place. The health activities at Epidaurus are an original example of the endeavor to cure a human being not by isolating him from the community but by aiding him to participate with others in activities which minister to the many different sides of his personality.

Or, if the citizen were not symptomatically ill but were sensitive enough to want to achieve greater self-knowledge and inner integration, he might go, as Socrates did, to the shrine of the god Apollo at Delphi. Socrates sought help in his endeavors to unmask hypocrisy, false piety, and self-deceit in himself and in others, faults which he believed were due to the fact that men did not honestly examine their inner motives. As a method for achieving this examination of motives he developed the "Socratic dialogue," which chiefly consisted (how like good therapy of any period!) of asking the right questions. The Socratic method of unmasking self-deceit and rationalization had at least three evidences of efficacy as a therapy: it enabled Socrates himself to become a model of probity and courage; it was of great help to Socrates' friends in their quest for inner integration; and it called forth the rabid anger and opposition of the conventional members of the populace of Athens. On his trip to Delphi, Socrates followed the custom of breathing the fumes which emerge from the fissure in the rocks at the shrine of Apollo (fumes which perhaps had a hypnotic effect). In the succeeding ceremony

1. Avenging spirits who pursue evil-doers and inflict madness; hence undoubtedly mythological symbols of guilt and remorse.

he was told by the god—so he relates in the *Apologia*—that he was the wisest man then living in the world, and he was given the famous injunction "Know thyself." The former encomium Socrates explained as being related to the fact that he publicly admitted his ignorance. What the god meant, then, was that the person who had broken through his need to pretend, the need to absolutize his beliefs, and had arrived at a humble, seeking attitude toward truth is the wise man. (This is, of course, parallel to one tenet of modern psychotherapy—a tenet often used for the unjustified criticism that therapy causes one to be "too introspective"—namely, that the wise and mature man is he who realizes that his motives never are entirely pure but always involve some rationalization, who tries to admit and work through this rationalization, but who nevertheless acts as best he can on his insights at the time.)

The dictum given currency by Socrates, "Know thyself," is one of those seminal phrases which psychologically avid people all through the ages have tried to interpret and reinterpret. For one example, Nietzsche in the nineteenth century wrote, "What did the God mean who gave the advice 'Know thyself!' to Socrates? Did it perhaps imply: 'Cease to be concerned about thyself! become objective!'?" Thus Nietzsche, with his customary psychological acuteness, suggests that objectivity is to be achieved as the end result of knowledge of one's self, that objectivity is arrived at, not by *suppressing* one's subjective interests, but only by knowing one's self so well that one can transcend the boundaries of subjectivity in favor of objective interest in the problem at hand. How self-knowledge, religion, and ethics are united in Socrates' attitude is shown in Kierkegaard's comment (1946):

"In the Socratic view each individual is his own center, and the entire world centers in him, because his self-knowledge is a knowledge of God. It was thus Socrates understood himself, and thus he thought that everyone must understand himself, in the light of this understanding interpreting his relationship to each individual, with equal humility and with equal pride. He had the courage and self-possession to be sufficient unto himself, but also in his relations to his fellowmen to be merely an occasion even when dealing with the meanest capacity. How rare is such magnanimity!" (p. 7).

The "knowing" in the Socratic dictum cannot be taken in an intellectualistic or rationalistic sense, for it means an endeavor to know one's self on the various levels within one's personality which in modern parlance would be termed unconscious levels. Socrates' idea (and later Plato's) was that every person, through intuition or dreams or fantasies, remembers truths which he learned in a previous existence. This is the doctrine of "reminiscence."[2] Shorn of its mythological character, this concept is simply a way of describing something which becomes clear in every psychoanalysis, that a person knows much more than he is consciously aware that he knows, that what Freud called the unconscious depths of personality contain not only impulses and desires but observations, previous learning, and past experience which have for various reasons been blocked off from the individual's conscious awareness. Furthermore, this "store of learning" is not to be thought of as the result solely of one's own past experience; there is in it much that is the residue of the teachings of the culture which the individual is unaware that he has learned.[3] As a person progresses in psychotherapy and gradually overcomes the anxiety which forced him to repress his awareness of certain things, it is not at all uncom-

2. The term "reminiscence," which is the usual English translation of the term in Plato's dialogues, is actually too passive a word to do full justice to the active uncovering of truth within one's self which Socrates was talking about. Kierkegaard's term when discussing this point in Socrates —"recollection"—is much better in that it suggests an active re-collecting of one's knowledge.

3. It is not necessary to accept Jung's hypothesis of the existence of archetypes in the collective unconscious (incidentally, a direct adaptation of Plato's theory) to agree that every individual has picked up considerable stores of experience and judgment which are the residue of his historical culture.

mon for him to arrive at a startling discovery and then say, "Well, I knew this all the time, but I never admitted it to myself."

Knowing one's self meant to Socrates a continuous, rigorous, and relentless, though joyful and immensely gratifying, endeavor to penetrate to deeper levels within one's self, and then to act on the basis of a unity of these levels with the conscious self. As he phrased it in his prayer at the conclusion of the *Phaedrus*, "May the outward and the inward man be at one."[4] He believed that ethics and value judgments must be based on this deeper self-knowledge; his picturesque term was that he had a *daimon* (conscience) within him which always told him what he should not do.

Indeed, the pilgrimage to Delphi and the ceremony there were religious practices designed to facilitate this arriving at his own deepest insights. It would obviously be a complete mistake to be misled by Socrates' terms (e.g., *daimon*) into assuming that his approach was authoritarian. Actually his attitudes, his manner of teaching, and his emphasis on the individual's arriving at truth through penetrating into himself are exactly the opposite to the authoritarian approach in religion or psychotherapy. His central point is that the individual, by rigorous honesty and by symbolic processes that go far beyond mere intellectualizing, is able to arrive at truth within himself, that this is the closest he can get to objective knowledge, and that his happiness depends upon his finding and following this inner truth. In Socrates self-knowledge and ethics are given a common base. A parallel in contemporary writing is Fromm's idea of conscience as "man's recall to himself" (1947).

The culture out of which the Greek dramatists and Socrates spoke was moving toward unity in its basic symbols in art, philosophy, science, and religion—a unity discernible particularly in the art of the Golden Age and the works of Plato and culminating in the thought system of Aristotle in the fourth century B.C. But in the decline of Hellenic society which began shortly thereafter, following the conquest of Greece by Alexander and later by the Romans and the dispersion of Greek culture to Asia Minor and to Rome, this unity was progressively lost.

The citizens of Hellenistic society, particularly in the second and first centuries B.C., no longer supported by an integrated culture, were thrown on their own, as it were; and psychological insecurity and anxiety, together with attitudes of cynicism and hopelessness, are much more discernible than in the earlier periods. Gilbert Murray speaks of this period of the second and first centuries B.C. as the time of the "failure of nerve," a phrase which might well characterize the condition of citizens of any social period which is in the process of disintegration and basic change. A number of philosophical schools flourished during that period—the Stoics, Epicureans, Cynics, Cyrenaics, and Hedonists, together with the traditional Platonists and Aristotelians. What is significant about these diverse schools is that they take the form of psychological and ethical systems designed to help the individual find some source of strength and integrity to enable him to stand securely and gain some happiness in a changing society which no longer lent him that security. In this period, thus, the philosophical systems assume very much the character of methods of *overt* psychotherapy, good or bad as they may be.

The Stoics developed the doctrine of *apatheia*, meaning a passionless calm attained by the exercise of strong will. One should assert one's mastery over outward events, or if one could not do that, one should at least be unaffected by them.[5] Great individual strength was often produced by the beliefs and practices of Stoicism, but it was a strength gained at the price of suppression of all emotions, negative and positive alike. The Epicureans, on the other hand, sought to achieve tranquillity of mind by rationally balancing their pleasures—a doctrine called *ataraxia*—with special value placed on intellectual pleas-

---

4. The whole prayer is so beautiful, and so revealing of Socrates' emphasis on sound value judgments as intimately intertwined with psychological clarification, that we quote it *in toto*: "Beloved Pan, and all ye other gods who haunt this place, give me beauty in the inward soul; and may the outward and inward man be at one. May I reckon the wise to be the wealthy, and may I have such a quantity of gold as none but the temperate can carry."

ures. But again, as in the case of the Stoics, this in practice entailed an emasculation of dynamic urges; one writer of the period even refers to the Epicureans as eunuchs. The Hedonist tradition emphasized finding pleasure in sensual satisfaction. But one teacher, Hegesias, despairing of ever attaining happiness, became the philosopher of pessimism; and his lectures in Alexandria had to be prohibited by Ptolemy because they resulted in so many suicides.

These ancient methods of trying to avoid anxiety and attain happiness by repression of parts of one's experience are not at all foreign to us in the twentieth century, for they have their parallels (as we shall see) in the compartmentalization of emotion, will, and intellect in the nineteenth century which preceded the development of psychoanalysis.

From this brief glance at the parallels to modern psychotherapy in two phases of the ancient Greek period, it seems clear that the state of the culture, its relative unity or disunity,[6] is closely related to the character of the "therapeutic" activities in the society. In comparing the time of Socrates with the later period, we noted that in the former the therapeutic activities were much more intimately a function of the normal practice and expression of philosophy, religion, and drama in the society. One gets the impression in the earlier classic period of *education* more than *re-education*, of normal development of the individual toward integration rather than desperate endeavor to

overcome neurosis and attain reintegration. In Socrates there is the assumption that, if one develops in unity with his own deeper self, the problems which we normally call "neurotic" will be largely obviated. This kind of normal development is relatively more possible for the individual when his culture is moving toward, or has achieved, some unity. But in the later period of social change (the "failure of nerve" period), the individual was anxious and insecure, and his problems seem to be much more like those we would today term "neurotic."[7] Then the function of the systems of "therapy" (as we have noted in Stoicism and Epicureanism) is to help the person back to some unity, to help him *overcome* some unfavorable pattern, to give him *re-education* and *reintegration*, in contrast to education and integration.[8]

We now turn to the modern period. Psychological analyses of this period, which began in western Europe with the Renaissance and Reformation and of which we are direct

5. The writings of Epictetus, though he was Roman and lived in the first century A.D., are excellent examples of Stoicism attempting to perform services for the individual like those of some modern forms of psychotherapy.

6. We are not speaking chiefly of political unity and peace; the Hellenistic period, after the Roman conquest, had peace, and Greece, in the Golden Age in Athens, did not. Rather, we are speaking of the unity of a culture in terms of those symbols which give meaning to it: its artistic, philosophical, scientific, ethical, economic, and religious symbols. I realize the difficulty in defining specifically what one means by cultural unity without going into a wealth of historical data. But I assume the unity of the classic period in Greece and the disunity of the later centuries are so well accepted that they do not need to be proved here.

7. It is difficult to find discussions of anxiety (as distinguished from fear) in the Socratic period or in Plato or, for that matter, in Aristotle. It is not through they did not experience anxiety in the pervasive way we do in the twentieth century (see also Spinoza and the seventeenth century in this respect). But in the first centuries B.C. and A.D., one finds plenty of descriptions of anxiety: Plutarch paints a very vivid picture of an anxious man, and Epictetus describes anxiety-like states in detail. It is very clear that they knew in the Hellenistic period what anxiety was.

8. Though we shall make no endeavor here to explore the Hebrew or the Roman culture, it can be remarked in passing that these are both exceedingly important areas for research for the student who wishes to understand how human beings dealt with psychological problems in previous ages. The ancient Hebrew psychological approach avoided the dualism which became increasingly prominent in Greek thought; and in its emphasis on psychophysical interrelations, the Hebrew psychology was in many ways close to the modern emphasis. See Mowrer's discussion (1950) of the Hebrew psalms with reference to anxiety. One especially important period is the fifth century A.D., when Rome began to disintegrate and later fell. This also was a period of widespread psychological upheaval, as would be expected; and it produced, in Augustine, some of the most astute depth-psychological writing to be found before the modern

heirs, have been given elsewhere.[9] Hence we shall here only summarize some of the main points in the development of the modern period which bear on the present state of psychotherapy.

The disintegrating phase of medievalism, out of which the modern period was born, was marked by rampant anxiety, despair, and pessimism. It was a time similar in psychological mood to the "failure of nerve" period in the disintegrating phase of Greek culture. Anxiety about death and fears of the devil, sorcerers and witches were prevalent, particularly in the fourteenth and fifteenth centuries. During the previous centuries in the Middle Ages, an individual would have sought security, relief from anxiety, and answers to his psychological and ethical problems in the collective structure of the church and the feudalistic hierarchy. But in the phase of the "waning of the Middle Ages," multitudes of people believed in sorcery and witchcraft and apparently resorted to the sorcerer and witch to find answers to their problems. The religious practices likewise tended to become magical. The distinction between the spiritual meaning of a religious sacrament and objective fact was increasingly lost. Not only was the use of symbols rampant, but the symbols either became empty and without emotional meaning for people at large or on the other hand were identified with objective reality. In the sacrament of the mass, for example, the tendency was to consider the bread the real body of Christ. The practice of indulgences grew apace, not only because it was a good way for the papacy to raise money, but because people were so anxious about their sins that they were always willing to try to buy off some future punishment. The need of many persons to go to confession more and more frequently tended to become obsessional. These religious practices illustrate the deteriorated, disunified state of the culture at that time, with the church seen as one aspect of the culture (an ecclesiastical deterioration which Catholic scholars readily admit, and which was followed by a partial reformation within the Roman church.[10]

A radical change occurred with the Renaissance and Reformation in the form of belief in the power of the individual, together with a new concrete and empirical concern with physical nature. These changes had as one of their obvious psychological results the increase of the individual's confidence that problems could be overcome by his own courage, by knowledge that he could obtain by his own study and travel, and by following the guidance of his own conscience in religious and ethical matters. The method which became the tool of

period. Augustine, for example, held that it is possible for the individual to arrive at a level within himself in which objectivity and subjectivity are not opposite but are united.

9. See May (1950b), chaps. ii and vi; also "The Historical Roots of Modern Anxiety Theories," chap. i in Hoch and Zubin (1950). For a similar sociopsychological analysis to which I am indebted, see Fromm (1941). Abram Kardiner has written a brief description of the cultural history from a psychodynamic viewpoint (1945).

10. Cyril Richardson, to whose historical studies I am indebted for part of the above material, proposes the thesis that one can discover the chief anxiety-allaying methods of a historical period by noting what the reformers in the subsequent period attacked. This interesting hypothesis strikes me as being exceedingly fruitful for further study. Thus, Luther and the other leaders of the Protestant Reformation attacked the reliance on external sacramentalism of late medieval Catholicism, and the leaders of the Renaissance attacked the scholastic symbolism and corporate authority of medievalism as opposed to their new individualism and naturalism. Thus, the reformers following the disintegrating phase of Hellenistic culture (for example, the early Christians) attacked the vapid and arid rationalistic philosophies of the Hellenistic time. I should only add to Richardson's hypothesis that it seems to me that the central "motif," the particular "genius" or "charter" (in Malinowski's sense) of a given historical period, will be what, in deteriorated form, is obsessively clung to at the time of disintegration of the period. With regard to the present period, we shall indicate below that the dependence on science as a form of magic is what many persons in our day cling to as a method of allaying anxiety and may well be what the next age will attack. These propositions are suggested not as answers but as hypotheses for future psychocultural investigations.

the new devotion to knowledge and individual reason was mathematics, Arabic mathematics having been introduced into western Europe after the crusades in the thirteenth century. The understanding and control of physical nature became Western man's dominant concern, an enterprise greatly expedited by Descartes' dichotomy between mind and body, with its corollary that the body and physical nature could be understood by mathematical, mechanical laws.

In the late Renaissance (the sixteenth century) there are several writers who, though unfortunately rarely studied in connection with modern psychological developments, presented germinal ideas for the modern period. One is Giordano Bruno (later to be burned at the stake by the Inquisition) whose idea of Creation as concentric circles with the self at the center gave the original philosophical orientation for modernism. Another is Jacob Boehme, a German mystic and precursor of Protestant thought, who wrote with amazing insight about the relation between anxiety and individual creative effort. And a third is Paracelsus, a physician in the Renaissance who emphasized the influence of the patient's own will (decision) in the achievement of health. It is with Paracelsus, according to Tillich, that the physician began to take over in modern culture the role which the priest had played in medievalism.

The systematization of the philosophical viewpoints which were to dominate most of the modern period occurred in the seventeenth century. This century—the time of that group of seminal thinkers of modernity including Spinoza, Descartes, Leibnitz, Locke, Galileo, Newton, and others—is the classical phase of the modern period as the fifth century B.C. was of the Greek period. An excellent example of the use of the dominant concepts of the day in the service of overcoming problems of fear and hatred is seen in Spinoza, who used mathematical reason as a basis for a theory of the emotions and the ethical life. "Reason" in that day did not at all mean arid intellectualism coupled with the repression of emotion, which the term often connotes in both academic and popular circles now. For Spinoza, reason was an "ecstatic" term;[11] it meant a general attitude toward life which penetrated below the customary distinction between subjectivity and objectivity and included emotions and decision for action as well as thinking.[12]

We have elsewhere pointed out that Spinoza does not discuss anxiety as the term is used in modern psychotherapy.[13] Given the cultural milieu in which he lived, it seems that his confidence in individual reason served him satisfactorily. That was a time, again parallel to the fifth century in ancient Greece, when the culture was moving toward unity in its basic symbols. Thus the citizens found in their society more psychological support. One has the impression that the problems which we in the twentieth century describe as calling for therapy were met more by the natural, spontaneous processes of education and religion in the society of the seventeenth and eighteenth centuries.

The disunity which became apparent in the middle and second half of the nineteenth century and became much more extensive in the twentieth century has also been described elsewhere.[14] We wish here only to emphasize that this disunity went hand in hand with the great progress which had been made in the application of mathematical reason and mechanical laws to physical nature. The far-reaching achievement of the physical sciences, with the promise of making Nature man's servant, together with the vast progress of industrialism and its promise of meeting human physical needs, gave ample support for the great confidence which had been placed in the endeavor to understand and control Nature by mechanical laws. By the nineteenth century the earlier confidence in individual reason as related to all aspects

11. The term "ecstatic" in this use is a technical one, coming from the Greek *ecstasis* (a standing out from). It implies the kind of activity in which a person is wholly caught up or absorbed.

12. A close parallel in this use of "reason" as involving ethical and emotional factors is seen in our day in the writings of Fromm (1947).

13. May (1950a and 1950b).

14. May (1950b).

of life had changed to an emphasis on techniques and the application of reason more and more exclusively to technical problems. There was no common view of man except those of the various sciences, and these different sciences had no basis of unity with each other. Cassirer points out that this disunity with respect to views of man was a grave "threat to the whole extent of our ethical and cultural life."[15]

The psychological aspect of this disunity lay in the compartmentalization of the personality, the tendency to see man as consisting of different "faculties"—e.g., reason, emotion, and will power. The nineteenth century man was supposed, like a successful businessman or industrialist, to make decisions by practical reason and then to enforce these decisions by his strong will power. It was as though the citizen of the nineteenth century were trying to solve his personal psychological problems by the same methods which had been so effective in mastering physical nature and so successful in the industrial world. This process meant in practice a repression of the emotions and the irrational aspects of experience. In the nineteenth century, penetrating thinkers like Kierkegaard, Nietzsche, and Dostoievski saw the psychological havoc that was to result from this compartmentalization. They tried to find a new basis for individual action which would involve a unity of reason and emotion and would include the dynamic aspects of experience which had previously been repressed. These thinkers were centrally concerned with ethics, and ethics not consisting of repression of emotion to fit bourgeois mores but rather of actions proceeding from an individual who had inner unity and integrity.[16]

The psychological disunity and conflict resulting from nineteenth century compartmentalization underlay in general the symptoms for which people came to Freud. His genius was that he took the central emphases of our period, the methods of science, and made them applicable to the areas which previously had been excluded, namely the dynamic, so-called irrational, unconscious aspects of human experience. The radical distinction between our age and previous ages, with respect to therapy for people's problems, is that for the first time in history we have methods for dealing with emotional problems which are partially objective (in the scientific sense) and thereby communicable.

In this brief historical survey we have noted several points, which we suggest here as tentative conclusions. Whereas people in different historical ages and presumably in all ages have the problems which in our own day bring them to the therapist, the degree of these problems, both in the extension of psychological difficulties throughout the society and in the "overtness" and articulateness of the problems, varies at different phases of a given historical period. We observed that, when the culture is moving toward unity and integration, as in Greece in the fifth century B.C. or in the seventeenth century in the modern period, anxiety and psychological disunity are less discernible and the functions of "therapy" seem more to be taken care of by the normal functions of education, art, religion, philosophy, and the like in the society. But in the phases of the period when the culture is involved in basic change and disunity or disintegration, as for example in the later centuries of the Greek period, the last of the Middle Ages, and the later nineteenth and in the twentieth centuries in our own period, *anxiety, isolation, pessimism, and despair are much more in evidence*. The individual is driven within himself to find security and integration. The problems which we would term "neurotic" and the specific functions of therapy in the society become more overt and articulate, more to be described as re-education and reintegration than as education and integration.

We also noted that in all ages, with the partial exception of our own period from Freud to the present, people went for help on their problems to the ethical and religious leaders in their society. That is to say, psychotherapy historically has been until the modern period a function of philosophy, ethics, and religion.

15. See his excellent discussion in chap. i of *An essay on man* (1944).
16. See Nietzsche's concept of the "transmoral" conscience, in *Beyond good and evil*.

As indicated earlier, the chief values of a historical perspective are that it frees us from being blindly determined by our given historical position, it enables us to avoid universalizing a viewpoint which is actually relative to and a product of our own particular stage in history, and it enables us to correct the particular biases and errors of our culture in the light of the wisdom and learning of previous periods in history.[17] The perplexing difficulty is that the chief constructive contribution of any period and the particular biases of that period will be intertwined, since they both arise from the dominant motif of the culture.

The great contribution of our period has been the applying of science to psychological and personal problems. But that also involves our greatest danger of error unless we can free ourselves from two tendencies. One is the widespread tendency in our society to place a magical faith in the powers of science. The fact that "Dianetics" swept the country is a staggering and sobering testimony to this tendency. It seems to me that "Dianetics" bears a relation to modern science similar to the relation of witchcraft and sorcery to the religion of late medievalism. "Dianetics" illustrates how the faith of large numbers of persons in our age of science tends, in a time of anxiety, to cling to a practice which has all the external markings and all the claims to power of science but none of its inner meaning, and that is as good a definition as any of what constitutes magic.

Another danger from which we must free ourselves arises from a particular conception of science which has dominated our society since Descartes introduced his dichotomy between body and mind in the seventeenth century. We must find new methods which will not involve the disunity arising from that dichotomy. Medicine, for example, has made great and laudable progress in the past century, chiefly because its methods have fitted the traditional emphasis in our historical culture. But the tendency to try to stretch the methods of medicine to fit all problems of health, emotional and psychological as well as physical, is to fall into the error of universalizing a method which actually is relative and specific. The methods which have been traditionally dominant in academic psychology have in general been taken over from the methods of the physical sciences; and, like medicine, they are a product of the traditional dichotomy between subjective and objective phenomena. Hence they cannot serve as a basis for a new unity. Though Freud so clearly saw these points, it is fairly widely recognized that his chief error also was in uncritically taking over some of the dominant concepts of the Newtonian mechanics and physics of the nineteenth century, as particularly illustrated in his physio-chemical libido theory.

It is our task, as therapists and investigators in psychotherapy in the middle of the twentieth century, to appropriate the gains and insights not only of our own period but of previous ages as well, that we may correct the particular errors to which our period is heir, and that we may find a new basis for therapy which will as effectively as possible fit the particular needs of persons in our day....

The ethical aspect of therapy

...Value judgments and ethical standards are inextricably interwoven with the process and the goals of therapy. By "value judgments" we simply mean the conviction, for example, that it is better for the human

17. In my judgment, Kardiner illustrates the error of universalizing a viewpoint which is actually historically relative when he states that he takes "modern science as an absolute base" (1945) from which to study and criticize other periods. Kardiner uses this base particularly to criticize the absolutism of the Middle Ages, but actually his own method is parallel to that absolutism. The difference is one of symbols—he uses for his absolute base the symbol of "science," instead of which the medieval scholar would use "the Church" or "God." But both are used as absolutes. The fact that the term is "science" rather than the medieval "God" doesn't make either symbol the less relative to a point in history. The sound scientific approach, I submit, is to see all our presuppositions as relative to our position in history and as our approximations to truth. The only tenable absolute from the scientific viewpoint is that the quest for truth is worth making.

being to expand in his capacities, to be free, to love, and to be happy than not to be and do these things. And we define ethics for the present purpose as the application of such value judgments to one's interpersonal relations—ethical behavior thus being ways of acting which affirm the growth, freedom, and happiness of others in the community as well as one's self.

The progress of psychoanalysis in the last decade could be judged, on one side, by the increasing recognition that it is an illusion for the analyst to suppose that he can avoid value judgments. This recognition is explicit, to mention only a few examples, in the writings of Fromm and Horney, and implicit in the work of Fromm-Reichmann, Kubie, Alexander, and French. Among the psychologists who are concerned with practicing or testing therapy, the same conclusion is being reached. In a very pertinent article on this point, Hunt (1949) notes that it has been generally "claimed that values do not belong to the subject matter of science." He remarks that he endeavored to devise instruments for the measuring of therapeutic results which would not involve value judgments, and then he writes these significant words:

". . .but after over four years of work . . . I have reluctantly come to the conclusion that the scientist cannot avoid the value assumptions merely by deciding to do so. Precisely because casework and psychotherapy are directed toward helping people with their problems of adjustment and adaptation which involve value concepts, the instruments designed to measure the results in behavioral or situational change must inevitably take human values into account. I contend, therefore, that the theory of measuring instruments in this frontier area should be explicit not only about the fact that values are involved, but about *whose* values are taken into account in each instrument" (p. 125).

The only question we would raise about Hunt's excellent statement is his curious use of the word "reluctantly" in the first sentence quoted above. It is as though those of us in the field of social science in the modern day still assume that it would be "better" if we did not have to make value assumptions, and as though the necessity to take "human values into account" is a kind of concession we have to make to the imperfections of knowledge and human nature. But is not our "reluctance" clearly a product of the Cartesian dichotomy of which we are heirs, and the particular compartmentalization of human experience which occurred in the nineteenth century as a final outworking of this dichotomy? The long historical perspective is at this point a most persuasive corrective to our contemporary distortions: all through history until about the last seventy-five years it has been recognized that value judgments are a central aspect of an individual's interpersonal clarification. From Socrates and Isaiah down to Spinoza and Kierkegaard, it has been repeatedly stated that the problems of how a human being is to overcome hate, anxiety, and guilt and to achieve some psychological freedom and capacity to love and to use his power in creative productivity involve ethical attitudes and decisions. Our contemporary problem, therefore, is not merely that we must "bring back" value judgments into consideration, but rather to ask why we ever in the first place attempted to separate elements which are in reality inseparable. For if therapists or social scientists endeavor to deal with a human being—who is of necessity continuously engaged in making decisions which affect his welfare as well as that of others—without taking into consideration the value judgments on which these decisions are based, they are dealing not with a living human being but an abstraction which has reality only in the subjective categories in the mind of the therapist or scientist.

The upshot of this discussion is not at all that there should be less emphasis on the specifically scientific techniques in therapy, but rather that these techniques can and should go hand in hand with a clarification of the value judgments and the ethical aspects of therapy. One of the most insidious illusions in much of the therapy of two and three decades ago was the supposed "neutrality" of the process of therapy on ethical questions, with the implication that it doesn't matter very much what value judgments the analysand or therapist makes. It was not seen that this attitude is actually not at all neutral but is based on a particular ethical viewpoint, namely that of a fairly complete relativism. Ethical and value judgments are inescapably present whenever one deals with living human beings. To try to suppress these judgments only tends to confuse the goals of the therapy or results inadvertently in the therapist's value judgments being impressed rigidly on the patient or produces a vapid and undynamic form of therapy.

The practical problem, therefore, is to be openly aware of the presence and significance of ethical aspects in therapy. By this open awareness, several pitfalls can be best avoided. First, the person in therapy can then find a sound basis for distinguishing neurotic guilt feelings from real guilt feelings, and he can thus avoid being blocked in his development by the former.[18] Secondly, the client or analysand need not fall into the pit of unconsciously taking over the superficial mores of his culture, which may not be productive of his best development. And third, the therapist is helped to realize that his particular value judgments and ethical standards are not absolute, and do not *ipso facto* constitute the universal goals of mankind's development. Just as the therapist can avoid projecting his own resentments, for example, into his relation with the subject by being aware of these resentments, so he can avoid projecting his particular ethical judgments on the patient only by being consciously aware of what his judgments are. Particular and specific forms of value judgment will, of course, vary with the diverse problems and configurations of different clients and analysands. Certain sexual actions may represent genuine and constructive values for one person and not for another; or, to learn to apply himself persistently in work may represent an important value for the passive individual, but for the compulsive person the capacity to say "no" to the demands of his work may be equally important as a specific value. We shall not endeavor here to go into the problem of the relation between immediate value judgments in a given culture and the long-term, underlying ethical meaning in human relations. Suffice it to say that the customary ethical relativism or authoritarian absolutism are not the only alternatives; there are the classical ethical traditions in Western history as well as in the history of other cultures, and there are the common needs of man in his human relations upon which we have much more light since the development of depth-psychological techniques. We suggest the problem of the relation of the various ethical approaches to psychotherapy as one of great fruitfulness for future students of the field who can utilize the contemporary understanding of unconscious motivations.

It should be obvious in this discussion that we are not suggesting that explicit—and certainly not theoretical—discussions of ethics as such will come up in the therapeutic hour. After the initial agreement on the goals of therapy, it may well be that not much specific reference will be made to value judgments as such. We mean, rather, to emphasize that ethical aspects will always be part of the *presuppositions*, part of the context, of therapy, not only with respect to the goals of therapy but also with respect to the relation between the therapist and the other person. The therapist's aim, with regard to ethical standards, is to help the other person to remove distortions and the various forms of neurotic contradictions within himself that he may arrive at and choose freely the value judgments and ethical standards which are most constructive for him. This ability to be a "midwife," to use Socrates' word, is not easy of attainment, and it can well be a goal toward which a therapist works in his own development year in and year out. As Kierkegaard remarked about Socrates, "how rare the magnanimity" of a helper who can be sufficiently concerned with the other person's self-realization and sufficiently free of his own need to dominate that he is willing to be merely an "occasion" for the other's achievement of his own values.

18. For discussions of the distinctions between neurotic and real (objective, constructive) guilt feelings, see Fromm (1947) and May (1950b).

Carl R. Rogers

PSYCHOTHERAPY TODAY

OR WHERE DO WE GO FROM HERE?

In reviewing the current situation in the field of psychotherapy, Rogers makes abundantly clear the lack of agreement about the nature of good therapy. If similar goals were accepted by most therapists, reaching agreement would be a matter of determining facts: which method is most successful? This question could then be answered by research, because to agree on goals is to agree on what constitutes success. But Rogers finds little agreement on the goals themselves. He argues for an emphasis on facts, rather than faith in a doctrinaire point of view, and is optimistic about a future in which curious and skeptical younger minds, freed from dogmatism, will pursue new therapeutic knowledge anchored in sound experimental studies and empirical observations. We can certainly share the view that objective data will reconcile many differences and advance the field. But we must keep in mind the problem of value choices and ask whether facts alone will enable us to choose among the different kinds of goals that Rogers and the other authors represented in this book have identified.

The germ of this paper started to develop more than four years ago, at the first workshop of the American Academy of Psychotherapists. I had, for many reasons, looked forward eagerly to this workshop. Among my reasons, as I realized later, was the implicit belief that experienced therapists, no matter how divergent their orientations, certainly had in common their *experience* of what constituted helpfulness. Hence if they could observe and participate together in a therapeutic *experience*, it would be a very important stride in the direction of ironing out their verbal and ideological differences. So it was very exciting that we were able to arrange to have patients interviewed by different therapists, the rest of us observing.

But then came the jolt. The very portions of those interviews which to me seemed obviously moments of "real" therapy, were experienced by other members as non-therapeutic or even anti-therapeutic. And the moments which some others regarded as clearly of a healing nature, I experienced as meaningless or ineffectual, or worse. At the time this was a hard blow to assimilate. It meant that our differences ran far deeper than I had presumed. I had supposed that we were all talking about the same *experiences*, but attaching different words, labels, and descriptions to these experiences. This was clearly not true. I have been mulling over this fact ever since.

I believe there is little question but that it *is* a fact. Let me mention some of the diverse and occasionally amusing incidents which support this statement—that what seems therapeutic to one seems anti-therapeutic to another.

Recently I participated in a diversified group of therapists in which a well-qualified analyst presented a portion of one of his cases. The central point was the way he had encouraged his patient to speak up to his boss and give the boss a solution to a problem which was troubling the company. To him, this encouragement seemed clearly therapeutic. The group felt, almost unanimously, that he had kept the man from making an important personal, existential choice, that he had robbed the incident of its therapeutic potential.

A prominent therapist, who would, I believe, term himself a practitioner of existential therapy, listened to a tape recording of a therapeutic interview conducted by two well-known members of the American Academy of Psychotherapists, which I am sure they regarded as helpful. Afterwards his comment was that the two therapists ought to refund the patient's money. "The only good elements in the interview were the bird songs in the background!"

This same existentialist played one of his taped therapeutic interviews and was particularly pleased with the way he had dissuaded his patient, a young woman, from going home for the weekend, a trip which he believed would have been regressive. I was surprised at his comments, for in listening to the interview I had felt that his persuasion was the one clearly anti-therapeutic portion of the interview.

A young therapist of my acquaintance was highly successful with a deeply disturbed hospitalized psychotic man. He feels that one of the crucial therapeutic moments occurred when he shouted at the man, who was engaged in rambling intellectualized incoherencies, the one word, "Bulluhit!" Other therapists listening, however, have often been shocked, and feel not only that such a term is not proper therapeutic technique, but that it was not therapeutic in this instance.

Similarly unconventional, a serious paper was given at the recent Convention of the American Psychological Association on "The Dog as Co-Therapist" (Levinson, 1961). The idea was born when the therapist's dog was by accident in his office and a very difficult problem child refused to return unless the dog was to be there. Since then he has found that his child clients use the dog as a confidant, fellow conspirator, companion, and scapegoat, and also as a "person" who may be loved, safely and without losing face. The dog can be the embodiment of "the bad me" which can be

From *American Journal of Psychotherapy*, 1963, Vol. 17, pp. 5-16. Reprinted by permission of the author and the Journal.

tolerated, then accepted, even loved. But curiously (or not so curiously) some of those who listened to the paper thought this was ridiculous poppycock, and that his idea had no place among serious therapists.

Thus far I have spoken of these incidents as though they existed at arm's length. But in myself I have often had strong feelings when listening to tapes of therapeutic interviews, or even stronger feelings when, at workshops or in other situations, I have sat in on a therapy interview as an observer. My feeling in that situation has often been, "Move out of that chair and let me take over! This person needs therapy, not what you're giving him!" I suspect others among us have experienced similar feelings.

One more example. In the Standal and Corsini book on *Critical Incidents in Psychotherapy* (1959), a therapist reports, anonymously, a critical or difficult situation in one of his cases, and a panel of experienced therapists give their individual reactions and comments in writing, each panel member ignorant of the comments being made by his fellows. The views expressed are often almost diametrically opposed. Here is one sample. A therapist describes a very difficult and dramatic episode in his therapy with a 19-year-old college girl. The content of the episode need not, for our purposes, concern us. Here are sample reactions, from five experienced therapists, to this interview:

"The first has a completely negative reaction, and says, 'It appears that the therapist realizes to some degree the serious implications of his seductiveness.'

"The second speaks very favorably, and says 'This incident throws light on what therapy is — namely, living with a person on a real basis in an understanding relationship through the most awful moments of fear or disorganization.'

"The third indicates his attitude by saying, 'Had I stumbled into such a predicament. . .' and adds, 'This incident is an excellent example of what can happen when a therapist fails to perceive a schizophrenic's "parataxic distortions." '

"The fourth says that this interview 'I found most distressing to read about' and amplifies this negative statement.

"The message of the fifth contains such statements as 'This event was therapeutic'; 'a lot of growth was demonstrated.' "

I hope I have made my point that our differences as therapists do not lie simply in attaching different labels to the same phenomenon. The difference runs deeper. An experience which is seen by one therapist as healing, growth-promoting, helpful, is seen by another as none of these things. And the experience which to the second therapist is seen as possessing these qualities is not so perceived by the first. We differ at the most basic levels of our personal experience.

Some people may feel that though we differ regarding specific incidents, as I have indicated, nevertheless in our goals and in our general directions there is much agreement, and much unity. I think not. To me it seems that therapists are equally divergent in these realms.

For the past two years I have encouraged my seminar of psychiatric residents to discuss goals of therapy, either in general, or in regard to a particular client we are considering. Such discussions reveal the most profound differences. We are not agreed on whether the goal is removal of symptoms, reorganization of personality, curing of a disease, or adjustment to the culture. When we try to pin down our goals to those specific behaviors in a specific client which we would regard as evidence of "success," the divergence is almost equally great. In my experience the only therapists who agree on goals of therapy are those who have been strongly indoctrinated in the same dogma.

Not only is there divergence in what we mean by success, but the conference of the American Academy of Psychotherapists, on "Failure in Psychotherapy," has demonstrated that we do not agree on what constitutes failure. There is even difference of opinion as to whether the suicide of a client or patient in therapy is necessarily a failure.

But what about the direction in which we should move? Is there agreement in this realm? A vigorous and growing group, particularly among psychologists, is the group which in one way or another bases its therapy upon learning theory as studied in the psychologic laboratory. They regard this as the only scientific direction in which to move, and look with scorn upon the so-called dynamic approaches. This scorn is returned by the majority of therapists who regard themselves as "dynamic." Each group feels positive that the other is moving in a fruitless, if not ridiculous, direction.

One of the more extreme forms of learning-theory approach is the operant conditioning carried on by B. F. Skinner and his group (see Lindsley, 1956). Although as yet it has had little practical impact upon psychotherapy, it will be heard from. Fundamentally the hypothesis is that deviant human behavior can be "shaped up" into normal behavior by the same principle of properly scheduled immediate rewards which transform everyday pigeons into ping-pong players. Yet a large group of therapists would find this aim and this hypothesis definitely unacceptable.

In some ways closely related is the view of Eysenck that all "dynamic therapies," and their attempts to deal with "underlying complexes," are completely unfounded. His own theory is that "there is no evidence for these putative complexes, and symptomatic treatment is all that is required" (Eysenck, 1957, pp. 267-268). I feel sure that Wolpe (1958) and various other therapists within the learning-theory stream of thought would join him in this statement. Yet at least an equal number of practicing therapists would hold a deeply opposed point of view.

In regard to the approach which has been developed by the so-called client-centered group, the situation is the same. Some therapists comment on the promise and significance of the direction in which we are moving. On the other hand, a serious-minded therapist and researcher said (privately) "Rogers has set back clinical psychology and psychotherapy by two decades!" And while I am deeply engaged in a research in client-centered therapy with psychotics, I come across a statement by a client-centered therapist in which he says, "I would question whether a clinic which uses a client-centered approach exclusively is prepared to accept psychotic clients" (Snyder, 1959, p. 59).

If we look at the new trends coming over the horizon—the growing development of a phenomenological existentialist point of view, the interest in Zen Buddhism, and the like—we find the same situation. The differences over such trends are just as strong as those I have cited. To some these appear to be important and promising directions, while others regard them as mystical dead ends. A reviewer, attempting to be objective, states that the effect of all such writings is "to obfuscate and impede the orderly development of a science."

Even within the fold of psychoanalysis, the original entrant in the field, there is the same divergence within the group, and about the group. There is strong evidence that though analysts may still talk in relatively orthodox terms, what they do in the practice of therapy in their offices bears little or no resemblance to classical analysis. Time magazine reports that "The original Freudian concept of analysis . . . is going out of style" (Time, 1961). Some students of the professional culture believe that the analytic movement is well into its declining phase. Yet even in regard to psychotherapy of the psychoses a reviewer (with freudian background, to be sure) says "Psychoanalytic theory overshadows all other approaches, and appears to be most fruitful."

It is, I believe, clear that were I to close my paper at this point, a one-sentence summary would be, "The field of psychotherapy is in a mess." Therapists are not in agreement as to their goals or aims in therapy. They are in deep disagreement as to the theoretical structure which would contain their work. They cannot agree as to whether a given experience for a client is healing or destructive, growth-promoting or damaging. They are not in agreement as to what constitutes a successful outcome of their work. They cannot agree as to what constitutes failure. They diverge sharply in their views as to the promising directions for the future. It seems as though the field is completely chaotic and divided.

I am sure that some must look back nostalgically to the situation which existed two or three decades ago. The small number of professionals who were then engaged in the field lived and worked within a comfortable and secure framework of freudian theory and practice. They knew what psychotherapy was, what its goals were, and the procedures by which to reach those goals. By contrast the field of psychotherapy today is fractionated in a hundred different ways, and the comfortable feeling of unified assurance has all but vanished.

In spite of the contradictions and confusions I have tried to describe, I find this a very exciting and hopeful period in the development of psychotherapy. It is a burgeoning period when new theories, new ideas, new methods of practice are being born at a startling rate. Psychotherapy is becoming a province of university departments, and hence its nature can be openly considered and discussed and criticized by professional workers whose daily livelihood does not depend upon defending a given point of view. Psychologists and psychiatrists are bursting forth with new conceptualizations of psychotherapy. I find this to be true even among graduate students. It is clear that the dogmatic views which held the profession in intellectual chains for many years have completely eroded and given way. Every worker in the field is now much more free to think his own thoughts, formulate his own views on the basis of his own experience, and put forth his own hypotheses. I regard this as a thoroughly healthy flowering of thought, even if a confusing one.

I believe I might bring this conceptual diversity alive if I try to indicate, even in over-simplified terms, the essence or core of the therapeutic experience as it seems to various therapists today. Suppose we were to ask today's wide variety of therapists, what is the essential moment of therapy? Granted that there are many background conditions and elements and proce-dures of therapy, what is the essence of the moment of change? What is the nature of those episodes in therapy where one feels that some real change has occurred, where it seems that one's client or patient has in some significant way altered in his personality, his self-organization, or his behavior? Recognizing that there is much that precedes such a moment, and much that must follow it if therapy is to be complete, what is the *crucial* core, without which no lasting change could take place?

Years ago one would have received primarily one answer to such a question. Now it seems to me there are dozens of answers, often overlapping answers to be sure, but still perceptibly different. I should like to give some of these answers as I have been able to understand them. I am sure no one individual will be satisfied with the formulation regarding his own point of view, both because it will be brief and oversimplified, and because of my own failure correctly to understand the nuances of each view. Nevertheless it may help to suggest the multiplying ways in which psychotherapy is now being perceived.

The traditional answer from the analytic group would, I believe, be this: That the moment of change is the moment in which there is an experience of insight or understanding of one's self in relation to one's past, usually following upon a well-timed interpretation.

But let us sample some of the many other answers. For the operant conditioning group I believe the statement would be something like this: The moment of change in therapy involves no necessary conscious element at all; it is simply a slight alteration of behavior which occurs when the subject's verbal or other behavior varies by chance to a form which is slightly closer to the goal which the experimenter has chosen, and is immediately rewarded. I do not call the participants therapist and client or patient. because I believe this group would prefer the more scientifically oriented term of experimenter and subject. I hope I have, however, satisfactorily described the essential unit of change as they perceive it. This is the way in which the individual's behavior would gradually be "shaped up."

Let us again choose a contrasting view. For the Atlanta group—Whitaker, Warkentin, Malone, and others (1959)—the essence of therapy seems to be those moments in which the patient and therapist(s) live together in a deeply experienced fantasy relationship having little or nothing to do with the real world, but where the unconscious of one individual interacts with the unconscious of the other.

I trust it will be clear that the three formulations I have given are challengingly different. They cannot all be equally true, unless they represent three sharply different kinds of change, with sharply different outcomes. But let us add more.

Alexander (Alexander & French, 1946) and many neo-Freudians would see the essential moment of change in therapy as a corrective emotional experience, in which some crippling experience from the past is newly experienced in a new context and with different meaning.

On the other hand, George Kelly (1955) sees the key experience of therapy as one in which the individual recognizes that the way he has construed some aspect of his life is loosening or collapsing, and some reconstruing and some rebuilding of personal constructs is necessarily occurring.

The adlerian therapist would see the critical moment in a somewhat similar way—as one in which the patient, thanks to the interpretation and teaching of the therapist, sees the mistaken concepts he has had regarding himself and his life, and changes these erroneous conceptions.

With an even stronger cognitive emphasis, Ellis (1962) sees the moment of change as being that moment when the individual is convinced by the therapist that the rational structure by which he has been functioning is in some respect erroneous, and that the structure suggested by the therapist is more correct.

For myself and the group that clusters around the client-centered focus, the moment of therapy is still differently defined (Lewis, Rogers, & Schlien, 1959).

It is the immediate and complete experiencing by the client, in a psychologically safe relationship, of a feeling which has hitherto been too threatening to experience freely.

Many of the learning theorists would feel that the unit of change in psychotherapy is the counter-conditioning of anxiety. The moment in which the subject or patient experiences anxiety simultaneously with a comfort situation which is incompatible with anxiety is the moment of change.

Other psychologists whose views develop from Festinger's theory of cognitive dissonance (Festinger, 1957) see it somewhat differently. For them the essence of change is the client's acceptance of the therapist's view of him, a view dissonant from his own, but made acceptable by the high status and credibility of the therapist. It is essentially a moment of reduction of cognitive dissonance in the client.

The psychotherapists who start from an existential base would have a sharply divergent view. For them the core of therapy is the instantaneous subjective encounter of two separate individuals, an event which cannot be planned for, but which can be *allowed* to occur—an I-Thou moment of relationship.

We could go on and on with these differing conceptions of the crucial moment in therapy. For those interested in family therapy, it is the reliving of the family relationship in a new context provided by the therapist. For the person interested in Zen, the crucial moment may be one of psychologic shock, as it was to the suicidal student who was enlightened and cured by the "thundering cry" of a Zen master (Sato, 1958).

Perhaps I have said enough to indicate that this rank growth of theory and practice in therapy has led to many diverging views as to what constitutes the essential moment of therapy, views which in some instances overlap, but in others seem quite completely irreconcilable. If there were "thirty-six therapies" when Robert Harper wrote his book (1959), there seem to me to be closer to one hundred today.

What is the meaning and significance of all these variations in view, the confusion, the contradictions, the differences? What are the implications for the whole realm of psychotherapy? I should like to give my views on this, but with a clear recognition that I have no special gift of prophecy, and that I may be greatly mistaken.

It means, I believe, that we are backing off and taking a fresh look at the basic problem of our profession, with no inhibitions, few preconceptions, and no holds barred. We can ask again the central question, "How may constructive change in the behavior and personality of the troubled or deviant person be facilitated?" The variety of answers being given will, I believe, help us to open our minds to possibilities which we have not dreamed of before.

Another implication is that for the time being it will be a young man's field. The curiosity and skepticism, the vigor and creativity of younger minds are freed by this chaotic situation. No longer is it governed by the heavy hand of supposedly wise elders. Young men are free to go at the problems freshly, without the sense of being rebels.

I am sure that because of this situation of confusion, various means of altering human behavior will be proposed and tried which will seem to some of us as unethical, unsound, ineffective, and philosophically indefensible. In this respect it will be a difficult period for experienced therapists. But ways of working will also be proposed and tried which will stretch our imaginations, open new vistas of effectiveness, challenge our complacencies, cut through our verbal elaborations, and produce new means of assistance to human beings.

I believe that the present variations in thought and practice mean that the day of systems, of schools of thought, of dogma, is over. Institutions and organizations which indoctrinate therapists in one point of view only are pure anachronisms in today's situation. I do not say this casually. I believe that psychoanalytic institutes—of whatever brand—with their cultish type of training, are on the way out. I would say exactly the same about university departments which expose their students only to training in client-centered therapy, or in any other single approach to therapy. I know how hardy organizations are, and I am well aware that such narrow institutions may continue to function for a long time, but I believe their day of vital influence on thoughtful individuals is past.

In this connection I believe that an organization such as the American Academy of Psychotherapists will increasingly come into its own. I think its instigators—and I can speak freely, because I was not one of that group—were even wiser than they knew. It is one of a very few organizations I know in this field in which a central purpose is to provide a forum for all points of view in therapy, with every approach equally welcome as long as the therapist himself is a broadly qualified professional person. Certainly the distinctive hallmark of our meetings and workshops has been the directness and deep honesty of our interchanges, whether we are in full agreement or profound and almost violent disagreement. This quality of communication is helping to set a pattern for the future in which free and open consideration can be given to every serious new way of working in this field.

There is one final implication of this flowering diversity in psychotherapy. I wish to examine several facets of this implication. It is that of necessity we must move toward looking at the *facts*. And to look at the facts means moving toward research. We are beyond the point where differences will be resolved by the voice of authority or by commitment to an essentially religious type of faith in one point of view as against another. To buttress our theory by quotations from Freud, or by pointing to the precision of our logic, or even by appealing to the depth of our own inner conviction, will not be enough. The public and the profession will want, in the words of the TV detective, "just the facts, please, ma'am, just the facts."

But how will we obtain these facts? First of all, perhaps, by a great extension of naturalistic observation. We need to *look* at therapy, in each of its various forms, and consider, openmindedly and thoughtfully, the events which are occurring. We need to do this individually, as we live with another person in a meaningful therapeutic relationship. We also need to do this as a profession. Here the Academy or some similar group might play a vital role. If the organization set as its goal one complete recorded case from each therapeutic point of view, what an astonishing difference this could make. The organization could furnish the recorder, the tapes, and a sympathetic person with the technical know-how to set up the recording in a satisfactory manner. Any serious therapist who was willing to have his work recorded, whether member or non-member, would receive this service. Perhaps some day one of the major requirements for membership would be the submission of a complete recorded case.

This material, available for thoughtful study by any qualified professional person, would be a great stride forward. Its value would be multiplied if it contained two follow-up interviews at least one year after the conclusion of therapy, one conducted by the therapist, and one conducted by an unbiased worker skilled in evoking responses to a series of survey questions which would be used with all clients.

Another way of getting at the facts is the empirical study of observed behaviors in therapy. This means the testing of theory-based hypotheses by means of pre-therapy and post-therapy tests, and by measures of in-therapy behaviors on the part of both therapist and client. Most psychotherapy research to date has been of this type, but such studies could be greatly extended.

A third way of getting at the facts will be the use of laboratory situations. When an issue regarding psychotherapy has been clearly identified in its essential form, it will often be possible to develop a laboratory situation which contains the issue in simplified form, and to test it at the laboratory level. Some very valuable beginnings have already been made along this line. "Conflicts" have been created by hypnosis, and then treated by differing procedures. In another study one group of clients talked to an understanding therapist, while another group talked to a tape recorder. In still another, clients were, under hypnosis, given different mind-sets as to the congruence or genuineness of their therapist. The differences in process under these different conditions have been studied. Such laboratory studies, much further developed, should teach us much about therapy.

But perhaps the most important means of getting at the facts will be an increasing skill and sophistication in measuring the subjective. A young psychologist (Bergin, n.d.) recently showed me a paper of his, as yet unpublished. Its title says a great deal. It is "Worknotes Toward a Science of Inner Experience." In this paper he describes the encouraging progress being made in coming to grips with the crucial problem of measuring the subjective feelings which occur in one's personal experience. Little by little the strictly behavioristic approach is modifying its rigid resistance to the study of inner subjective problems. Ways are being discovered — phenomenological descriptions, Q-sorts, semantic differentials — by which subjective feelings can be respectably and accurately put into operation and quantified. It is entirely possible that from this trend toward measuring the subjective will come not only new light on the complex processes of psychotherapy and personality change, but also a modification of our current philosophy of science. In any event this trend is already beginning to supply us with objective measurement of very subtle inner experiences. We can measure the changes which occur over therapy in the meaning of such concepts as mother, good, self, and therapist, as these concepts move in the "semantic space" of the client. We can reliably measure the degree of immediacy in the client's experiencing, or the perception of the therapist's genuineness by the client. Such beginnings are extremely promising for the future.

All of these various channels of fact-finding will, I believe, be called into service as we try to determine objectively the changes which occur in different modes of therapy, and the subtle pre-conditions which are associated with these changes. Such fact-finding processes are an inevitable part of the future of our field if it is to move forward. They need not interfere with the subjective personal quality of therapy itself — but they are essential if we are to find our way out of the present confusing Babel of voices, each with its own "truth."

Summary

Psychotherapy at the present time is in a state of chaos. It is not however a meaningless chaos, but an ocean of confusion, teeming with life, spawning vital new ideas, approaches, procedures, and theories at an incredibly rapid rate. Hence the present is a period in which the most diverse methods are used, and in which the most divergent explanations are given for a single event. This situation makes inevitable the development of a new fact-finding attitude — a more objective appraisal of different types of change in personality and behavior, and a more empirical understanding of the subtle subjective conditions which lead to these changes. Only on the basis of such facts can the therapist of the future select the way of working which is most effective in achieving his own deeper aims of those of his client. Only out of such a fact-finding attitude can a reasonable order again emerge in this crucially significant area, and bring us again to some clarity in our understanding of ways by which constructive personality change may be facilitated.

C. H. Patterson

THE PLACE OF VALUES IN COUNSELING

AND PSYCHOTHERAPY

"The accepted point of view has been," Patterson points out, "that the therapist's values should be kept out of the therapeutic relationship." But, as he goes on to show in his review of research and opinion on the value problem, this view is changing. It is becoming clear that values cannot be avoided in the therapeutic context. Furthermore, the values held by counselors and therapists influence the client's behavior. The fact of this influence raises an ethical problem—a problem which requires close critical examination. Patterson argues that though the counselor will influence the client, it is not justifiable for him "to attempt conscious, direct manipulation." Now we would hope that the therapist, whatever he attempts to do, acts consciously rather than unconsciously. Whether he acts directly or indirectly is a question of method—if direct action is more effective, it is more appropriate. So the question is whether manipulation is justified, and we are led to wonder how manipulating the client differs from influencing him. In either case one is changing the client's behavior, and change is, after all, the goal of therapy. Perhaps a better approach is to ask: should the client be influenced without his knowledge, or should he be made aware sooner or later of the goals and procedures of the therapist?

The place of values in psychotherapy has been receiving increasing attention recently. The accepted point of view has been that the therapist's values should be kept out of the therapeutic relationship. Wilder, (in Ginsburg & Herma, 1953) commenting upon a paper by Ginsburg puts it as follows: "It has been taken for granted that the analyst must not try to impose his value systems on the patient," and he adds: "and I still think this to be true." In line with this "hands off" approach, therapists have been exhorted to become aware of their value systems, for the purpose of keeping their own values out of the therapy and to avoid deliberate or unconscious indoctrination of the client (Ginsburg & Herma, 1953).

Perhaps few therapists feel that values should not be *dealt* with in psychotherapy. As Green (1946) has pointed out, therapists *must* deal with values, since they are part of the personality of the patient, and the source of many of his problems. That some therapists still are uncomfortable in doing so seems to be indicated by Zilboorg's (1950) defense of subjectivity.

Recently there has been developing the realization that the therapist's own values cannot be kept out of the therapeutic relationship.

How values affect counseling and psychotherapy

Besides the fact that many of the client's problems involve values and value conflicts, there are other ways in which values affect the therapeutic relationship.

Values and counseling ethics

Values and ethics are related; the ethics of individuals and groups reflect their values. In fact, ethics might be considered as an expression of a group's values, an attempt to represent or express them in a systematized form. This is no doubt why Sutich (1944) became involved in values in his discussion of ethics. Bixler and Seeman (1946) state that "ethics are principles of action based on a commonly accepted system of values," thus relating professional ethics to social values. The APA code of ethics (APA, 1953, p. 49) states that a cardinal obligation of the psychologist "is to respect the integrity and protect the welfare of the person with whom he is working." This is clearly an expression of the value of the individual in our society, as is recognized in Principle 1.13: "The psychologist should express in his professional behavior a firm commitment to those values which lie at the foundation of a democratic society, such as freedom of speech, freedom of research, and respect for the integrity of the individual" (APA, 1953, p. 10).

Philosophy of counseling

From ethics and values to philosophy is only a short step. A philosophy is an integration of values, usually resulting in statements of postulates and assumptions, or principles.

It is only natural, and to be expected, that philosophies of counseling and psychotherapy should reflect the philosophies of the societies in which these activities operate. The prevailing philosophy of our society is a democratic one. This is more than a political term, although Meehl and McClosky (1947) would make it primarily such. Democratic principles and values have permeated our economic, social, educational and occupational institutions and relationships. And as Sutich (1944) points out, "It is evident that modern therapeutic and analytical principles have their roots in democratic principles. And it is equally evident that most American psychologists are committed to the support of democratic principles throughout the entire range of human behavior."

What are the democratic principles which

From *Journal of Counseling Psychology*, 1958, Vol. 5, No. 3, pp. 216-223. Reprinted by permission of the author and *Journal*. This paper is part of a chapter in *Counseling and Psychotherapy: Theory and Practice* by C. H. Patterson, published by Harper & Row, 1959.

are accepted by counselors and psycho-therapists? Bixler and Seeman (1946), in their discussion of counseling ethics, present the postulates of Hand (1942), which succinctly express these principles:

1. The belief that human life, happiness and well-being are to be valued above all else.

2. The assertion that man is master of his own destiny, with the right to control it in his own interests in his own way.

3. The determination that the dignity and worth of each person shall be respected at all times and under all conditions.

4. The assumption of the right of individual freedom; the recognition of the right of each person to think his own thoughts and speak his own mind.

The philosophy of the client-centered approach to counseling appears to many counselors to be an expression of this democratic philosophy in the counseling relationship. Rogers (1951, p. 5), speaking of the development of client-centered therapy, writes that "some of its roots stretch out ... into the educational and political philosophy which is at the heart of our American culture." Green (1946) feels that client-centered therapy is supported by the "democratic-liberalistic idealogy."

The philosophy of client-centered counseling is expressed in the attitudes which the client-centered counselor holds and expresses toward his clients. These basic attitudes may be stated simply. The client-centered approach to counseling and psychotherapy is based on the following attitudes toward others, whether as clients or persons in other relationships with the counselor:

1. Each person is a person of worth in himself, and is therefore to be respected as such.

2. Each individual has the right to self-direction, to choose or select his own values and goals, to make his own decisions.

These, as simple as they seem, express the philosophy of client-centered counseling. They would probably not be disagreed with by most counselors today. Nevertheless, the extent to which these attitudes are implemented in counseling varies tremendously.

Goals of counseling and psychotherapy

Goals are influenced by our values, and therapeutic goals are no exception. The therapist has goals, either specific or general, and these are influenced by his values. Since no complete cure is possible, according to most therapists, what constitutes "tolerable conflict" is a matter of the therapist's values (Ginsburg, 1950).

Concepts of mental health vary. Adjustment has often been conceived as the goal of counseling and psychotherapy. However, there has been increasing dissatisfaction with this concept. The question must be raised, "adjustment to what"? It is evident that adjustment to certain situations is undesirable—the conditions should be changed. And if everyone were adjusted, change and progress would cease. Therapeutic progress or even success can be achieved while the client remains unadjusted to his environment, or to some aspects of it. The concept of adjustment is static. It leads to a subjective interpretation, influenced by the bias of the evaluator, or to a mass, statistical interpretation leading to the definition of adjustment as non-disturbing behavior.

Integration is another concept applied to the goals of psychotherapy. This places the stress on the internal state of the client, rather than on his adjustment to a particular environment. Presumably an individual can be integrated as a person and at the same time be in conflict with his environment. But it has been pointed out that a paranoiac may be integrated but yet not be mentally healthy.

Realizing the inadequacy of adjustment and integration, alone or in combination, as criteria of mental health, Jahoda (1950, 1953) and Smith (1950) have added to them a third, which they call "cognitive adequacy," or the perceptual adequacy for testing reality, thus proposing a triple criterion. Jahoda (1950, p. 213) examined five criteria of mental health: absence of mental disorder or symptoms, normality of behavior, adjustment to the environment, unity of the personality, and the correct perception of reality. The first two were discarded, since symptoms are normal or abnormal depending on the cultural context, and it is difficult to define what is normal. Also, recognizing that adjustment may be "passive acceptance of social conditions to the detriment of ... mental health," she proposes a criterion of active adjustment, or "mastery of the environment, involving a choice of what one adjusts to, and a deliberate modification of environmental conditions" (1950, p. 216). Integration, or self-consistency, is not acceptable alone, since it doesn't imply freedom from conflicts with the environment. Correct perception of reality, both of the world and of oneself, while difficult to establish, since the majority judgment is not necessarily correct, is still useful as a criterion. No one criterion is adequate by itself.

While it is thus difficult to define mental health, counselors and psychotherapists have stated various goals of psychotherapy. Adjustment, integration, and an adequate perception of reality usually are included in these goals. One of the most extensive lists of the goals of therapy is that of Maslow (1954, Chap. 12) in his study of the characteristics of normal, healthy, "self-actualizing" people." This list includes most of the goals mentioned by other authors. Included is the goal of adequate interpersonal relations stressed by Sullivan, who writes that "One achieves mental health to the extent that one becomes aware of one's interpersonal relations" (1947, p. 102).

There has been concern on the part of some regarding such goals as independence, spontaneity, and self-actualization. These goals seem to emphasize the individual to the detriment of society, and to encourage anti-social or asocial behavior. Mowrer (1953a,b) has criticized psychoanalysis for its emphasis on freeing the id from the rule of the superego, and suggests that psychotherapy should strengthen the superego. Actually, self-actualization depends on other people. The individual is dependent on the esteem and regard of others for his own self-esteem—for his mental health. He is thus dependent on satisfactory interpersonal relations. This means that mature, responsible behavior is essential. In the goals listed by Maslow there is this concept of responsibility, as well as independence. Mowrer (1953a,b) also has emphasized responsibility. Shoben (1953) has suggested the "development of responsible individuals capable of maintaining and advancing a democratic society" as the goal of student personnel work, involving the "dual commitment to the worth of the individual and the furtherance of democracy."

The goal of psychotherapy might well be thought of as the development of a responsible independence. Counseling and psychotherapy thus would attempt to facilitate the development of individual independence in a client who takes responsibility for himself, his behavior, his choices and decisions, and his values and goals. This would be consistent with the democratic concept of the freedom of the individual, and also with the concept of the responsibility which accompanies freedom. Such a goal is clearly an expression of the value of a democratic society.

There may seem to be the possibility of a conflict between the attitudes and goals of the counselor and the desires or wishes of the client. Should the counselor be committed, as Meehl and McClosky (1947) state "to help the client achieve the client's end," whatever it is? Most counselors would say no. Almost every therapist, and not only the client-centered counselor, is prepared "to thwart the momentary motivations of his client, apparently in terms of long-time goals, which are assumed to be mutually acceptable" (Meehl & McClosky, 1947). The counselor's ethics, values, and philosophy determine his goals in counseling, and he should not be required to compromise these if he does not choose to do so. The client who does not wish to work under these conditions is not compelled to do so. He has the freedom to accept or reject any counselor and his services. To the charge that the counselor is putting himself in the position of thinking he knows best what the goals of counseling should be, the answer can only be one of "Guilty"—the counselor must be free to choose his own goals for the counseling process. Actually, counselors and therapists have always done so. Psychoanalysts have insisted on the goal of personality reorganization as opposed to symptom relief.

Therapeutic methods

It should be obvious that if values influence, or even determine, the goals of therapy, they also influence methods and techniques, which are means toward the goals. The APA code of ethics recognizes that "the psychologist's ethical standards and his professional techniques are inseparable" (APA, 1953, p. 37). Methods and techniques will not be dealt with here; it is sufficient to point out their relationship to therapeutic goals. Techniques are not chosen primarily on the pragmatic basis of whether they provide relief to the client, but in terms of their appropriateness to the ultimate goal of therapy. If this goal is client responsibility and independence, then it would appear to follow that all techniques should be consistent with this goal. The client learns responsibility by practicing it, and this should begin in psychotherapy, not at its conclusion.

Influence of the counselor's values on the client

We indicated earlier that the generally accepted point of view has been that the counselor's values should be kept out of the counseling relationship. In addition to Wilder, others have stressed this avoidance of influencing the values of the client (Deutsch & Murphy, 1955, p. 33). Therapists have been exhorted to become aware of their value systems, and those of the society and culture in which they work, to better avoid impressing them upon the patient. Some writers have insisted that the client's value system cannot be influenced by psychotherapy, or that only those values which are consistent with his existing value system will be accepted by him.

But is it possible for the therapist to avoid influencing his client? There is growing opinion, and some evidence, that he cannot. Ingham and Love (1954, pp. 75-76) express this conviction. Wolberg (in Ginsburg & Herma, 1953), commenting on Ginsburg's paper, states that "No matter how passive the therapist may believe himself to be, and no matter how objective he remains in an attempt to permit the patient to develop his own sense of values, there is an inevitable incorporation within the patient of a new superego patterned after the character of the therapist as he is perceived by the patient. There is almost inevitably an acceptance by the patient of many of the values of the therapist as they are communicated in the interpretation or through direct suggestion, or as they are deduced by the patient from his association with the therapist." Parloff (1957) states that "The disclosure of many of the therapist's values is inevitable," and "such disclosure and communication may occur without the therapist being aware of it." It might be expected that the therapist, by reason of his position and prestige, would become an example to the client, and that the client would tend to imitate him, consciously or unconsciously, in terms of his perception of the therapist. The APA statement quoted earlier continues by saying that "the attitudes, values, and ethical concepts of the psychologist are expressed in his clinical relationships and very directly influence the directions taken by his client" (APA, p. 37).

There is some evidence that what these writers claim happens actually does. Rosenthal (1955) studied 12 patients presenting a wide variety of diagnoses, and ranging in age from 18 to 46, who had from three weeks to one year of psychotherapy. It was found that, in general, patients' scores on a moral values test changed during therapy, with those patients rated as improved becoming more like their therapists; while those rated as unimproved tended to become less like their therapists.

In another study, Parloff and his associates (Parloff, Iflund, & Goldstein, 1957) had observers list topics discussed during therapy by two schizophrenic patients. The patients and the therapist then ranked the topics from most to least important. While both patients differed from the therapist's values, as indicated by agreement in their rankings of topics, at the beginning of therapy, they came closer to the therapist's values as therapy progressed, though one patient came no closer after the first six weeks of treatment.

There is also some clinical evidence that the therapist influences the patient's values without consciously attempting it or being aware of it. Parloff (1957) refers to the well-known fact that patients conform in their verbalizations to the terminology and theories of the therapist. If therapists value dreams, patients dream; if the therapists value sexual material, patients produce it, etc. "The literature is replete with examples of patients unwittingly adapting their productions and even use of symbols to the particular psychodynamic theories and preferences of their therapist" (1957).

The mechanism of such influence is suggested by some interesting experiments of Greenspoon (1954) and Verplanck (1955, 1956). In these studies it was found possible to control the subjects' verbal behavior by means of operant conditioning, without awareness on the part of the subjects. In the case of psychotherapy, it is easy to imagine the effect on the client of such responses of the therapist to the patient's verbalization as a trace of a smile or a pleased look, an incipient nod of the head, or other mannerisms indicating his attitude, favorable or unfavorable, toward the patient's productions. And all this may be unknown to the therapist and the patient. Parloff (1957) presents some evidence that the therapist's responses may be classed by observers as "approving" or "disapproving," and that these responses were related to the therapist's ranking of the topics responded to in terms of their importance. This occurred without the therapist being aware of the differential nature of his responses as "approving" or "disapproving."

Conscious influence of the client's values

As has been indicated above, it has been generally agreed that the therapist should not consciously attempt to manipulate the patient's values. Recently, however, there have been what Wilder (in Ginsburg & Herma, 1953) refers to as "rising voices to the effect that the analyst not only does but should transmit his own value system to the patient." Taylor (1956), in a letter to the editor taking issue with the writer of an article making a plea for the abandonment of guidance in counseling, suggests that there are common, general patterns of human conduct which are ethically "good," and that counselors are justified in introducing them in guidance. Weisskopf-Joelson (1933) proposes that the inculcation of a philosophy of life be considered as one of the objectives of psychotherapy.

Gardner Murphy (1955) has recently asked: "Shall personnel and guidance work. . .attempt to impart a philosophy of life?" While admitting that "no one knows enough to construct an adequate philosophy of life," he suggests that "it is not true that the wise man's sharing of a philosophy of life is an arrogant imposition upon a defenseless client." He feels that the young need help and advice from those who have thought things through. But he warns counselors not to "attempt the arrogant and self-defeating task of guiding men and women without a rich, flexible, and ever-growing system of values of your own."

There is some slight evidence, in the studies of Rosenthal (1955) and Parloff (1957; Parloff et al., 1957) that those clients who improved, or improved most, tended to approach most closely to their therapists in values. This, if true and borne out by other studies, might appear to be an argument for direct intervention toward influencing the values and philosophies of clients. However, it must be remembered that this result occurred where no overt or direct attempt was made to influence the client. It might not hold where direct influence was attempted. Indeed, every counselor well knows the resistance that often develops where direct influence is attempted, and the resistance that often follows the attempt to fulfill a direct request of the client for advice or other help.

Granted that the counselor will influence the client, whether he desires or directly attempts to do so, is it therefore justifiable to attempt conscious, direct manipulation? The present writer believes not. There are a number of reasons for this.

First, while there are no doubt some generally, or even almost universally, accepted principles or ethical rules, these do not constitute a philosophy of life. One may even question how much agreement there is on ethical principles or rules of behavior. Each individual's philosophy is different, unique, and something which is probably not adequate for any other individual.

Second, it is too much to expect all counselors to have a fully developed, adequate philosophy of life ready to be impressed on the client. All counselors are not, to use Murphy's term, wise men.

Third, the counseling relationship is not, in the opinion of the writer, the appropriate place for instruction in ethics and a philosophy of life. The home, the church, and the school are more appropriate sources for such instruction.

Fourth, an individual does not develop a system or code of ethics, or a philosophy of life, from one source, or in a short interval of time. It is a product of a long period of time and many influences.

Fifth, it would appear to be best for each individual to develop his own unique philosophy, and not be deprived of the experience of doing so. Such a philosophy will probably be more meaningful and effective than one adopted from someone else, no matter how wise a man he be.

Sixth, we must still accept the right of the client to refuse to accept any system of ethics, or any philosophy of life.

Now this does not mean that the counselor refuses to discuss ethics, values, or philosophy. It does not mean that he is not concerned about the influence he has on the client in these areas. He recognizes this, and attempts to be a constructive influence. But he does this not by attempting to manipulate the client in the counseling process. He does it by being himself. As Murphy suggests (1955), "A great deal of what you communicate to your client is not what you say but what you are." Further than this, the counselor on some occasions must express his own values. He may do so on the request of the client. But he carefully identifies these expressions as his own, perhaps only opinions, and avoids imposing them on the client, or implying that the client ought to feel the same way.

There may also be times when the counselor, whether on the request of the client or not, feels it necessary or desirable to inform the client of the attitudes, standards, or values of society, or the ordinary or generally accepted rules of ethics and morality.

The counselor should not strive to be an amoral, ethically neutral individual. Such a goal would be impossible of achievement—all of us have values, merely by being living human beings. Nor should the counselor attempt to pretend that he is amoral. It is unlikely that he could successfully give this impression to his clients, but it is also undesirable that the counselor attempt to appear to be other than he actually is. Furthermore, the attempt to appear to be neutral as regards social and ethical standards may lead to the danger of appearing not only to accept the client's unethical or immoral behavior, but of approving or condoning it. Counselors are not indifferent to social and moral standards, and should not attempt to appear to be so.

Biestek (1953) presents an excellent discussion of the behavior of the counselor in the area of ethics and standards. He points out that while the counselor may judge the attitudes, standards, or actions of the client in terms of his own or prevailing standards, he does not judge the client himself. He further states that "this judgment is preferably made non-verbally; the client usually is able to make such appraisals of himself in the security of an accepting relationship." He suggests that the counselor cannot be indifferent to social, legal, or moral wrong, and must favor the good: "In the non-judgmental attitude the (counselor) does not relinquish his own sense of values, his personal and social ethics. He cannot remain interiorly indifferent to standards contrary to his own if he is to maintain the integrity of his own personality. He must remain true to them. He does not become moralistic, but he has a right to his own sense of social, moral, and spiritual values, personally and professionally" (1952).

Ingham and Love (1954, p. 77) add a second reason for avoiding indoctrination of moral standards to the usual one. This reason is that the therapist might fail. "And trying to impress moral values in psychotherapy without success interferes with the freedom of the participants' communication and the strength of their relationship."

The point of view expressed above may appear to be a departure from the client-centered framework. Like many other therapists, the client-centered counselor has professed neutrality, and has in many cases at least felt that he has achieved this. But, actually, he has perhaps been no more successful than have other therapists. De Grazia (1952, pp. 152-158) gives examples of the expression of counselor moral attitudes and values from published type-scripts of client-centered interviews.

The proposal that the counselor not only should be aware of, and has a right to have, his own moral attitudes and values, but should sometimes express them in the counseling relationship, is consistent with recent developments in client-centered thinking. Stressing that the therapist should be himself in the relationship between himself and the client, Rogers (1956) suggests that he should express his own feelings as he experiences them.

Summary

The approach to values in counseling as outlined in this paper appears to have several advantages. By recognizing that the counselor's moral attitudes and values do enter into counseling, it prevents the counselor from erroneously believing that he is neutral. Freed from this belief, and the feeling that it is necessary or desirable to be neutral, the counselor is better able to recognize and accept his own values. He then can be aware of them in the counseling relationship, and, when he feels that the counseling relationship would be improved or furthered by his expressing his own attitudes and feelings, he can do so. That is, he can freely be himself, without guilt about doing so, or without feeling that he should not have any feelings. Finally, this approach contributes to the openness of the counseling relationship, without violating its client-centeredness. In fact, the relationship is probably more client-centered. That is, where the counselor's attitudes and feelings are unexpressed, even unrecognized by the counselor, they may, and apparently do, have a pressuring influence on the client. Where they are expressed by the counselor and labeled as representing his own values, feelings, attitudes or point of view, or identified as those of others, or society in general, there is less coerciveness about them. While there are some who would sanction the counselor acting as a representative of society in prescribing moral or ethical values or standards (De Grazia, 1952), the majority of therapists, including client-centered therapy, still insist that the client must freely accept or reject such values, and develop or construct his own ethical system or philosophy of life. Some apparently fear that the client when given such freedom will choose wrongly or adopt an unethical or immoral course of behavior. The client-centered counselor would respect the client's right to do so. He would not feel that the counseling relationship is the place to teach moral or ethical standards, or a philosophy of life. He is confident, as apparently some are not, that the client in the therapeutic relationship will be aware of and influenced by social realities. He will leave to the family, the church and the school, as institutions representing the moral and ethical standards of society, the teaching of such standards.

Lucy Freeman

FIGHT AGAINST FEARS

This is an excerpt from Freeman's account of her experience in therapy. In simple and lucid style, her introspective report describes the various objective and subjective changes she experienced while undergoing psycho-analysis. Note particularly the shifts in her value system, her increased awareness of hitherto unconscious components of her personality, and the improved integration of her values, aspirations, and actions. Was the therapist neutral, or did he feel that certain kinds of behavior are better than others? To what extent was her psychotherapy an education rather than an indoctrination to a particular viewpoint? Did she adopt new attitudes and values on faith, or did she treat them as hypotheses to be tried out and accepted only if they worked?

Pain forced the decision.

Standard routine reeled off by doctor after doctor had not eased agony.

"Get plenty of sleep and eat regular meals."

Trouble is, I can't sleep.

"Here are some pills, then."

How can I eat when everything upsets my stomach?

"Take these pills."

What about the splitting headaches?

"More pills."

Or: "It's the war, this dreadful war. Get away from your work for a few weeks. Relax."

One day war ended, World War II, that is. Another illness struck and again doctors could not help.

Then came a point in pain where I either had to accept suffering and give up all else or try to find a different way to stop torment.

Psychoanalysis was my way.

The following description applies just to my own analysis. I can write only of what I know.

This is not a photograph of my life. It is but parts of my life as they unreeled before me. Not all that I felt or thought lies in this book. Many things I cannot write and never intend to write, but the reader who knows his own heart will know them. I have chosen certain ideas, abandoned others, sometimes deliberately, sometimes unconsciously.

Some know what they feel. I did not dare know. Analysis for me was continuous discovery, sometimes shocking discovery. I felt like the intended victim in a murder, with the analyst as hero-detective trying to rescue me from a life of inner terror.

It is dangerous, in a way, to quote the analyst so extensively. The inaccuracy of one word could change the meaning of his thought. It is difficult, too, without appearing dramatic or didactic, to compress five years of analysis into numbered pages.

But this is risk I must take. I have relied on training as reporter and the copious notes I scribbled after each session, part of my fight against fear. If at times the analyst seems abrupt, challenging or like a lecturer, it is because I have quoted in one place what he may have said different times in different ways.

No book can catch the sound of a voice. It was not what he said so much as how he said it. His voice was always even, compassionate, rich with wisdom — truly an invitation to trust.

I have gone a long way and have a long way to go.

In the beginning there was only fear. Then moments occurred when terror took a holiday as I learned to trust John in spite of my senses which told me he was another human being and, therefore, not to be trusted.

I started, then, to trust myself to know what I did not know.

The tragedy in my life was that I thought I knew myself. No one could have told me I did not determine my fate, miserable though it might be.

I was one of those who shouted to the world, "I don't need help, I *know* what my problems are," but my twisted life showed I did not know. I had been unable to search deeply into my life, for I was afraid of what I might find. Headlines told of murder by other men; I feared the murder I might do should I ever lose control.

It was not easy to admit to the world or myself, "I am ill." If limb or lung were infected, I would not deceive myself or try to deceive the world that a physical, tangible section of me was diseased. But emotional illness (truly dis-ease, non-ease) gave itself more readily to deceit. I could forever blame all else and thus escape the stigma sometimes attached to emotional illness which arises, as do most stigmas, from man's fear. . . .

The first day I walked into John's office I would have sworn my childhood was happy. Then I started to feel it was horrible. I came to know it was neither extreme but in the middle. It possessed both the desirable and undesirable in life.

As an adult I tried to nourish myself on

the indigestible belief I had been a happy child. That was the greatest fallacy of all, for if I had been happy as a child, I would have grown into a happy adult.

"Look at the child and you see the adult; look at the adult and you see the child," John said.

I remembered only flight from unhappiness. I forgot feelings underneath that caused the flight; forgot them, but never forgot them—that was the rub. As they surfaced I knew that growing up sometimes felt so intolerable I had to pretend it was wonderful.

Some (unanalyzed, of course) charge analysis kills ability to feel. For me it heightened awareness of self and others, allowing me to feel with more assurance instead of groping with confusion.

I felt more comfortable with myself and, therefore, with all others who inherited the earth to do with as they wish. I accepted the world more as it was, merged with both its misery and merriment. Browning wrote, "When the fight begins within himself, a man's worth something." I felt the fight was being waged more within me, less with those around me.

I no longer blamed misfortune or bemoaned what happened. I was finding out, as Thomas Tusser wrote in the sixteenth century:

Except wind stands as never it stood,
It is an ill wind turns none to good.

Analysis, which some might think ill wind, paid off in many ways. The illness which drove me to seek help disappeared as did other physical pain that never, in wildest dream, had I hoped to be lucky enough to lose. . . .

When skeptics ask what I "got" out of analysis, I tell them it cured the sinus. This they understand, for it is a tangible result. They will accept a symptom where they will not accept the illness that causes it.

The sinus, like all else, disappeared slowly. During the first months of analysis I breathed easier for the few hours that followed each session. After a day's work the nose again ached. But today the sinus stands completely banished. My tears set free my nose.

Colds forsook me. I sailed through two years without catching one, whereas, before analysis, I suffered a series of serious colds all winter. They would begin by dizziness, proceed to sore throat, loss of voice, chest pain, racking cough. With each attack I wished I were dead (the cold, part of the unconscious wish) but I always lived long enough to catch another. . . .

I rid the medicine chest of pills accumulated for two decades. I felt less need for painkillers as I felt less need for pain. I took care of my body, respecting it more. If I felt a slight temperature I remained home from work, something I never did before.

I became less of a hypochondriac. A small cut did not send me scurrying for the nearest iodine bottle. Instead I thought, "My body will mend this, since it is not too disastrous." No longer was I so consciously afraid of death. . . .

Nightmares tortured me less; no longer did I wake sobbing. I took no more sleeping pills, and although occasionally tossed away nights without sleep, did not worry. (I would not die just because I did not sleep.) Before analysis I wallowed in ten hours a night. Now I felt content with seven or eight.

I acquired a different physical as well as psychological feeling, a change in body-tone. My pulse beat slower, I breathed more calmly, I stood straighter. . . .

Some friends remarked, "You're no different today from the way you were five years ago, except you're a little calmer."

But that marks quite a difference, I thought. A little calm, where before no calm existed, denotes much control.

It was not easy for me to slow up. I moved slower in comparison to the once breathless dash through house, street and city. I strolled leisurely along the sidewalk, thinking. This is what it is like to walk. I deliberately pulled back on pace. Instead of hurling myself from bed I rested a few minutes after the alarm's ring.

"So do we put our life into every act," wrote Emerson. I could tell by the way I lit a cigarette, or let others light it for me, how much my life changed. . . .

I was acquiring a new ally. My unconscious now helped to save my life as once it worked to destroy me because I overburdened it with too much fear. As I gradually eased its load, consciously able to tolerate more of myself, it could work more in harmony with the conscious, allowing me to think more freely. . . .

My unconscious was also producing in dreams some of the more dangerous material it once had been forced to suppress, now offering me important clues for conscious consideration. It was helping me know the truth. I could probably never know the entire truth but I could learn more of it so I would be less afraid.

No longer did I feel I must be perfect. Some will try nothing, fearing they will not be perfect. Others, like me, who try to be perfect in everything, writhe in agony each time they fail.

My parents had expected me as a child to do things right the first time. I felt stupid if I made a mistake. If I kept my father waiting, he might rage at me. I might bother Mother at a moment when she struggled with shopping and I would feel I had chosen the wrong time to talk—wrong, wrong, wrong.

In later life I felt I must be right or draw wrath. I chose a job where it was important to be right, unconsciously perpetuating the need for punishment and the feeling of the familiar. On the paper I must get things right the first time; too many errors would cost me my bread and butter.

I felt I must always be perfect because I felt so imperfect. But I also knew that to err is human. Therefore, I felt inhuman, wretched.

"I wanted to die when I made a mistake," I told John.

"Nobody is perfect," he said.

He chuckled, added, "Maybe it's lucky. A perfect person would have a hard time living with the rest of us."

That was heartening to hear. I remembered it when it appeared as if I had committed a mistake on an important story, the White House Conference on Children and Youth, by omitting mention of a resolution. The old feeling of shame started to shake me. Then I thought, I guess I'm entitled to one or two boners. I'm only human after all. But I proved right. No error, this time.

One day my train was five hours late to St. Louis where I was bound to cover an American Prison Association convention. Because of the delay, I faced missing my first deadline.

Five years before I would have felt like hurling myself off the train in suicidal despair. Now I thought, This train is late because of an accident on the line. People may have been hurt. This is not conspiracy on the part of the railroad crew to wreck your career.

Besides, who cares if you are late? What happens if you do miss the deadline? The paper gets too much copy from correspondents, anyhow. Send a telegram, saying you will try to make the second edition. Don't be egotistical enough to think they will hate you if you do not produce a story. You are not that important. You have a job to do but if an emergency occurs over which you have no control, do what you can. Do not fret about what you cannot do.

I sent the office a telegram from Indianapolis explaining the situation. The first edition appeared without my story, the second edition ran it. No one knew the difference. No one cared. I had saved myself much torment.

As I expected myself to be less perfect I became more thoughtful. I stopped leaving things behind. I remembered to pick up packages, pocketbooks, cigarettes. I did not unconsciously need to rid myself of parts of me.

I took life not less seriously but less personally. In one way I had always taken myself too seriously, in another not seriously enough. I had overrated the danger to my life, too busy unconsciously fighting death to know I had as much right as any other person to my own likes and dislikes, decisions and opportunities. . .

I felt more confident of my own ability. I discovered when I sought favors from people they were more likely to give them if I did not appear upset. Hysteria frightens. People then fight fear with anger, which may take the form of the word "no." If I asked in fear and trembling, I was apt to be turned down. If I asked in calm, I was more likely to get my wish. No wonder nothing succeeds like success, for the successful are apt to feel and inspire confidence.

As I demanded less of myself in one way, I demanded more in another. I saw how much I needed self-discipline, for I had lived a hedonistic, almost psychopathic life.

I could not have everything I wanted. I could want many things and the wanting of them I could not help, but I had to learn to say no to myself. Willingness to give up without anger some things I desired showed maturity.

I had complained to John that I found myself covering an early morning assignment before I had a chance to gulp coffee.

"I *must* have a cup of coffee before I do anything else in the morning," I said.

"My, you are spoiled," he commented.

I had not thought of myself as spoiled; I felt the opposite—deprived. In one way, though, I had expected the world. I wanted to eat all the meals, yet never wash a dish. I had been overindulged, as though my parents wanted to make up to me for some of their feelings. Children need not indulgence but direction and good example, John said. . . .

Discipline differs from rigidity or puritanism, John explained. Discipline is conscious, arising from wise choice. Rigidity stems from an unconscious that feels excessively wicked and would like nothing better than a little conscious indulgence.

Accusation of people as "indulgent" and "lazy" indicates only fear, John pointed out, fear of assuming responsibility, fear of attempting to think. If I were "spoiled," I was more to be pitied than scorned. Nature meant me to contribute to the world in some productive form in order to know a satisfaction forbidden to me if I remained "spoiled" and "lazy."

Part of my increasing happiness was due to feeling less lazy underneath. My energy had masked a desire to stop dead. During analysis, I heard with envy of one patient, not John's, who found his real wishes so devastating he gave up his job and went to bed every day following his analytic session.

Laziness was part of the feeling I was not worth anything to anyone so why bother to move? It also served my anger—I do not care, therefore I will do nothing. My feelings of laziness became intensified when away from John for several days. I would feel psychically and physically paralyzed. After seeing him, after fear ceased, I could work more productively.

Some would do less, others more, if they were not so frightened. It heralded happiness when I could do less. Before analysis, in addition to work I forced myself to keep social engagements for lunch, supper and after work, to collapse in depressed exhaustion before going to bed, then wonder why I could not sleep. Now I saw few people during the day except in connection with work.

At the same time I could do more when it was required of me. A friend called up one day to ask a favor at a time she knew I was busy.

"I'm sorry," she apologized. "I know how rushed you are but this is important to me."

"It's all right," I said. "For you it's a labor of love." I added, just finding it out, "A labor of love is no labor when it's love."

In order to contribute most fully to the world we should feel we like the world and ourselves enough to want to give. Many who are unhappy give, but suffer in the giving. Would, perhaps, they gave less to the world and more to themselves. What was the use of life to Van Gogh, no matter how many wonderful pictures he painted, if he ended it in madness? Perhaps he would have painted even greater pictures had he been happier. Who can know?

As I felt less lazy, a whole new world opened before me, one in which I could take my time. I began to use my eyes which, fogged by fear, had never seen very clearly. I had felt the world with my other senses rather than observing it with my eyes.

The details which I had always ignored started to take shape. (I despised those games where you are given two minutes to study a complicated picture and are then expected to name all the objects in it. My mind would go blank.)

Now I knew I must be specific to be able

to understand myself or others. The generalization was derogatory. It kept me from granting to each one the dignity of his life.

I remembered many more of the details of my life, particularly the house in which I grew up and in which I started to run away from feelings. I could walk once more up the red brick steps, onto the porch, past the carved chest, into the hall with its terracottaed walls, fashionable in the thirties, on which hung an etching of a ship, drawn by one of Dad's partners, artist as well as lawyer.

Then, into the parlor, to face the fireplace and a painting of Lake Placid's Mount Whiteface. On the walls also hung etchings of castles and street scenes in England and the portrait of a lady with a snake draped around her bare bosom. No wonder I had forgotten that; what a devastating picture to place before a hungry child—snake and bare breasts!

The bookcases bulged with red books of knowledge, green O. Henry's and one volume that will forever haunt me, titled *The Yellow Room*. After someone borrowed ours, I never found another copy of it, to rediscover how the killer committed murder in an apparently locked room. That is one forgotten detail lost forever. . . .

Before analysis I had dissipated so much energy fighting fear I had little left to savor life. Now I sought to follow John's suggestion that the aim of life be "to enjoy whatever you do, work or play, to relax while you do it, the way a happy child relaxes at play."

When I asked how I could be sure of enjoying life, he replied, "By not making sure."

"What does that mean?" I demanded.

"By not gritting your teeth and being determined to enjoy it, but just by accepting yourself."

Happy people do not need continual achievement and excitement, he said. They do things not because they have to but because they want to. Occasionally they run risks, but the risks are calculated, like those taken by trapeze performers who seem to jeer at death as they swing through perilous space but who know exactly the measure of the chance they take.

I enjoyed more of the "simple things," those that required more thought from me. I needed the escape of movies less. When depressed, formerly I lurched into a double feature, willing to sit through anything except a Western. My record for one day reached five—two doubles and a single and *that* night of the year 1944 I slept. I would sink back in the lush chairs, lose myself in the splendor of the fantasy before my eyes as others dreamed for me. But now, instead of going to the movies just for the sake of going, I go to enjoy the good ones.

I read fewer murder mysteries. As my unconscious need to murder decreased I needed less stories to feed my fantasies of murder. I found myself rereading Shakespeare, the Bible.

I even dared to paint. Strictly from the subconscious, I splashed bright oils on canvas—all feeling, no technique—and liked what I produced. . . .

I am aware that, in analysis, I absorbed much of John's philosophy as my own. But before analysis, I held few values that helped in living that was one reason I was ill, I was in search of values, always questioning others as to their values. I accepted many of John's because I liked them. They seemed kind, wise.

Human nature can be changed. I believe my nature is more human. I found the difference between being nice to people to save my oversensitive skin and truly caring for them.

No longer did I have to woo men or placate women to reassure them I did not want the men. I need fear nobody. People did not belong on pedestals, any more than my father did. It was colossal egotism on my part to place them there, then worry about what they thought of me, if they thought of me at all.

Now that I was not so terrified of people I saw some as far more wonderful than I ever dreamed they could be. Some were so hurt and yet contributed so much to so many. Some fought their fear so valiantly.

I had never really seen anyone. I looked at people through the haze of associations.

I liked or disliked them according to the way I felt about them (manner like my father, eyes like my mother, stance like my brother). This is prejudice, judgment of another on the basis of emotions, judgment from the unconscious, judgment devoid of reason.

The words I used indicated my feelings toward myself and others. As a child I felt tortured because of certain words my parents flung out to tell me what they thought of me — silly, crazy, dopey, stupid, lazy. No matter how ardently they tried to deny the words by hugs and kisses, I held the feeling all my life, until analysis, that I was silly, crazy, dopey, stupid, lazy.

But when I no longer thought of myself in such words, my thinking about others changed. I thought of some not as "stupid" or "weak" or "phony" but as "frightened" and "angry," for that was how I thought of myself.

Because I was kinder to myself, I could be kinder to others. . . .

My life had been so full of search for someone to be kind to me I had not thought of the possibility of my being kind to someone else. Or if I had, it was a kindness for which I would get something in return.

Real kindliness expects little reward, John said. Yet the kindly people usually receive the most in return. The unkind demand most but receive least.

I turned slowly from admiring those who could put up a fight to admiring those who did not need to fight because they possessed compassion. This is, perhaps, the most highly developed of man's feelings because so much acceptance of self and others must go into it. There are many who possess all the qualities to make them fine human beings except compassion. They are brilliant, affectionate, sensitive — but not compassionate.

Compassion belongs to the one who can think of others. The cynic, for instance, can afford to feel only for himself. He cannot be compassionate; his bright, knifelike wit masks an unending flow of self-pity.

Compassion also possesses realism as an essential. While I might feel sorry for, and try to understand, a murderer as an emotion-ally disturbed person, I must know that other men must be protected from him. I want to help the weak, but not at the expense of the strong.

Compassion for an enemy is proof of strength. At one point John quoted a proverb that advised, "Embrace thine enemy."

"I'd spend all my time embracing," I muttered, then feeling everyone was enemy.

As I felt less like my own enemy I realized, if one wants to conquer, one should embrace an enemy, show him another way, if it is a better way than his. He will then want to copy you because he likes you.

In compassion lies true strength, the strength to yield when necessary. I had envied the strong, rather than admired them, because I felt so weak. In a crisis, the strong bend, the weak break. The strong may also attack when they feel justified. But the weak must always defend; by building up defenses against perpetual fear, they destroy their strength to attack.

As I could feel more compassionate I found I did not want to hurt people, did not want them to be hurt. Once I had to pry into everyone's life because I did not dare pry into my own. I learned to keep things to myself. Talking of someone's misery had been an unpleasant way of avoiding my own.

A friend called to tell me of the divorce of a couple we knew. "Isn't it dreadful?" she gasped.

"I'm sorry to hear it," I said. Formerly, I, too, would have gasped, "Oh, no — I don't believe it!" wanting very much to believe it but not daring to confess it.

"Aren't you shocked?" she asked.

"Not shocked, but sorry for them." Once I would have felt shocked on the surface, delighted underneath. Because I had suffered, I wanted others to suffer. But now I felt sorry for unhappiness, not envious of happiness.

When someone spilled a cup of coffee over my best black suit I smiled, I believed it to be an accident instead of thinking, He has deliberately chosen me as target. Perhaps, unconsciously, he did not like my hat or I reminded him of his mother. I had been all too ready to believe the worst of others because I had believed the worst of myself.

I met a friend one night whom I had not seen in years. She was brittle, sharp, sarcastic. Instead of throwing back wisecracks at her, I spoke gently, feeling sorry she needed to make cutting remarks. Wisecracks mean just that — a crack, even though wise, at the other fellow. I learned to watch my sarcastic remarks, to know they were not kindly.

There seemed to have been a number of important "c's" in analysis, far more important than the three r's ever were. In addition to compassion and control, there was "conviction." In my carload of emotions once nary a conviction rode. I had made decisions on the basis of fear, never daring to take a firm stand on any question. I was one of those who claimed to see both sides but were merely confused. A happy person may see both sides but also may possess convictions about one of them, John said.

I had to learn the feel of a conviction. At times I thought I grasped one but would soon know otherwise.

Once I said to John, "I think my fear of death is tied up with fear of sex because I always felt wicked, as though I deserved to die, because of sexual feelings. Is that right?"

"Do you really believe that, or are those just words?" he asked.

"Just words," I sighed. "But I keep trying." I knew when I sounded glib.

Convictions came after asking many "whys," after seeing the relationship of many things. Men start wars. Why? To expand, to get more land, more natural resources, more seaports. Why? To get money. Why? To raise the standard of living. Why? Because they are not satisfied with what they have. Why? They are not happy within themselves. Why? What they have is not enough. Why? They are not content. Why? They are angry. Why? They fear. Why? All men have an unconscious. Why and why and why. And there are no final answers.

Once I had been dogmatic. Now I might possess convictions if I used reason. . . .

Then there was the word "consistency," something my life had lacked, except for the consistency of complaining. I experienced flashes of feeling rather than any consistent flow of feeling-thinking combined. If I wanted happiness, I would have to be consistently aware I held feelings of murder, hatred and jealousy, not pleasant feelings but ones that, in terms of the past, I could not help but hold. Like the acne scars imbedded in my face, these feelings would serve to remind me of my tempestuous childhood and of the different direction in which I now headed. The acceptance of these feelings, John said, is basic for relief of them.

"Calmness" was another word beginning with "c" that held new meaning for me. The Lord, or Nature, seems to pay dividends for calmness, I thought. The devil takes his due from disturbed people. Was not "possessed by the devil" one of the first descriptions applied to the psychotic?

Anger destroys as all unkind qualities destroy. Calmness increases inner peace which, in turn, may add years to life. It was almost a matter of self-preservation, then, for me to be calm, for I would live longer.

Gains achieved from calmness differed from those I had been taught to seek. Calmness put priority not on fame or need for the world's attention, as I once needed my parents, but on peace, self-liking, ability to like others. These were the rewards of repose.

Then there was the word "compromise" against which I had always rebelled, for I could never afford to do it agreeably. I could only appease, with resentment.

But as I acquired the strength of a few convictions I learned the value of compromise. Only the strong are able to do it; the weak dare not. Matthew Green's eighteenth century advice still holds true:

Happy the man, who, innocent
Grieves not at ills he can't prevent;
His skiff does with the current glide,
Not puffing pulled against the tide.

Poet Green also composed two other lines I found gratifying, because while on the surface I had always given in to impulse, underneath I possessed a strong conscience:

Though pleased to see the dolphins play,
I mind my compass and my way.

There was also the word "courage." Courage and wisdom differ. I had neither. The frightened and the brave may both own courage but wisdom belongs to the brave alone, for wisdom accompanies security and ability to choose. Some ardent crusaders possess courage but lack wisdom, John said. Perhaps the suspicion that some do-gooders are up to no good is not altogether unwarrented, I thought.

One reason I felt such a crusader in my youth was because again I copied my father. He sent me to a progressive college. I felt he approved of slight rebellion.

Once, he told me with pride, he had run away from home.

"When?" I asked, awed. That was more than I dared do.

"One night after a quarrel with my mother."

"Where did you go?"

"The Williams Club."

I was not quite so impressed. I expected him to have set forth immediately for Calcutta.

"For how long?"

He sounded even more abashed. "Just overnight. Father came and persuaded me to go home."

"What did you fight about?" My hopes of my father as a real rebel were slowly being dashed.

"A plate of soup."

"What?" I was horrified.

"Something about soup," he admitted. "Mother wanted me to eat it. I didn't want to. I got up and left."

But now I knew a plate of soup could be the most important thing in the world should it swirl with the anger of the one who eats or the one who prepares.

I became less of a rebel, no longer convinced I could save the world, John said. The need to play God rages strong in many of the unhappy. For one thing, they may feel so much like the very devil inside, they try to compensate by acting the opposite on the outside. They also may unconsciously feel

if they are God, no one can harm them; finally they are out of reach of parents. Too, they may be copying their parents in a display of tyranny originally launched against them.

"Save yourself, first," John advised. "Because only then will you be able to help anyone else. Real saving takes place in a quiet way."

"Neither a martyr nor a savior be." John's philosophy was the Golden Mean. Nature meant us all to be in the middle, he said.

At first I made fun of him. "The middle path!" I said scornfully. "That's for fence-sitters."

Then I saw the middle path was actually the hardest path for some of us who are troubled. We veer off to the right and the left. We dare not trust temperance. The fanatic cannot accept "a little" of anything. He wants the whole works because he feels so emotionally starved.

Everything that exists has a place in the world. Only man's emotional illness blows things up into disastrous proportion. Although the world holds both slums and sables there is a good deal in between. When enough of us care about ourselves and others, the slums may disappear.

As my rebellion against my parents became less severe, so did my rebellion against the world, which I felt less like changing because it did not look so threatening.

Those who insist on radical change are egotists, John said. They cannot bear the thought anything good might happen after they are gone. Real change, he said, is slow and gradual.

Then there was the word "cooperate." I could not cooperate with people when I felt frightened and threatened. Now I understood more of what John meant when he said the world would be happier if all men could work for the interests of all men, rather than one man for one man, or a special group for its own interest. As the individual man becomes stronger and able to work more effectively with others, the community becomes stronger, he said. The best warriors use not guns, but reason.

John was "for" things, rather than "against" them. He believed there was too much "anti" in the world, that when people joined "anti" groups, they were really raging "anti" their parents.

The healthy person is "for" something, he said. He stood for good emotional health, but that did not mean he ranted against bad emotional health. He knew he could not make me happier by inciting hate in me.

His approach was constructive (another "c"). "Nobody is entirely wrong," he said. He started with what was right in me. He helped build up, never once tore me down.

Everyone possesses the potentiality to be a decent human being, he believed. This I have always felt, too. A child, whether born in jungle hut or asphalt jungle, is a piece of clay to be molded by parents and community. Potentials may never be developed, blocked by fear, but they exist.

One of the great lessons John taught me was to try to be tolerant of intolerance. Not to like it, but to understand the reason for its existence so that, just as with my own intolerance, I might work for tolerance.

In my life I had failed to grant others the right to their prejudices, at the same time demanding the right to mine.

"They're just stupid and weak," I would scoff at those prejudiced against Catholics, Jews, Negroes.

"Everybody has strength but often they are just too angry to use it," John said.

I tried to be more tolerant. When someone made a rude remark, I no longer assumed he did it to offend me; I took into account the possibility that he protected himself against his fear with rudeness. My being hurt was just incidental.

Others were entitled to defenses, too. Some must help, whether asked or not, while some must never offer help. Some must always hurt, while others must always be hurt. Some must be dependent, some must dominate. Dependency and domination stem from the same source, an inability to trust self or others, John said. The dominating person, who cannot bear that anyone disagree with him, trusts no one, though he needs the support of others too much to antagonize them, as I should well know. The healthy person uses judgment after giving consideration to the opinion of others. He surrenders when he believes others wiser but sticks to his own decision when he feels himself right.

Women I once condemned as selfish I now thought of as frightened little girls, using as best they knew how the protective devices acquired from their parents, unable in their fear to think of anyone but themselves. Opportunists turned into the unloved who lived by wit and stratagem because this was the way they knew best as children.

If I truly liked people I would try to be not vulnerable but valiant. I could not use anyone emotionally to live more easily but only share with them those moments they wanted to give.

As I expected less of others, I also expected them to expect less of me, in one sense. There was really little I could do for those who wanted more psychologically from me than I was able to give.

I now sought those who could, perhaps, see more of the world as it was, not as they wished it to be, as I hoped I was doing. I tried to select those less likely to hurt me or to be hurt by me.

I found it easier to hurt though, if necessary, to save deeper hurt later, as a doctor operates to prevent more serious illness. (It is better, of course, not to have to hurt at all.) Once when I broke off with a man I wailed to John, "How can I hurt him like this?"

"He was hurt long before you came along," John said. "It happened in childhood." His mother did the job, I thought.

Now I did not mind so much occasional hurts from others. After all, who was I to demand constant thoughtfulness?

"You can ask—but don't expect," John said.

One day I asked another reporter to take a message to a friend attending a convention he was covering.

"I won't have time," he said rudely.

For the moment his reply shocked me. I had always gone out of my way to do things when others asked. Then I thought, This reporter has his troubles. Everyone has to live—even the people who cannot be nice. I will dislike them less, perhaps, if I know they, too, are struggling to survive.

Once I complained to John someone called me at 2 A.M. waking me out of sound sleep. "What a nasty thing that was for him to do," I raged. "Doesn't he know I have trouble enough getting to sleep? I was awake for the rest of the night."

"Don't you accept that some are like that?" John said. "Some do not and cannot care about anyone else."

I had set too high standards for myself, and it follows, as the night the day, I had set them too high for others. When I found they could not possibly live up to these inhuman standards, I felt rejected, not knowing I was rejecting myself.

As I could be less rigid in my life, I could be less rigid with others. When I had to keep stern watch over my behavior I insisted the behavior of others be guarded. I would allow no one a freedom not allowed me. I made my own fantastic rules. I could break them any time I wished but no one else could.

I no longer needed to "hate" anyone. I had spit out hatred at others only when I could not admit self-hatred.

The things I belittled had held special meaning for me. My jealousy had caused me to criticize. I thought, What I want and cannot have, nobody else can have either.

My scorn for women whose lives revolved around dishes and babies was sheer envy. When I said "dirty dog," in scornful voice, I was thinking of all the natural functions of a dog that, to me, had become so unnatural—I was envious of a dog who did not need to hide feelings about his body.

As I liked people more I was willing to depend on them. Independence had been very important to me when I felt dependent. As I became more independent, I could know the importance of interdependence. I wanted to trust people, not flee them.

I took a lesson from Dr. Brock Chisholm, the Canadian psychiatrist, who heads the World Health Organization. One day he and another psychiatrist sped in an airplane across desolate stretches of Canada. The pilot was forced to fly low to see their only guide, a narrow-gauge railroad track visible through the fog only at intervals.

Tense and worried because of the perilous flight, the other psychiatrist was astounded to see Dr. Chisholm lean back in his chair and fall asleep.

When Dr. Chisholm woke up, the other asked in wonder, "How could you sleep at a fearful time like this?"

"Why not?" replied Dr. Chisholm. "The pilot undoubtedly thinks as much of his life as I do of mine."

Such trust in another had not been mine to hold. I could not even trust the engineer on a train. This time, we might have a wreck, I would always feel before stepping aboard nervously.

Now I could trust more. I even trusted taxi drivers to make their own choices—lucky, too, what with traffic today a systematic snarl. I no longer pushed along the cab with my stomach. The days of "Why did he choose this jammed street?" or "Why did he get in back of this Jersey jerk?" disappeared. I gave the driver my destination, settled back for a smoke. Formerly I talked a blue streak. By the time I ended a ten-block ride I had learned how the driver felt about politics, sports and family life. Now I gazed out the window at city scenes, discouraged conversation.

But when I chose, I could listen. I had spent my life listening to people but not really "hearing." Now I wanted to find out what they were trying to tell me.

I felt as though sometimes I talked a different language, what someone called the dialogue of the unconscious and described as far more powerful than the spoken word.

I listened to how things were said, undertones and overtones, as well as what was not said. Some joked about what disturbed them; others dared not mention their troubles even in jest. Some would not tell immediately how they felt but eventually needed to pour it out.

A friend of mine, most vocal in his distrust of analysis, wound up a frantic day's work with the comment, "I don't know why I'm so happy when I really feel so unhappy." He was confessing he covered up his unhappiness, though he would never admit it in those words.

Often what some said did not bear out their deeds. So I started, too, to look at deeds, rather than just accept words. The spoken word had been so threatening in my life I never dared investigate beyond it. Now I saw that many kind words hid unkind deeds and harsh words often masked kind deeds. "Handsome is as handsome does," indeed.

I noticed the difference that often existed between what I did, what I thought, what I said and what I felt. The more opposed these were without my being conscious of the opposition, the unhappier I was.

"We are what we feel," said John, "whether the feelings are repressed or expressed. 'As a man thinketh in his heart, so is he.'"

Finally I could face how much I owed those who gave comfort throughout life, who were and are on my side. Many helped me live, helped me find jobs, helped me get ready to go to the analyst.

One aunt kept encouraging me to write, to learn more about myself, to play golf, to get thin, even leading me to a reducing salon. Her husband, too, seemed to admire me for my struggles.

Another uncle made me feel I could do no wrong, even the writing of this book, always invited me to his home for summer vacation just like my grandmother did in the winter. An aunt, the mother of Merlin, often shopped with me and talked to me eagerly for hours. An uncle by adoption, before he died, insisted I keep writing and sent copies of my early newspaper articles to prominent men, friends of his who wrote back in praise (they had to or lose his friendship). I consider several aunts good friends, as I do my father's second wife and daughter.

I am still deceiving myself and probably will continue to do so, but the deceiving, I hope, will become less and less. Perception possesses depths. For instance, when the truth of self-hatred first came up, I dismissed the thought in fear. A few months later I dared take it up again, accept a little more of it. Months later, I knew it more deeply and could actually face some of my suicidal impulses.

Now I know I must keep examining what upsets me, for it is important. What makes me irritable? Why? Always the why of it, but a different why than before—a why with meaning and purpose. I never had difficulty asking questions but they were rarely thoughtful.

I know more what John meant when he said there really are no questions. The answers were always there if I could have but stopped to think them through. I must keep practicing thinking about what I feel. Some must practice feeling what they think.

I no longer argue about psychoanalysis with those who attack it. Analysis is not witchcraft which destroys the spirit, neither does it clear up unhappiness like magic, saving lives in a twinkling of the psychic eye. It is a long, slow process involving guidance by a man who knows himself well and determined effort by the one who seeks help. Anger, the leech of fear, is one of the hardest things in the world to shake off.

The only mysterious thing about analysis to me was how on earth I managed to set up such strong defenses against fear—I lacked no frailty when it came to self-preservation. Analysis to me was the discovery of the obvious, the things I felt as a child but covered up with civilization's concrete layers of "thou shalt not's."

I believe psychoanalysis is part of today's struggle for survival, that unless man concentrates more on what John called the atom bombs exploding in his mind, he may be blown off the earth.

But others need not believe this. I know some are more terrified of analysis than I was. I respect their terror. Man will select the lesser of his fears every time. Some may endure the pain of operation after operation for recurring ulcers rather than face a psychoanalyst, although ulcers are accepted as one of the chief psychosomatic illnesses.

For some, the psychological wounds may drive deep. The surgical knife is less terrifying than opening up other wounds. The scar (the defense) may be very thick, covering up for layers the depth of the wound (the fear). Some would rather not risk reopening a deep wound but prefer to live with the scab even though poisons in the wound may slowly destroy them.

The perils of psychoanalysis were preferable to the knife of the surgeon for me. I feared an operation on my nose more than the thought of lying on a couch and dissecting my life. But I had to deceive myself, mistaking symptoms for causes. I thought life would be fine if only I could get rid of the sinus or if only I could get married. I could not ask why I had the sinus or why I had not been able to get married until I lost the sinus and got married and still suffered.

When someone charges analysis is a racket, I remember, too, that as I felt a little better, as I could breathe once more through my nose, sometimes I resented the money I was paying.

It took a long time to know that if I had an unhappy childhood the only way I would get happiness was by paying for it, just as I paid for all else I lacked and desired. I would not get something for nothing in life and to expect it was to deceive myself further. Because I had it hard emotionally I screamed I must have life easy. I had not been strong enough to know this is a world of work and to him that has shall be given

more. The great American gamble might pay off in the Kentucky Derby — though never to me — but not in the field of human relations.

There I had to pay for a skill known as psychoanalysis, combination art and science, that would give me a chance to face myself. Seek and ye shall find. Analysis was one long search into self.

It was expensive but all the money in the world could not pay for what it brought me — peace of mind. There is no shortcut to peace, either in time or money. Peace is always expensive. Chaos is cheap. Those who think in terms of easing human suffering know peace is cheap, chaos expensive.

To those critics who demand "proof" of the success of analysis, I can only say, echoing John's words, "There is no proof except in one's heart for the important things."

How can you prove the cause of a tear?
How can you prove a spark of hatred?
How can you prove the warmth of love?

Joseph Wood Krutch

GENIUS AND NEUROTICISM

The relation between genius and neuroticism is not clear. Perhaps research can resolve the ambiguity. If neuroticism is really an attribute of genius, we are confronted with a value dilemma. If poor adjustment is the basis of discontent, and discontent is the challenge a creative genius rises to meet—the stimulus to his effort—then the choice is between creative or adjusted personalities. And this choice in turn depends on which we value more. The problem is hypothetical in the sense that we do not know if adjustment and creativity are incompatible, but it exemplifies the value dilemma in a specific and compelling way. In a practical sense, the problem is not hypothetical at all, because we cannot withhold therapy until all the facts are known. In practice, decisions based on incomplete evidence must be made. Is it possible, Krutch suggests, that in some instances the disorder may be better than the cure?

Psychoanalysis is now one of the taken-for-granted tools of the biographer and critic, whether "serious," middle-brow, or even low. It seems to me, nevertheless, that one fundamental question has never been satisfactorily answered. Exactly what is the relation between a writer's complexes, obsessions, or neuroses and his genius? An ancient gag used to run "Photographers don't have to be crazy, but it helps." Are we compelled to say the same thing about artists?

Back in the late teens and early twenties when Freudianism first became a fad, an affirmative answer to this question was often implied or even given. The argument ran something like this: Closely examined, most great men turn out to have been at least a little bit queer; therefore, genius is necessarily queer. In fact, queerness and genius are the same thing. The artist's gift is the neurosis he exploits.

With shame I must confess that I was guilty of seeming to accept this absurdity in the first book I published (not counting a doctoral thesis). It was a biographical-critical study of Edgar Allan Poe, who was, among other things, a perfect sitting duck for the amateur psychoanalyst. And I chose him for that very reason. I laid great stress on his sadistic fantasies, his obsessive concern with death and dissolution, and with what seemed to be in his own life a desperate determination not to become sexually involved with any of the women whom he professed to love; also on his "Philosophy of Composition," which maintained, despite conclusive evidence to the contrary, that he deliberately chose the macabre effects which were in fact the only ones he could produce.

I am still ready to argue that the theory I evolved concerning Poe's personality is consistent. I still believe also that the *"frisson nerveux"* which Baudelaire discovered and celebrated in Poe is a neurotic shiver. But in my enthusiasm I went far beyond this. I said, or at least strongly implied, that Poe's neuroses *were* his genius and that, if we could get all the facts, such was usually the case with great imaginative writers. They are always neurotic. Unfortunately I

neglected to ask why, if all geniuses are neurotic, all neurotics are not geniuses.

What I am asking now is simply this: Granted the extravagance of any mere equating of genius with mental disorder, what actually is the relation between them, especially in extreme cases like that of Poe where at least much of the unique character of the work obviously is profoundly influenced by these disorders? That great art is essentially sane I am convinced. But it often is the product of minds which seem to be more rather than less disturbed than those of ordinary men.

Perhaps the reason why the contemporary critic seems rather disinclined to face this question is simply that he (and all of us) have come to believe that what used to be called "abnormalities" are part of the psychic make-up of nearly everybody and that the genius sometimes seems more abnormal than most men simply because he gives us a better opportunity to see his mind at work. But, even so, I think my question is not completely answered. To take again the extreme case of Poe, it seems certain enough that if he had been less neurotic his work would have been quite different from what it is. Would it have been better or would it have been less original, less interesting? What would be the answer to the same question if it were asked about some other writer much less obviously "unhealthy"?

Shortly after my own indiscretion was published, I received a letter from Dr. Beatrice Hinckle, translator of Jung and then (next at least to the Freudian, A. A. Brill) the best-known practicing psychoanalyst. She approved my diagnosis and said she had met a number of cases where the pattern was the same as Poe's. But she added a vehement protest. The neurotic genius was a genius in spite of his neuroses, not because of them. Mental illness was never anything but a handicap. This seemed to me then, and still does, as much an overstatement as my own opposite thesis. Poe

From *Saturday Review*, January 19, 1963, pp. 12-14. Reprinted by permission of the author and *Saturday Review*.

would certainly not have written what he did if he had been "normal." It's there that the problem arises.

Since Dr. Hinckle was engaged in the attempt to cure neurotics she was perhaps reluctant to admit that she might sometimes be doing them and the world a doubtful service. A few years later Dr. Alfred Adler revealed in conversation that he, at least, was quite aware of this possibility. I have told the anecdote at more length elsewhere but the nub of it has to be repeated. I had accused him of a non sequitur by pointing out that more than one of his books had first set out to show how abnormal the great men had been but had then concluded with the exhortation, "Therefore, let us all try to be as normal as possible." Adler hedged and I asked the direct question, "Suppose that a creative artist was functioning effectively; would it be dangerous for him to submit to a psychoanalysis?" He replied with cagey pomposity: "I would not like to answer that question directly. But I will say this. Dr. Freud and I are the only two leading psychoanalysts who have never themselves been analyzed . . . and I think we have made the greatest contributions to the science."

The whole question comes to my mind again because I have just been reading several reviews of the new 1,400-page edition of Beethoven's letters, many of which had never before been accessible and which, so the reviewers all seem to agree, are painful reading for those who admire Beethoven the man no less than the music he wrote.

Here is a case far more complicated than that of Poe; the relation between the man and his abnormalities is far less simple. "Ligeia" and "The Fall of the House of Usher" (to say nothing of such astonishing productions as "Berenice" and "The Pit and the Pendulum") obviously bear so close a relation to their author's own neurotic fancies that the one seems a direct expression of the other. Though Poe has given artistic form to his obsessions, they and the stories they inspired are qualitatively almost identical. But whatever the Ninth Symphony may express, no one would be likely to call it obviously "sick" in the sense that Poe's

writing usually is. On the basis of the works alone, the understandable image of Beethoven has been of a heroic figure struggling manfully against a cruel fate and transmuting his agony, sometimes into tragedy, sometimes into a joy that transcends the suffering over which an abounding vitality triumphs.

This is the way in which he has usually been pictured by admirers who assumed (and wanted to assume) that the man and the music were identical. That element of stormy protest which is so different from anything to be read into the cheerful Haydn or even into the plaintive discontent sometimes audible in Mozart is sometimes explained in terms of a changed sociopolitical atmosphere. Haydn accepted the position of the musician as merely that of one of the higher servants of the nobility; Mozart, for all his nascent vision of democracy and brotherhood, was too gentle to be moved to anything approaching rage. But Beethoven was the child of a revolutionary era. He was less contented than either of his two great predecessors because he could not, like them, accept the status quo. Hence he spoke out violently with the voice of the genuinely committed rebel.

But whatever truth there may be in this picture, it is not the whole truth. The letters are said to confirm abundantly what some of the more recent biographers have maintained; namely, that the man whose utterances are so "noble" was in his own character and personality a sort of distressing parody of his musical utterances. It is not merely that he was quarrelsome, pettish, and given to throwing dishes at the cook. His relations with his scamp of a nephew —conventionally pictured as proof of his loving patience—actually included a dishonorable attempt to separate this nephew from his mother and to become in effect a mother himself. The lonely titan aspiring toward fulfilment in the love of the several women he worshiped but was denied, seems, not entirely unlike Poe, to have seen to it himself that any promising relationship was broken off. All this, together with the grotesque possessiveness of his attitude toward the incorrigible nephew, invite the psychoanalyst to explore some pretty dark corridors. But even that is not all. Though it may seem odd to speak of a truly great artist as suffering delusions of grandeur, Beethoven seems to have been close to paranoid in both his sense of his own greatness and in what amounts to delusions of persecution. The fact remains that what were mere delusions in the artist are somehow transformed into convincing realities in the works which he created. Listening to them we believe what he believed about himself; reading the letters we still see a relationship between the man and his work. But it is by no means an identity.

Perhaps the best of the reviews I have read (that by Albert Goldman in *The New Leader*) puts it thus: "No one who has read the Sterbas' book ["Beethoven and his Nephew"] will ever forget the terrible image it contains of the great Beethoven living constantly in a kind of emotional squalor, his imagination periodically inflamed by fantasies of a paranoidic order in which he figures as the noble and innocent victim of base and evil persecutors. And no one who knows Beethoven's music could fail to connect these dreadful distortions of reality with the mythopoetic content of his compositions — allowing, of course, for the idealization of fantasy in art."

This describes, perhaps, as well as possible, what seems actually to have happened. But it does not answer the question (possibly unanswerable) how anything so improbable *could* have happened. Some critics dodge the question by insisting that in the case of any work of art one should always fix one's exclusive attention on the work itself; that all "background," whether biographical, historical, sociological, or what not is both irrelevant and misleading; that it not only tends to explain away rather than explain, but may also make it actually impossible to take the work in question at face value — which is the only way in which a work of art can profitably be taken. We must not let Beethoven the man get between us and the works. It is only they that we have any business concerning ourselves with. Too much biography and there is danger that we will hear in the Ninth Symphony only the paranoid ragings (which are not actually there) and miss the grandiose triumph of a joyously achieved victory over cruel fate (which very decidedly is there).

Such an attitude defines one approach to criticism and possibly the most fruitful one. But if — as seems to be the case — we must remove Beethoven from the category of the "normal" and "healthy" artist where we once pigeonholed him along with Haydn and Handel, then we must put him among the neurotics and raise again the question with which we started: What is the relationship between works of art and the neurotic afflictions of their creators?

What is the power, which Beethoven had and Poe did not have, of using but transcending delusions of grandeur and of persecution? Would this question lead to the conclusion (not too helpful, I admit) that it is wrong to say either that neurotic abnormality is genius or that, as Dr. Hinckle protested, it is merely a disability over which the artist triumphs? Would it enable us to grant that most geniuses are neurotic and at the same time explain why all neurotics are not geniuses? Genius, in this conception, does not consist in the abnormality but in the power to transform it, and Beethoven was a far greater genius than Poe just because he could make a sane image out of what was in itself not entirely sane. Such an explanation is perhaps no explanation at all. It leaves "genius" as mysterious as ever. But it does enable us to recognize the troublesome fact that great works are often created by men less great than they, while, at the same time, it removes the temptation to fall into the error of believing that art itself is not "sane" and "healthy."

Those who read Havelock Ellis in pre-Freudian days will remember that he was concerned with our problem in a rather old-fashioned way at a time when the "abnormality" of genius was most likely to be attributed to physical causes. Max Nordau in his once famous but now mostly unread "Degeneracy" argued that most modern literature was indeed neurotic and therefore simply bad art. But others were far from ready to accept this simple solution. Did the febrile excitement characteristic of the tubercular contribute to the glow of Keats's poetry? Did a moderate colony of *Spirechaeta pallida* act as a stimulus in Swift, Nietzche, and Beethoven, all of whom were suspected of playing host to it? Were geniuses most likely to appear in families some members of which were mentally subnormal, and did this suggest that the creative spirit was more closely related to feeble-mindedness than to insanity?

Any theory that the artist is in some sense sick (note, by the way, that Thomas Mann seems to have at least toyed seriously with this thesis) raises a practical problem which becomes more pressing as "planning" is more and more talked of and is coming to include artificial insemination in the interests of eugenics, as Sir Julian Huxley has only recently proposed. One of Havelock Ellis's theories might suggest that syphilis should not be stamped out completely; some psychological theories that all neuroses should not be nipped in the bud. Now we are back to Alfred Adler. Perhaps Beethoven would never have written any of his major works if he had been psychoanalyzed in time.

For the present, most of these are, fortunately, only theoretical questions. But there is a related and very practical one. No age before ours has been so determined to give children "all the advantages" of a good education and a happy, normal childhood. Yet the lives of great men all (or at least in numerous instances) remind us that they frequently had none of these good things and that overcoming difficulties was a stimulus, not a deterrent. Either God or Nature seems to work in a mysterious way. Whom the Lord (or Mother Nature) loveth he chastiseth.

Who is to take the responsibility for planning these difficulties and attempting, for the benefit of humanity at large, to thrust painful greatness upon some of those about to be born? Had I been asked as I was reaching the age of discretion whether or not I wanted to be Beethoven at the price he paid, I am afraid I might have said: "No, thank you. I'd rather be 'normal' or even just 'average.'" But think what the world might have lost had Beethoven been given that choice.

Carl R. Rogers and B. F. Skinner

SOME ISSUES CONCERNING THE CONTROL OF HUMAN BEHAVIOR: A SYMPOSIUM

Who should control the minds of men? To what ends and with what means? In this article two eminent psychologists take up the question of how scientific and public knowledge should be used. The issues raised in their discussion obviously apply to counseling and psychotherapy, and the importance of values or goals can be seen in the emphasis both authors place on them. Rogers argues that commitment to fixed and final goals would be stultifying and premature. He suggests instead a concern with the process of acquiring values and attitudes. As men become more self-directing, more aware of the evidence of their senses, and less rigid, they become, according to Rogers, better able to work out their own values and more capable of flexible, responsible adaptation to new realities. Skinner maintains that survival is the "ultimate criterion," and that there are values which he and many of us embrace — happiness, security, productivity, creativity — toward which people (patients) can be conditioned. Thus self-determination is promoted by Rogers, "shaping" of desirable behavior by Skinner. For Skinner, the psychotherapist is a benevolent authority charged with the responsibility of conditioning patients for their own betterment and for the betterment of humanity. For Rogers, the counselor is a custodian of public knowledge and skills which are used to increase self-awareness so that the client can arrive at independent, self-directed choices. Perhaps the most important aspect of this confrontation is that, like the article by Lowe, it makes clear the depth of the value problem and the difficulty of reconciling differences.

I — Skinner

Science is steadily increasing our power to influence, change, mold—in a word, control—human behavior. It has extended our "understanding" (whatever that may be) so that we deal more successfully with people in nonscientific ways, but it has also identified conditions or variables which can be used to predict and control behavior in a new, and increasingly rigorous, technology. The broad disciplines of government and economics offer examples of this, but there is special cogency in those contributions of anthropology, sociology, and psychology which deal with individual behavior. Carl Rogers has listed some of the achievements to date in a recent paper (1956). Those of his examples which show or imply the control of the single organism are primarily due, as we should expect, to psychology. It is the experimental study of behavior which carries us beyond awkward or inaccessible "principles," "factors," and so on, to variables which can be directly manipulated.

It is also, and for more or less the same reasons, the conception of human behavior emerging from an experimental analysis which most directly challenges traditional views. Psychologists themselves often do not seem to be aware of how far they have moved in this direction. But the change is not passing unnoticed by others. Until only recently it was customary to deny the possibility of a rigorous science of human behavior by arguing, either that a lawful science was impossible because man was a free agent, or that merely statistical predictions would always leave room for personal freedom. But those who used to take this line have become most vociferous in expressing their alarm at the way these obstacles are being surmounted.

Now, the control of human behavior has always been unpopular. Any undisguised effort to control usually arouses emotional reactions. We hesitate to admit, even to ourselves, that we are engaged in control, and we may refuse to control, even when this would be helpful, for fear of criticism. Those who have explicitly avowed an interest in control have been roughly treated by history. Machiavelli is the great prototype. As Macaulay said of him, "Out of his surname they coined an epithet for a knave and out of his Christian name a synonym for the devil." There were obvious reasons. The control that Machiavelli analyzed and recommended, like most political control, used techniques that were aversive to the controllee. The threats and punishments of the bully, like those of the government operating on the same plan, are not designed—whatever their success—to endear themselves to those who are controlled. Even when the techniques themselves are not aversive, control is usually exercised for the selfish purposes of the controller and, hence, has indirectly punishing effects upon others.

Man's natural inclination to revolt against selfish control has been exploited to good purpose in what we call the philosophy and literature of democracy. The doctrine of the rights of man has been effective in arousing individuals to concerted action against governmental and religious tyranny. The literature which has had this effect has greatly extended the number of terms in our language which express reactions to the control of men. But the ubiquity and ease of expression of this attitude spells trouble for any science which may give birth to a powerful technology of behavior. Intelligent men and women, dominated by the humanistic philosophy of the past two centuries, cannot view with equanimity what Andrew Hacker has called "the specter of predictable man" (1954). Even the statistical or actuarial prediction of human events, such as the number of fatalities to be expected on a holiday weekend, strikes many people as uncanny and evil, while the prediction and control of individual behavior is regarded as little less than the work of the devil. I am not so much concerned here with the political or economic consequences for psychology, although research following certain channels may well suffer harmful effects. We ourselves, as intelligent men

From *Science*, November 30, 1956, Vol. 124, pp. 1057-1066. Reprinted by permission of the authors and publishers.

and women, and as exponents of Western thought, share these attitudes. They have already interfered with the free exercise of a scientific analysis, and their influence threatens to assume more serious proportions.

Three broad areas of human behavior supply good examples. The first of these —*personal control*—may be taken to include person-to-person relationships in the family, among friends, in social and work groups, and in counseling and psychotherapy. Other fields are *education* and *government*. A few examples from each will show how nonscientific preconceptions are affecting our current thinking about human behavior.

Personal control

People living together in groups come to control one another with a technique which is not inappropriately called "ethical." When an individual behaves in a fashion acceptable to the group, he receives admiration, approval, affection, and many other reinforcements which increase the likelihood that he will continue to behave in that fashion. When his behavior is not acceptable, he is criticized, censured, blamed, or otherwise punished. In the first case the group calls him "good"; in the second, "bad." This practice is so thoroughly ingrained in our culture that we often fail to see that it is a technique of control. Yet we are almost always engaged in such control, even though the reinforcements and punishments are often subtle.

The practice of admiration is an important part of a culture, because behavior which is otherwise inclined to be weak can be set up and maintained with its help. The individual is especially likely to be praised, admired, or loved when he acts for the group in the face of great danger, for example, or sacrifices himself or his possessions, or submits to prolonged hardship, or suffers martyrdom. These actions are not admirable in any absolute sense, but they require admiration if they are to be strong. Similarly, we admire people who behave in original or exceptional ways, not because such behavior is itself admirable, but because we do not know how to encourage original or exceptional behavior in any other way. The group acclaims independent, unaided behavior in part because it is easier to reinforce than to help.

As long as this technique of control is misunderstood, we cannot judge correctly an environment in which there is less need for heroism, hardship, or independent action. We are likely to argue that such an environment is itself less admirable or produces less admirable people. In the old days, for example, young scholars often lived in undesirable quarters, ate unappetizing or inadequate food, performed unprofitable tasks for a living or to pay for necessary books and materials or publication. Older scholars and other members of the group offered compensating reinforcement in the form of approval and admiration for these sacrifices. When the modern graduate student receives a generous scholarship, enjoys good living conditions, and has his research and publication subsidized, the grounds for evaluation seem to be pulled from under us. Such a student no longer *needs* admiration to carry him over a series of obstacles (no matter how much he may need it for other reasons), and, in missing certain familiar objects of admiration, we are likely to conclude that such *conditions* are less admirable. Obstacles to scholarly work may serve as a useful measure of motivation—and we may go wrong unless some substitute is found—but we can scarcely defend a deliberate harassment of the student for this purpose. The productivity of any set of conditions can be evaluated only when we have freed ourselves of the attitudes which have been generated in us as members of an ethical group.

A similar difficulty arises from our use of punishment in the form of censure or blame. The concept of responsibility and the related concepts of foreknowledge and choice are used to justify techniques of control using punishment. Was So-and-So aware of the probable consequences of his action, and was the action deliberate? If so, we are justified in punishing him. But what does this mean? It appears to be a question concerning the efficacy of the contingent relations between behavior and punishing consequences. We punish behavior because it is objectionable to us or the group, but in a minor refinement of rather recent origin we have come to withhold punishment when it cannot be expected to have any effect. If the objectionable consequences of an act were accidental and not likely to occur again, there is no point in punishing. We say that the individual was not "aware of the consequences of his action" or that the consequences were not "intentional." If the action could not have been avoided—if the individual "had no choice"—punishment is also withheld, as it is if the individual is incapable of being changed by punishment because he is of "unsound mind." In all these cases—different as they are—the individual is held "not responsible" and goes unpunished.

Just as we say that it is "not fair" to punish a man for something he could not help doing, so we call it "unfair" when one is rewarded beyond his due or for something he could not help doing. In other words, we also object to wasting reinforcers where they are not needed or will do no good. We make the same point with the words just and right. Thus we have no right to punish the irresponsible, and a man has no right to reinforcers he does not earn or deserve. But concepts of choice, responsibility, justice, and so on, provide a most inadequate analysis of efficient reinforcing and punishing contingencies because they carry a heavy semantic cargo of a quite different sort, which obscures any attempt to clarify controlling practices or to improve techniques. In particular, they fail to prepare us for techniques based on other than aversive techniques of control. Most people would object to forcing prisoners to serve as subjects of dangerous medical experiments, but few object when they are induced to serve by the offer of return privileges—even when the reinforcing effect of these privileges has been created by forcible deprivation. In the traditional scheme the right to refuse guarantees the individual

against coercion or an unfair bargain. But to what extent *can* a prisoner refuse under such circumstances?

We need not go so far afield to make the point. We can observe our own attitude toward personal freedom in the way we resent any interference with what we want to do. Suppose we want to buy a car of a particular sort. Then we may object, for example, if our wife urges us to buy a less expensive model and to put the difference into a new refrigerator. Or we may resent it if our neighbor questions our need for such a car or our ability to pay for it. We would certainly resent it if it were illegal to buy such a car (remember Prohibition); and if we find we cannot actually afford it, we may resent governmental control of the price through tariffs and taxes. We resent it if we discover that we cannot get the car because the manufacturer is holding the model in deliberately short supply in order to push a model we do not want. In all this we assert our democratic right to buy the car of our choice. We are well prepared to do so and to resent any restriction on our freedom.

But why do we not ask why it is the car of our choice and resent the forces which made it so? Perhaps our favorite toy as a child was a car, of a very different model, but nevertheless bearing the name of the car we now want. Perhaps our favorite TV program is sponsored by the manufacturer of that car. Perhaps we have seen pictures of many beautiful or prestigeful persons driving it—in pleasant or glamorous places. Perhaps the car has been designed with respect to our motivational patterns: the device on the hood is a phallic symbol; or the horsepower has been stepped up to please our competitive spirit in enabling us to pass other cars swiftly (or, as the advertisements say, "safely"). The concept of freedom that has emerged as part of the cultural practice of our group makes little or no provision for recognizing or dealing with these kinds of control. Concepts like "responsibility" and "rights" are scarcely applicable. We are prepared to deal with coercive measures, but we have no traditional recourse with respect to other measures which in the long run (and especially with the help of science) may be much more powerful and dangerous.

Education.

The techniques of education were once frankly aversive. The teacher was usually older and stronger than his pupils and was able to "make them learn." This meant that they were not actually taught but were surrounded by a threatening world from which they could escape only by learning. Usually they were left to their own resources in discovering how to do so. Claude Coleman has published a grimly amusing reminder of these older practices (1953). He tells of a schoolteacher who published a careful account of his services during 51 years of teaching, during which he administered: "...911,527 blows with a cane; 124,010 with a rod; 20,989 with a ruler; 136,715 with the hand; 10,295 over the mouth; 7,905 boxes on the ear; [and] 1,115,800 slaps on the head...."

Progressive education was a humanitarian effort to substitute positive reinforcement for such aversive measures, but in the search for useful human values in the classroom it has never fully replaced the variables it abandoned. Viewed as a branch of behavioral technology, education remains relatively inefficient. We supplement it, and rationalize it, by admiring the pupil who learns *for himself*; and we often attribute the learning process, or knowledge itself, to something *inside* the individual. We admire behavior which seems to have inner sources. Thus we admire one who *recites* a poem more than one who simply *reads* it. We admire one who *knows* the answer more than one who *knows where to look it up*. We admire the *writer* rather than the *reader*. We admire the arithmetician who can do a problem in his head rather than with a slide rule or calculating machine, or in "original" ways rather than by a strict application of rules. In general we feel that any aid or "crutch"—except those aids to which we are now thoroughly accustomed—reduces the credit due. In Plato's *Phaedrus*, Thamus, the king, attacks the invention of the alphabet on similar grounds! He is afraid "it will produce forgetfulness in the minds of those who learn to use it, because they will not practice their memories...." In other words, he holds it more admirable to remember than to use a memorandum. He also objects that pupils "will read many things without instruction...[and] will therefore seem to know many things when they are for the most part ignorant." In the same vein we are today sometimes contemptuous of book learning, but, as educators, we can scarcely afford to adopt this view without reservation.

By admiring the student for knowledge and blaming him for ignorance, we escape some of the responsibility of teaching him. We resist any analysis of the educational process which threatens the notion of inner wisdom or questions the contention that the fault of ignorance lies with the student. More powerful techniques which bring about the same changes in behavior by manipulating *external* variables are decried as brainwashing or thought control. We are quite unprepared to judge *effective* educational measures. As long as only a few pupils learn much of what is taught, we do not worry about uniformity or regimentation. We do not fear the feeble technique; but we should view with dismay a system under which every student learned everything listed in a syllabus—although such a condition is far from unthinkable. Similarly, we do not fear a system which is so defective that the student must *work* for an education; but we are loath to give credit for anything learned without effort—although this could well be taken as an ideal result—and we flatly refuse to give credit if the student already knows what a school teaches.

A world in which people are wise and good without trying, without "having to be," without "choosing to be," could conceivably be a far better world for everyone. In such a world we should not have to "give anyone credit"—we should not need to admire anyone—for being wise and good. From our present point of view we cannot believe that such a world would be admirable. We do not even permit ourselves to imagine what it would be like.

Government has always been the special field of aversive control. The state is frequently defined in terms of the power to punish, and jurisprudence leans heavily upon the associated notion of personal responsibility. Yet it is becoming increasingly difficult to reconcile current practice and theory with these earlier views. In criminology, for example, there is a strong tendency to drop the notion of responsibility in favor of some such alternative as capacity or controllability. But no matter how strongly the facts, or even practical expedience, support such a change, it is difficult to make the change in a legal system designed on a different plan. When governments resort to other techniques (for example, positive reinforcement), the concept of responsibility is no longer relevant and the theory of government is no longer applicable.

The conflict is illustrated by two decisions of the Supreme Court in the 1930's which dealt with, and disagreed on, the definition of control or coercion (Freund *et al.*, 1954, p. 288). The Agricultural Adjustment Act proposed that the Secretary of Agriculture make "rental or benefit payments" to those farmers who agreed to reduce production. The government agreed that the Act would be unconstitutional if the farmer had been *compelled* to reduce production but was not, since he was merely *invited* to do so. Justice Roberts expressed the contrary majority view of the court that "The power to confer or withhold unlimited benefits is the power to coerce or destroy." This recognition of positive reinforcement was withdrawn a few years later in another case in which Justice Cardozo (Freund *et al.*, 1954, p. 244) wrote "To hold that motive or temptation is equivalent to coercion is to plunge the law in endless difficulties." We may agree with him, without implying that the proposition is therefore wrong. Sooner or later the law must be prepared to deal with all possible techniques of governmental control.

The uneasiness with which we view government (in the broadest possible sense) when it does not use punishment is shown by the reception of my utopian novel, *Walden Two* (Skinner, 1948). This was essentially a proposal to apply a behavioral technology to the construction of a workable, effective, and productive pattern of government. It was greeted with wrathful violence. *Life* magazine called it "a travesty on the good life," and "a menace. . . a triumph of mortmain or the dead hand not envisaged since the days of Sparta. . .a slur upon a name, a corruption of an impulse." Joseph Wood Krutch devoted a substantial part of his book, *The Measure of Man* (1953), to attacking my views and those of the protagonist, Frazier, in the same vein, and Morris Viteles has recently criticized the book in a similar manner in *Science* (1955). Perhaps the reaction is best expressed in a quotation from *The Quest for Utopia* by Negley and Patrick (1952):

"Halfway through this contemporary utopia, the reader may feel sure, as we did, that this is a beautifully ironic satire on what has been called 'behavioral engineering.' The longer one stays in this better world of the psychologist, however, the plainer it becomes that the inspiration is not satiric, but messianic. This is indeed the behaviorally engineered society, and while it was to be expected that sooner or later the principle of psychological conditioning would be made the basis of a serious construction of utopia—Brown anticipated it in *Limanora*— yet not even the effective satire of Huxley is adequate preparation for the shocking horror of the idea when positively presented. Of all the dictatorships espoused by utopists, this is the most profound, and incipient dictators might well find in this utopia a guidebook of political practice."

One would scarcely guess that the authors are talking about a world in which there is food, clothing, and shelter for all, where everyone chooses his own work and works on the average only 4 hours a day, where music and the arts flourish, where personal relationships develop under the most favorable circumstances, where education prepares every child for the social and intellectual life which lies before him, where—in short—people are truly happy, secure, productive, creative, and forward-looking. What is wrong with it? Only one thing: someone "planned it that way." If these critics had come upon a society in some remote corner of the world which boasted similar advantages, they would undoubtedly have hailed it as providing a pattern we all might well follow—provided that it was clearly the result of a natural process of cultural evolution. Any evidence that intelligence had been used in arriving at this version of the good life would, in their eyes, be a serious flaw. No matter if the planner of *Walden Two* diverts none of the proceeds of the community to his own use, no matter if he has no current control or is, indeed, unknown to most of the other members of the community (he planned that, too), somewhere back of it all be occupies the position of prime mover. And this, to the child of the democratic tradition, spoils it all.

The dangers inherent in the control of human behavior are very real. The possibility of the misuse of scientific knowledge must always be faced. We cannot escape by denying the power of a science of behavior or arresting its development. It is no help to cling to familiar philosophies of human behavior simply because they are more reassuring. As I have pointed out elsewhere (Skinner, 1955), the new techniques emerging from a science of behavior must be subject to the explicit countercontrol which has already been applied to earlier and cruder forms. Brute force and deception, for example, are now fairly generally suppressed by ethical practices and by explicit governmental and religious agencies. A similar countercontrol of scientific knowledge in the interests of the group is a feasible and promising possibility. Although we cannot say how devious the course of its evolution may be, a cultural pattern of control and countercontrol will presumably emerge which will be most widely supported because it is most widely reinforcing.

If we cannot foresee all the details of this (as we obviously cannot), it is important to remember that this is true of the critics of science as well. The dire consequences of new techniques of control, the hidden menace in original cultural designs—these

need some proof. It is only another example of my present point that the need for proof is so often overlooked. Man has got himself into some pretty fixes, and it is easy to believe that he will do so again. But there is a more optimistic possibility. The slow growth of the methods of science, now for the first time being applied to human affairs, *may* mean a new and exciting phase of human life to which historical analogies will not apply and in which earlier political slogans will not be appropriate. If we are to use the knowledge that a science of behavior is now making available with any hope of success, we must look at human nature as it is brought into focus through the methods of science rather than as it has been presented to us in a series of historical accidents.

If the advent of a powerful science of behavior causes trouble, it will not be because science itself is inimical to human welfare but because older conceptions have not yielded easily or gracefully. We expect resistance to new techniques of control from those who have heavy investments in the old, but we have no reason to help them preserve a series of principles that are not ends in themselves but rather outmoded means to an end. What is needed is a new conception of human behavior which is compatible with the implications of a scientific analysis. All men control and are controlled. The question of government in the broadest possible sense is not how freedom is to be preserved but what kinds of control are to be used and to what ends. Control must be analyzed and considered in its proper proportions. No one, I am sure, wishes to develop new master-slave relationships or bend the will of the people to despotic rulers in new ways. These are patterns of control appropriate to a world without science. They may well be the first to go when the experimental analysis of behavior comes into its own in the design of cultural practices.

II — Rogers

There are, I believe, a number of matters in connection with this important topic on which the authors of this article, and probably a large majority of psychologists, are in agreement. These matters then are not issues as far as we are concerned, and I should like to mention them briefly in order to put them to one side.

Points of agreement

I am sure we agree that men — as individuals and as societies — have always endeavored to understand, predict, influence, and control human behavior — their own behavior and that of others.

I believe we agree that the behavioral sciences are making and will continue to make increasingly rapid progress in the understanding of behavior, and that as a consequence the capacity to predict and to control behavior is developing with equal rapidity.

I believe we agree that to deny these advances, or to claim that man's behavior cannot be a field of science, is unrealistic. Even though this is not an issue for us, we should recognize that many intelligent men still hold strongly to the view that the actions of men are free in some sense such that scientific knowledge of man's behavior is impossible. Thus Reinhold Niebuhr, the noted theologian, heaps scorn on the concept of psychology as a science of man's behavior and even says, "In any event, no scientific investigation of past behavior can become the basis of predictions of future behavior" (1955, p. 47). So, while this is not an issue for psychologists, we should at least notice in passing that it is an issue for many people.

I believe we are in agreement that the tremendous potential power of a science which permits the prediction and control of behavior may be misused, and that the possibility of such misuse constitutes a serious threat.

Consequently Skinner and I are in agreement that the whole question of the scientific control of human behavior is a matter with which psychologists and the general public should concern themselves. As Robert Oppenheimer told the American Psychological Association last year (1956a) the problems that psychologists will pose for society by their growing ability to control behavior will be much more grave than the problems posed by the ability of physicists to control the reactions of matter. I am not sure whether psychologists generally recognize this. My impression is that by and large they hold a laissez-faire attitude. Obviously Skinner and I do not hold this laissez-faire view, or we would not have written this article.

Points at issue

With these several points of basic and important agreement, are there then any issues that remain on which there are differences? I believe there are. They can be stated very briefly: Who will be controlled? Who will exercise control? What type of control will be exercised? Most important of all, toward what end or what purpose, or in the pursuit of what value, will control be exercised?

It is on questions of this sort that there exist ambiguities, misunderstandings, and probably deep differences. These differences exist among psychologists, among members of the general public in this country, and among various world cultures. Without any hope of achieving a final resolution of these questions, we can, I believe, put these issues in clearer form.

Some meanings

To avoid ambiguity and faulty communication, I would like to clarify the meanings of some of the terms we are using.

Behavioral science is a term that might be defined from several angles but in the context of this discussion it refers primarily to knowledge that the existence of certain describable conditions in the human being and/or in his environment is followed by certain describable consequences in his actions.

Prediction means the prior identification of behaviors which then occur. Because it is important in some things I wish to say later, I would point out that one may predict a highly specific behavior, such as an eye blink, or one may predict a class of behaviors. One might correctly predict "avoid-ant behavior," for example, without being able to specify whether the individual will run away or simply close his eyes.

The word *control* is a very slippery one, which can be used with any one of several meanings. I would like to specify three that seem most important for our present purposes. *Control* may mean: (i) The setting of conditions by B for A, A having no voice in the matter, such that certain predictable behaviors then occur in A. I refer to this as external control. (ii) The setting of conditions by B for A, A giving some degree of consent to these conditions, such that certain predictable behaviors then occur in A. I refer to this as the influence of B on A. (iii) The setting of conditions by A such that certain predictable behaviors then occur in himself. I refer to this as internal control. It will be noted that Skinner lumps together the first two meanings, external control and influence, under the concept of control. I find this confusing.

Usual concept of control of human behavior

With the underbrush thus cleared away (I hope), let us review very briefly the various elements that are involved in the usual concept of the control of human behavior as mediated by the behavioral sciences. I am drawing here on the previous writings of Skinner, on his present statements, on the writings of others who have considered in either friendly or antagonistic fashion the meanings that would be involved in such control. I have not excluded the science fiction writers, as reported recently by Vandenburg (1956), since they often show an awareness of the issues involved, even though the methods described are as yet fictional. These then are the elements that seem common to these different concepts of the application of science to human behavior.

1) There must first be some sort of decision about goals. Usually desirable goals are assumed, but sometimes, as in George Orwell's book *1984*, the goal that is selected is an aggrandizement of individual power

with which most of us would disagree. In a recent paper Skinner suggests that one possible set of goals to be assigned to the behavioral technology is this: "Let men be happy, informed, skillful, well-behaved and productive" (1955-56). In the first draft of his part of this article, which he was kind enough to show me, he did not mention such definite goals as these, but desired "im-proved" educational practices, "wiser" use of knowledge in government, and the like. In the final version of his article he avoids even these value-laden terms, and his implicit goal is the very general one that scientific control of behavior is desirable, because it would perhaps bring "a far better world for everyone."

Thus the first step in thinking about the control of human behavior is the choice of goals, whether specific or general. It is necessary to come to terms in some way with the issue, "For what purpose?"

2) A second element is that, whether the end selected is highly specific or is a very general one such as wanting "a better world," we proceed by the methods of science to discover the means to these ends. We continue through further experimentation and investigation to discover more effective means. The method of science is self-correcting in thus arriving at increasingly effective ways of achieving the purpose we have in mind.

3) The third aspect of such control is that as the conditions or methods are discovered by which to reach the goal, some person or some group establishes these conditions and uses these methods, having in one way or another obtained the power to do so.

4) The fourth element is the exposure of individuals to the prescribed conditions, and this leads, with a high degree of probability, to behavior which is in line with the goals desired. Individuals are now happy, if that has been the goal, or well-behaved, or submissive, or whatever it has been decided to make them.

5) The fifth element is that if the process I have described is put in motion then there is a continuing social organization which will continue to produce the types of behavior that have been valued.

Are there any flaws in this way of viewing the control of human behavior? I believe there are. In fact the only element in this description with which I find myself in agreement is the second. It seems to me quite incontrovertibly true that the scientific method is an excellent way to discover the means by which to achieve our goals. Beyond that, I feel many sharp differences, which I will try to spell out.

I believe that in Skinner's presentation here and in his previous writings, there is a serious underestimation of the problem of power. To hope that the power which is being made available by the behavioral sciences will be exercised by the scientists, or by a benevolent group, seems to me a hope little supported by either recent or distant history. It seems far more likely that behavioral scientists, holding their present attitudes, will be in the position of the German rocket scientists specializing in guided missiles. First they worked devotedly for Hitler to destroy the U.S.S.R. and the United States. Now, depending on who captured them, they work devotedly for the U.S.S.R. in the interest of destroying the United States, or devotedly for the United States in the interest of destroying the U.S.S.R. If behavioral scientists are concerned solely with advancing their science, it seems most probable that they will serve the purposes of whatever individual or group has the power.

But the major flaw I see in this review of what is involved in the scientific control of human behavior is the denial, misunderstanding, or gross underestimation of the place of ends, goals or values in their relationship to science. This error (as it seems to me) has so many implications that I would like to devote some space to it.

Ends and values in relation to science

In sharp contradiction to some views that have been advanced, I would like to propose a two-pronged thesis: (i) In any scientific endeavor—whether "pure" or applied science—there is a prior subjective choice of the purpose or value which that scientific work is perceived as serving. (ii) This subjective value choice which brings the scientific endeavor into being must always lie outside of that endeavor and can never become a part of the science involved in that endeavor.

Let me illustrate the first point from Skinner himself. It is clear that in his earlier writing (1955-56) it is recognized that a prior value choice is necessary, and it is specified as the goal that men are to become happy, well-behaved, productive, and so on. I am pleased that Skinner has retreated from the goals he then chose, because to me they seem to be stultifying values. I can only feel that he was choosing these goals for others, not for himself. I would hate to see Skinner become "well-behaved," as that term would be defined for him by behavioral scientists. His recent article in the *American Psychologist* (1956) shows that he certainly does not want to be "productive" as that value is defined by most psychologists. And the most awful fate I can imagine for him would be to have him constantly "happy." It is the fact that he is very unhappy about many things which makes me prize him.

In the first draft of his part of this article, he also included such prior value choices, saying for example, "We must decide how we are to use the knowledge which a science of human behavior is now making available." Now he has dropped all mention of such choices, and if I understand him correctly, he believes that science can proceed without them. He has suggested this view in another recent paper, stating that "We must continue to experiment in cultural design...testing the consequences as we go. Eventually the practices which make for the greatest biological and psychological strength of the group will presumably survive" (Skinner, 1955, p. 549).

I would point out, however, that to choose to experiment is a value choice. Even to move in the direction of perfectly random experimentation is a value choice. To test the consequences of an experiment is possible only if we have first made a subjective choice of a criterion value. And implicit in his statement is a valuing of biological and psychological strength. So even when trying to avoid such choice, it seems inescapable that a prior subjective value choice is necessary for any scientific endeavor, or for any application of scientific knowledge.

I wish to make it clear that I am not saying that values cannot be included as a subject of science. It is not true that science deals only with certain classes of "facts" and that these classes do not include values. It is a bit more complex than that, as a simple illustration or two may make clear.

If I value knowledge of the "three R's" as a goal of education, the methods of science can give me increasingly accurate information on how this goal may be achieved. If I value problem-solving ability as a goal of education, the scientific method can give me the same kind of help.

Now, if I wish to determine whether problem-solving ability is "better" than knowledge of the three R's, then scientific method can also study those two values but *only*—and this is very important—in terms of some other value which I have subjectively chosen. I may value college success. Then I can determine whether problem-solving ability or knowledge of the three R's is most closely associated with that value. I may value personal integration or vocational success or responsible citizenship. I can determine whether problem-solving ability or knowledge of the three R's is "better" for achieving any one of these values. But the value or purpose that gives meaning to a particular scientific endeavor must always lie outside of that endeavor.

Although our concern in this symposium is largely with applied science, what I have been saying seems equally true of so-called "pure" science. In pure science the usual prior subjective value choice is the discovery of truth. But this is a subjective choice, and science can never say whether it is the best choice, save in the light of some other value. Geneticists in the U.S.S.R., for example, had to make a sub-jective choice of whether it was better to pursue truth or to discover facts which upheld a governmental dogma. Which choice is "better"? We could make a scientific investigation of those alternatives but only in the light of some other subjectively chosen value. If, for example, we value the survival of a culture, then we could begin to investigate with the methods of science the question of whether pursuit of truth or support of governmental dogma is most closely associated with cultural survival.

My point then is that any endeavor in science, pure or applied, is carried on in the pursuit of a purpose or value that is subjectively chosen by persons. It is important that this choice be made explicit, since the particular value which is being sought can never be tested or evaluated, confirmed or denied, by the scientific endeavor to which it gives birth. The initial purpose or value always and necessarily lies outside the scope of the scientific effort which it sets in motion.

Among other things this means that if we choose some particular goal or series of goals for human beings and then set out on a large scale to control human behavior to the end of achieving those goals, we are locked in the rigidity of our initial choice, because such a scientific endeavor can never transcend itself to select new goals. Only subjective human persons can do that. Thus if we chose as our goal the state of happiness for human beings (a goal deservedly ridiculed by Aldous Huxley in *Brave New World*), and if we involved all of society in a successful scientific program by which people became happy, we would be locked in a colossal rigidity in which no one would be free to question this goal, because our scientific operations could not transcend themselves to question their guiding purposes. And without laboring this point, I would remark that colossal rigidity, whether in dinosaurs or dictatorships, has a very poor record of evolutionary survival.

If, however, a part of our scheme is to set free some "planners" who do not have to be happy, who are not controlled, and who are therefore free to choose other values, this has several meanings. It means that the purpose we have chosen as our goal is not a sufficient and a satisfying one for human beings but must be supplemented. It also means that if it is necessary to set up an elite group which is free, then this shows all too clearly that the great majority are only the slaves — no matter by what high-sounding name we call them — of those who select the goals.

Perhaps, however, the thought is that a continuing scientific endeavor will evolve its own goals; that the initial findings will alter the directions, and subsequent findings will alter them still further, and that science somehow develops its own purpose. Although he does not clearly say so, this appears to be the pattern Skinner has in mind. It is surely a reasonable description, but it overlooks one element in this continuing development, which is that subjective personal choice enters in at every point at which the direction changes. The findings of a science, the results of an experiment, do not and never can tell us what next scientific purpose to pursue. Even in the purest of science, the scientist must decide what the findings mean and must subjectively choose what next step will be most profitable in the pursuit of his purpose. And if we are speaking of the application of scientific knowledge, then it is distressingly clear that the increasing scientific knowledge of the structure of the atom carries with it no necessary choice as to the purpose to which this knowledge will be put. This is a subjective personal choice which must be made by many individuals.

Thus I return to the proposition with which I began this section of my remarks — and which I now repeat in different words. Science has its meaning as the objective pursuit of a purpose which has been subjectively chosen by a person or persons. This purpose or value can never be investigated by the particular scientific experiment or investigation to which it has given birth and meaning. Consequently, any discussion of the control of human beings by the behavioral sciences must first and most deeply concern itself with the subjectively chosen purposes which

such an application of science is intended to implement.

Is the situation hopeless?

The thoughtful reader may recognize that, although my remarks up to this point have introduced some modifications in the conception of the processes by which human behavior will be controlled, these remarks may have made such control seem, if anything, even more inevitable. We might sum it up this way: Behavioral science is clearly moving forward; the increasing power for control which it gives will be held by someone or some group; such an individual or group will surely choose the values or goals to be achieved; and most of us will then be increasingly controlled by means so subtle that we will not even be aware of them as controls. Thus, whether a council of wise psychologists (if this is not a contradiction in terms), or a Stalin, or a Big Brother has the power, and whether the goal is happiness, or productivity, or resolution of the Oedipus complex, or submission, or love of Big Brother, we will inevitably find ourselves moving toward the chosen goal and probably thinking that we ourselves desire it. Thus, if this line of reasoning is correct, it appears that some form of *Walden Two* or of *1984* (and at a deep philosophic level they seem indistinguishable) is coming. The fact that it would surely arrive piecemeal, rather than all at once, does not greatly change the fundamental issues. In any event, as Skinner has indicated in his writings, we would then look back upon the concepts of human freedom, the capacity for choice, the responsibility for choice, and the worth of the human individual as historical curiosities which once existed by cultural accident as values in a prescientific civilization.

I believe that any person observant of trends must regard something like the foregoing sequence as a real possibility. It is not simply a fantasy. Something of that sort may even be the most likely future. But is it an inevitable future? I want to devote the remainder of my remarks to an alternative possibility.

Suppose we start with a set of ends, values, purposes, quite different from the type of goals we have been considering. Suppose we do this quite openly, setting them forth as a possible value choice to be accepted or rejected. Suppose we select a set of values that focuses on fluid elements of process rather than static attributes. We might then value: man as a process of becoming, as a process of achieving worth and dignity through the development of his potentialities; the individual human being as a self-actualizing process, moving on to more challenging and enriching experiences; the process by which the individual creatively adapts to an ever-new and changing world; the process by which knowledge transcends itself, as, for example, the theory of relativity transcended Newtonian physics, itself to be transcended in some future day by a new perception.

If we select values such as these we turn to our science and technology of behavior with a very different set of questions. We will want to know such things as these: Can science aid in the discovery of new modes of richly rewarding living? more meaningful and satisfying modes of interpersonal relationships? Can science inform us on how the human race can become a more intelligent participant in its own evolution — its physical, psychological and social evolution? Can science inform us on ways of releasing the creative capacity of individuals, which seems so necessary if we are to survive in this fantastically expanding atomic age? Oppenheimer has pointed out (1956b) that knowledge, which used to double in millennia or centuries, now doubles in a generation or a decade. It appears that we must discover the utmost in release of creativity if we are to be able to adapt effectively. In short, can science discover the methods by which man can most readily become a continually developing and self-transcending process, in his behavior, his thinking, his knowledge? Can science predict and release an essentially "unpredictable" freedom?

It is one of the virtues of science as a method that it is as able to advance and implement goals and purposes of this sort as it is to serve static values, such as states of being well-informed, happy, obedient. Indeed we have some evidence of this.

Small example

I will perhaps be forgiven if I document some of the possibilities along this line by turning to psychotherapy, the field I know best.

Psychotherapy, as Meerloo (1955) and others have pointed out, can be one of the most subtle tools for the control of *A* by *B*. The therapist can subtly mold individuals in imitation of himself. He can cause an individual to become a submissive and conforming being. When certain therapeutic principles are used in extreme fashion, we call it brainwashing, an instance of the disintegration of the personality and a reformulation of the person along lines desired by the controlling individual. So the principles of therapy can be used as an effective means of external control of human personality and behavior. Can psychotherapy be anything else?

Here I find the developments going on in client-centered psychotherapy (Rogers, 1951) an exciting hint of what a behavioral science can do in achieving the kinds of values I have stated. Quite aside from being a somewhat new orientation in psychotherapy, this development has important implications regarding the relation of a behavioral science to the control of human behavior. Let me describe our experience as it relates to the issues of this discussion.

In client-centered therapy, we are deeply engaged in the prediction and influencing of behavior, or even the control of behavior. As therapists we institute certain attitudinal conditions, and the client has relatively little voice in the establishment of these conditions. We predict that if these conditions are instituted, certain behavioral consequences will ensue in the client. Up to this point this is largely external control, no different from what Skinner has described, and no different from what I have discussed in the preceding sections of this article.

But here the similarity ceases.

The conditions we have chosen to establish predict such behavioral consequences as these: that the client will become self-directing, less rigid, more open to the evidence of his senses, better organized and integrated, more similar to the ideal which he has chosen for himself. In other words, we have established by external control conditions which we predict will be followed by internal control by the individual, in pursuit of internally chosen goals. We have set the conditions which predict various classes of behaviors — self-directing behaviors, sensitivity to realities within and without, flexible adaptiveness — which are by their very nature unpredictable in their specifics. Our recent research (Rogers & Dymond, 1954) indicates that our predictions are to a significant degree corroborated, and our commitment to the scientific method causes us to believe that more effective means of achieving these goals may be realized.

Research exists in other fields — industry, education, group dynamics — which seems to support our own findings. I believe it may be conservatively stated that scientific progress has been made in identifying those conditions in an interpersonal relationship which, if they exist in B, are followed in A by greater maturity in behavior, less dependence on others, an increase in expressiveness as a person, an increase in variability, flexibility and effectiveness of adaptation, an increase in self-responsibility and self-direction. And, quite in contrast to the concern expressed by some, we do not find that the creatively adaptive behavior which results from such self-directed variability of expression is a "happy accident" which occurs in "chaos." Rather, the individual who is open to his experience, and self-directing, is harmonious not chaotic, ingenious rather than random, as he orders his responses imaginatively toward the achievement of his own purposes. His creative actions are no more a "happy accident" than was Einstein's development of the theory of relativity.

Thus we find ourselves in fundamental agreement with John Dewey's statement:

"Science has made its way by releasing, not by suppressing, the elements of variation, of invention and innovation, of novel creation in individuals" (Ratner, 1939, p. 359). Progress in personal life and in group living is, we believe, made in the same way.

Possible concept of the control of human behavior

It is quite clear that the point of view I am expressing is in sharp contrast to the usual conception of the relationship of the behavioral sciences to the control of human behavior. In order to make this contrast even more blunt, I will state this possibility in paragraphs parallel to those used before.

1) It is possible for us to choose to value man as a self-actualizing process of becoming; to value creativity, and the process by which knowledge becomes self-transcending.

2) We can proceed, by the methods of science, to discover the conditions which necessarily precede these processes and, through continuing experimentation, to discover better means of achieving these purposes.

3) It is possible for individuals or groups to set these conditions, with a minimum of power or control. According to present knowledge, the only authority necessary is the authority to establish certain qualities of interpersonal relationship.

4) Exposed to these conditions, present knowledge suggests that individuals become more self-responsible, make progress in self-actualization, become more flexible, and become more creatively adaptive.

5) Thus such an initial choice would inaugurate the beginnings of a social system or subsystem in which values, knowledge, adaptive skills, and even the concept of science would be continually changing and self-transcending. The emphasis would be upon man as a process of becoming.

I believe it is clear that such a view as I have been describing does not lead to any definable utopia. It would be impossible to predict its final outcome. It involves a step-by-step development, based on a continuing subjective choice of purposes, which are implemented by the behavioral sciences. It is in the direction of the "open society," as that term has been defined by Popper (1945), where individuals carry responsibility for personal decisions. It is at the opposite pole from his concept of the closed society, of which *Walden Two* would be an example.

I trust it is also evident that the whole emphasis is on process, not on end-states of being. I am suggesting that it is by choosing to value certain qualitative elements of the process of becoming that we can find a pathway toward the open society.

The choice

It is my hope that we have helped to clarify the range of choice which will lie before us and our children in regard to the behavioral sciences. We can choose to use our growing knowledge to enslave people in ways never dreamed of before, depersonalizing them, controlling them by means so carefully selected that they will perhaps never be aware of their loss of personhood. We can choose to utilize our scientific knowledge to make men happy, well-behaved, and productive, as Skinner earlier suggested. Or we can insure that each person learns all the syllabus which we select and set before him, as Skinner now suggests. Or at the other end of the spectrum of choice we can choose to use the behavioral sciences in ways which will free, not control; which will bring about constructive variability, not conformity; which will develop creativity, not contentment; which will facilitate each person in his self-directed process of becoming; which will aid individuals, groups, and even the concept of science to become self-transcending in freshly adaptive ways of meeting life and its problems. The choice is up to us, and, the human race being what it is, we are likely to stumble about, making at times some nearly disastrous value choices and at other times highly constructive ones.

I am aware that to some, this setting

forth of a choice is unrealistic, because a choice of values is regarded as not possible. Skinner has stated: "Man's vaunted creative powers ... his capacity to choose and our right to hold him responsible for his choice—none of these is conspicuous in this new self-portrait (provided by science). Man, we once believed, was free to express himself in art, music, and literature, to inquire into nature, to seek salvation in his own way. He could initiate action and make spontaneous and capricious changes of course.... But science insists that action is initiated by forces impinging upon the individual, and that caprice is only another name for behavior for which we have not yet found a cause" (1955-56, pp. 52-53).

I can understand this point of view, but I believe that it avoids looking at the great paradox of behavioral science. Behavior, when it is examined scientifically, is surely best understood as determined by prior causation. This is one great fact of science. But responsible personal choice, which is the most essential element in being a person, which is the core experience in psychotherapy, which exists prior to any scientific endeavor, is an equally prominent fact in our lives. To deny the experience of responsible choice is, to me, as restricted a view as to deny the possibility of a behavioral science. That these two important elements of our experience appear to be in contradiction has perhaps the same significance as the contradiction between the wave theory and the corpuscular theory of light, both of which can be shown to be true, even though incompatible. We cannot profitably deny our subjective life, any more than we can deny the objective description of that life.

In conclusion then, it is my contention that science cannot come into being without a personal choice of the values we wish to achieve. And these values we choose to implement will forever lie outside of the science which implements them; the goals we select, the purposes we wish to follow, must always be outside of the science which achieves them. To me this has the encouraging meaning that the human person, with his capacity of subjective choice, can and will always exist, separate from and prior to any of his scientific undertakings. Unless as individuals and groups we choose to relinquish our capacity of subjective choice, we will always remain persons, not simply pawns of a self-created science.

III — Skinner

I cannot quite agree that the practice of science *requires* a prior decision about goals or a prior choice of values. The metallurgist can study the properties of steel and the engineer can design a bridge without raising the question of whether a bridge is to be built. But such questions are certainly frequently raised and tentatively answered. Rogers wants to call the answers "subjective choices of values." To me, such an expression suggests that we have had to abandon more rigorous scientific practices in order to talk about our own behavior. In the experimental analysis of other organisms I would use other terms, and I shall try to do so here. Any list of values is a list of reinforcers — conditioned or otherwise. We are so constituted that under certain circumstances food, water, sexual contact, and so on, will make any behavior which produces them more likely to occur again. Other things may acquire this power. We do not need to say that an organism chooses to eat rather than to starve. If you answer that it is a very different thing when a man chooses to starve, I am only too happy to agree. If it were not so, we should have cleared up the question of choice long ago. An organism can be reinforced by — can be made to "choose" — almost any given state of affairs.

Rogers is concerned with choices that involve multiple and usually conflicting consequences. I have dealt with some of these elsewhere (Skinner, 1953) in an analysis of self-control. Shall I eat these delicious strawberries today if I will then suffer an annoying rash tomorrow? The decision I am to make used to be assigned to the province of ethics. But we are now studying similar combinations of positive and negative consequences, as well as collateral conditions which affect the result in a lab-

oratory. Even a pigeon can be taught some measure of self-control! And this work helps us to understand the operation of certain formulas — among them value judgments — which folk-wisdom, religion, and psychotherapy have advanced in the interests of self-discipline. The observable effect of any statement of value is to alter the relative effectiveness of reinforcers. We may no longer enjoy the strawberries for thinking about the rash. If rashes are made sufficiently shameful, illegal, sinful, maladjusted, or unwise, we may glow with satisfaction as we push the strawberries aside in a grandiose avoidance response which would bring a smile to the lips of Murray Sidman.

People behave in ways which, as we say, conform to ethical, governmental, or religious patterns because they are reinforced for doing so. The resulting behavior may have far-reaching consequences for the survival of the pattern to which it conforms. And whether we like it or not, survival is the ultimate criterion. This is where, it seems to me, science can help — not in choosing a goal, but in enabling us to predict the survival value of cultural practices. Man has too long tried to get the kind of world he wants by glorifying some brand of immediate reinforcement. As science points up more and more of the remoter consequences, he may begin to work to strengthen behavior, not in a slavish devotion to a chosen value, but with respect to the ultimate survival of mankind. Do not ask me why I want mankind to survive. I can tell you why only in the sense in which the physiologist can tell you why I want to breathe. Once the relation between a given step and the survival of my group has been pointed out, I will take that step. And it is the business of science to point out just such relations.

The values I have occasionally recommended (and Rogers has not led me to recant) are transitional. Other things being equal, I am betting on the group whose practices make for healthy, happy, secure, productive, and creative people. And I insist that the values recommended by Rogers are transitional, too, for I can ask him the same kind of question. Man as a process of becoming—*what?* Self-actualization—for what? Inner control is no more a goal than external.

What Rogers seems to me to be proposing, both here and elsewhere (Rogers, 1956), is this: Let us use our increasing power of control to create individuals who will not need and perhaps will no longer respond to control. Let us solve the problem of our power by renouncing it. At first blush this seems as implausible as a benevolent despot. Yet power has occasionally been foresworn. A nation has burned its Reichstag, rich men have given away their wealth, beautiful women have become ugly hermits in the desert, and psychotherapists have become nondirective. When this happens, I look to other possible reinforcements for a plausible explanation. A people relinquish democratic power when a tyrant promises them the earth. Rich men give away wealth to escape the accusing finger of their fellowmen. A woman destroys her beauty in the hope of salvation. And a psychotherapist relinquishes control because he can thus help his client more effectively.

The solution that Rogers is suggesting is thus understandable. But is he correctly interpreting the result? What evidence is there that a client ever becomes truly *self*-directing? What evidence is there that he ever makes a truly *inner* choice of ideal or goal? Even though the therapist does not do the choosing, even though he encourages "self-actualization"—he is not out of control as long as he holds himself ready to step in when occasion demands—when, for example, the client chooses the goal of becoming a more accomplished liar or murdering his boss. But supposing the therapist does withdraw completely or is no longer necessary—what about all the other forces acting upon the client? Is the self-chosen goal independent of his early ethical and religious training? of the folk-wisdom of his group? of the opinions and attitudes of others who are important to him? Surely not. The therapeutic situation is only a small part of the world of the client. From the therapist's point of view it may appear to be possible to relinquish con-trol. But the control passes not to a "self," but to forces in other parts of the client's world. The solution of the therapist's problem of power cannot be *our* solution, for we must consider *all* the forces acting upon the individual.

The child who must be prodded and nagged is something less than a fully developed human being. We want to see him hurrying to his appointment, not because each step is taken in response to verbal reminders from his mother, but because certain temporal contingencies, in which dawdling has been punished and hurrying reinforced, have worked a change in his behavior. Call this a state of better organization, a greater sensitivity to reality, or what you will. The plain fact is that the child passes from a temporary verbal control exercised by his parents to control by certain inexorable features of the environment. I should suppose that something of the same sort happens in successful psychotherapy. Rogers seems to me to be saying this: Let us put an end, as quickly as possible, to any pattern of master-and-slave, to any direct obedience to command, to the submissive following of suggestions. Let the individual be free to adjust himself to more rewarding features of the world about him. In the end, let his teachers and counselors "wither away," like the Marxist state. I not only agree with this as a useful ideal, I have constructed a fanciful world to demonstrate its advantages. It saddens me to hear Rogers say that "at a deep philosophic level" *Walden Two* and George Orwell's *1984* "seem indistinguishable." They could scarcely be more unlike—at any level. The book *1984* is a picture of immediate aversive control for vicious selfish purposes. The founder of *Walden Two*, on the other hand, has built a community in which neither he nor any other person exerts any *current* control. His achievement lay in his original *plan*, and when he boasts of this ("It is enough to satisfy the thirstiest tyrant") we do not fear him but only pity him for his weakness.

Another critic of *Walden Two*, Andrew Hacker (1955), has discussed this point in considering the bearing of mass conditioning upon the liberal notion of autonomous man. In drawing certain parallels between the Grand Inquisition passage in Dostoevsky's *Brothers Karamazov*, Huxley's *Brave New World*, and *Walden Two*, he attempts to set up a distinction to be drawn in any society between conditioners and conditioned. He assumes that "the conditioner can be said to be autonomous in the traditional liberal sense." But then he notes: "Of course the conditioner has been conditioned. But he has not been conditioned by the conscious manipulation of another *person*." But how does this affect the resulting behavior? Can we not soon forget the origins of the "artificial" diamond which is identical with the real thing? Whether it is an "accidental" cultural pattern, such as is said to have produced the founder of *Walden Two*, or the engineered environment which is about to produce his successors, we are dealing with sets of conditions generating human behavior which will ultimately be measured by their contribution to the strength of the group. We look to the future, not the past, for the test of "goodness" or acceptability.

If we are worthy of our democratic heritage we shall, of course, be ready to resist any tyrannical use of science for immediate or selfish purposes. But if we value the achievements and goals of democracy we must not refuse to apply science to the design and construction of cultural patterns, even though we may then find ourselves in some sense in the position of controllers. Fear of control, generalized beyond any warrant, has led to a misinterpretation of valid practices and the blind rejection of intelligent planning for a better way of life. In terms which I trust Rogers will approve, in conquering this fear we shall become more mature and better organized and shall, thus, more fully actualize ourselves as human beings.

Anne Roe

MAN'S FORGOTTEN WEAPON

Roe calls attention to the fact that man, through his capacity for awareness of himself and the world around him, is able to control and direct his destiny consciously and deliberately. It is therefore up to us either "to develop our capacities or to choose not to." In general, this responsibility for shaping the future is a challenge to find the good life; for abnormal psychology it raises a specific challenge: Can psychological disorders be prevented? It can hardly be overemphasized that prevention is the only meaningful and practical resolution to the problem of mental and emotional disorders. Roe suggests that expanding our self-awareness should be a fundamental goal: "Awareness of our own needs and attitudes is our most effective instrument for maintaining our own integrity and control over our own reactions." Implementing such a program would no doubt involve enormous difficulties, but they would perhaps be no more staggering than those we face in attempting to treat today's psychological casualties. More crucial is the fact that if awareness leads to improvement, it necessarily leads to change in our institutions, values, and ways of life. Change is usually difficult, painful, and actively resisted. We might recall that hemlock was the rebuttal to an earlier statement of the injunction "Know thyself."

When I gave a title to this paper, several months before I wrote it, I was thinking primarily in terms of defense: defense against subtle invasions of personal privacy, defense against our national enemies, defense against the destruction of man. Several additional months of brooding over the issues have led me to see my thesis in a somewhat broader framework. The issue of an adequate defense remains; but there is a greater issue, and that is a constructive one.

The forgotten weapon to which I have reference is also our potentially most effective device for constructive advance. It is, simply, awareness, consciousness, man's awareness of himself and of the world around him. It is my thesis that we can, and must, deliberately exploit this characteristic, that its intentional development and use is as essential for our survival as men as it has been for our evolution into man. Consideration of the role that this has played in biological evolution in the past may give us some background for discussing its possibilities in the biological and cultural evolution of the future.

Such consideration is also particularly appropriate in this centenary of the publication of the *Origin of Species*. Since Darwin, the modern theory of evolution has incorporated the discoveries of paleontology and of genetics. Now the fact of evolution is beyond serious dispute, and not only the broad outlines of the history of life, but the mechanisms by which its myriad forms have evolved are well established.

Although it is clear that evolution has had neither plan nor purpose, it is meaningful to speak of many of the changes that have taken place as progressive. Some of these changes have particular bearing on our considerations. They have been discussed extensively by Simpson (1949) in the *Meaning of Evolution;* what follows is largely paraphrased from that book.

A major element in evolutionary progress has been change in the direction of increased awareness and perception of the environment and increased ability to react accordingly. At higher levels this involves increasing complexity and specialization of sensory organs, nervous systems, and other coordinating mechanisms, and the trend has culminated in man who has incomparably the best perceptual, coordinating, and reacting apparatus so far evolved. In the new sort of evolution now characteristic of man, that of transmitted learning and social structure, these organic receptors have been supplemented with inorganic receptors of enormous range and delicacy invented by man.

The new sort of evolution, the evolution of culture, is specifically human, and it is vital for us to appreciate its relation to and differences from organic evolution. One of the basic contrasts between them lies in the way in which mutations arise. In organic evolution, these arise without any relation to the needs or desires of the organism and their fate is not under the control of the organisms carrying them. In the new evolution, new factors arise as elements in consciousness, and in relation to the needs and desires of individuals. They arise in consciousness, but are influenced by and sometimes directly produced by elements in the unconscious. Their fate is not mechanistically determinate but is subject to the actions, values, judgments, and decisions of the group.

This means that the new evolution becomes subject to conscious control. "Man, alone among all organisms, knows that he evolves and he alone is capable of directing his own evolution." Certainly his control is neither rigid nor absolute; he must work with the changes that arise and disseminate these by existing or newly developed mechanisms. New ideas do not always arise at precisely the most useful moment; when they do arise, their dissemination is often blocked by inertia and active opposition. "But we do not conclude that man cannot control floods because he cannot make rain fall upward." We do have a measure of conscious control over what becomes of us, and it is our responsibility and ours alone to choose to develop our capacities or to

From *American Psychologist*, 1959, Vol. 14, pp. 261-266. Reprinted by permission of the author and the American Psychological Association.

choose not to. We must supply our own purposes, and our decisions as to what these purposes should be must be based on human evolution.

Of other biologists who have also commented that man now has the power of choosing the direction of his own social evolution, Huxley (1957) has been most insistent in pointing out that man has in fact new responsibilities whether he likes it or not. He says that man is now, in effect, made "managing director of the business of evolution," without warning and without the possibility of refusing the job. Whether he approaches the job by first finding out what the possibilities of human nature are, as he has been exploring the physical possibilities of the world, or whether he lets things drift without any conscious attempt at control, he is still responsible. Huxley notes the unrest in the world resulting from the discovery by the economically underprivileged nations that people need not be underprivileged, and the current difficulties arising from their reasonable desire for a fair share of the world's goods. He feels that this must be resolved, but that the same sort of unrest will emerge when people realize that no one need be denied the satisfactions of learning, of beauty, and of full self-development, but that this unrest, too, will be resolved and that in a reorganized world the underprivileged will disappear.

Now I, for one, find the logic of these arguments inescapable, and so must ask not only what responsibility I have as an individual, but what obligation is laid upon me as a psychologist. This obligation I find a very grave one, and I am attempting in some slight measure to meet it in this paper. There is no need to belabor the point that only man is a danger to man. Surely, then, it is incumbent upon us as students of man, as well as upon other social scientists, to reassess our roles, and if need be to redirect our activities. I do not decry our past preoccupations, but I confess to a great weariness with the present concentration upon technical minutiae, with better and better research design for matters of less and less importance. Indeed, it often seems that the correlation between goodness of design and importance of project is remarkably high, and negative.

Since as individuals or as a species we cannot evade our responsibilities and remain men, let us cast up our assets and liabilities, let us make some decisions, let us at least not lose the world by default. But what guides can we use? Let me suggest two basic propositions: first, that it is good for the species man to continue to inhabit the earth; and, second, that the ideal towards which we should strive is that every individual on earth should have the possibility of realizing his greatest potentialities, his own potentialities, not those that someone else thinks he should have. At first glance, these propositions may sound obvious and unobjectionable, but let us examine some of the hidden assumptions.

The survival of *Homo sapiens* does not mean that any of his present institutions, governmental, religious, social, must survive unchanged. On the contrary, all of these *must* change if man is to survive; and, if we do not understand this and accept it, we are lost. Must Communist institutions change? Yes, but so must ours. Must Mohammedanism change? Yes, but so must Christianity.

There are those who would argue that it would be better for mankind to perish than to relinquish old beliefs and old attitudes. Political or religious or any institutions that cannot evolve with man, that cling to old, now irrelevant doctrines rooted in earlier misconceptions, but that claim absolute truth or absolute authority, these would sacrifice mankind rather than themselves. This is a real and present danger. It can only be dealt with if we are fully aware of it, if we know what it would cost us to cling to the past, to refuse to see the present for what it is.

The flat statement that every man should have the opportunity to realize his own potentialities has behind it an assumption of major importance. That is, that, in the over-all picture, these potentialities will be good. This, too, is unacceptable to many. I shall not take time to defend this position now; it has been ably done by many, and by many of our own profession. I now want only to make the implications explicit.

If you will accept these premises, at least for the sake of the argument, what then? It is only so far as we are aware of our beliefs and of our prejudices that we can evaluate our behavior, and can make reasonably rational choices. Awareness of our own needs and attitudes is our most effective instrument for maintaining our own integrity and control over our own reactions. This is not new. Most therapists, whatever their technical schools, would, I think, agree with Kubie (1957) that

". . .greater mental health is achieved whenever important areas of life can be brought under the domination of conscious and preconscious processes (never exclusively, but to a major degree). Therefore, the goal of therapy is to shrink those areas of life which are dominated preponderantly by the inaccessible unconscious processes."

I submit that this is of such importance that it should be a major goal of all education, not a last resort for the ill.

In the last 10 years or so there has been a tremendous swing of interest back to the self, to ego-psychology, to conscious and rational processes; but we are only beginning to get a hint of the tremendous possibilities in the deliberate development of consciousness. In clinical circles the time when only the unconscious was a fit subject for discussion seems to have passed. But preoccupation with the unconscious has now developed, somewhat jejunely, in other circles. Most so-called motivation research, as well as subliminal perception, is aimed at exploitation of unconscious needs. The alarm and shock which has been a general public reaction to revelation of such techniques has not been alleviated by the fact, generally unpublicized, that there may not be much in the way of real evidence of their effectiveness, at least in their present forms. Naylor and Lawshe (1958) have recently concluded, following a rigorous review of the evidence, that

". . .there does not appear to be substantial evidence for subception as a distinct phenomenon. Until someone can demonstrate in an experiment which has complete and adequate controls that subception exists, the concern of many seems slightly premature."

But there is genuine concern over other possibilities of devious manipulation. The popularity of such a book as *The Hidden Persuaders* is evidence of such concern. On a technical level, there was the Rogers-Skinner debate (1956)* of a few years ago, where essentially the same issue was raised. There is no question but what great political use has been made of manipulation of emotions. That there is, however, a potent weapon against all of this which is within reach of any who dare to use it has not been understood nor publicized. This weapon, again, is self-awareness. The perfect defense against the possibility of manipulation, whether by politicians, priests, or advertisers, through appeal to unconscious processes is to be thoroughly conscious of one's basic needs and attitudes. You cannot be easily manipulated if you know more about yourself than the would-be manipulator does.

Awareness of these needs and attitudes is not only a defense against manipulation by others, it is a defense against misperception and bias in oneself. Such misperceptions and biases among scientists have always existed, but never before have they been of crucial importance for society. There is no possible doubt that the successful research scientist, of whatever variety, is deeply ego-involved in his work, although this involvement may be of various sorts. Furthermore, within some limits, it is true that the greater the degree of ego-involvement, the greater the possibility of creative advance. But this carries the corollary that an intensely biasing effect in the scientist's perception of his own work as well as that of others is practically inevitable. This can only be mitigated to the extent that he is aware of it.

That such ego-involvement may result in

*[This article appears in the present volume. Ed.]

significant distortions, even of the ordinary psychophysical scales, has been experimentally demonstrated. It affects such things as the recording of responses in accordance with personal belief in or rejection of the hypothesis being tested. It must surely be a factor in the remarkable differences in data reported by physicists who do and physicists who do not believe in fall-out danger—to use only one example of the social importance of the phenomenon. I would go so far as to say that no man, on whose opinion grave decisions rest, should dare to offer that opinion without knowing well what personal significance the issue has for him. He must be sure, for example, that it is not the protection of his own theory or discovery that motivates an insistence that a certain line be followed, and the public has a right to expect that he has considered this possibility seriously. The difficulty of course is that this is a private matter, and only he can be sure; but the public should demand that he be sure. Yet is there anything in any scientific curriculum which not only demonstrates to the student the inevitability of bias, but also gives him any basis for dealing with it in himself?

We psychologists are not free of such biases. I suggested some years ago that our ideas of what constitute the mature personality were very possibly biased by our own personalities and to a considerable extent are an ego-ideal which we have generalized into an ideal for society. Nor do our limitations stop with that. We are well aware of perceptual selectivity, but not very willing to open ourselves to determination of just wherein our own individual bases for selection lie, even though this might greatly improve our professional competence, in addition to personal gains. For example, even among psychologists who have led in this, the therapist who makes transcripts of unselected hours available to others for study, as well as to himself, is very rare. Most of us cannot relax our defenses to that extent. Yet I think we must do so.

Some time ago I devised what I called the Dyad Refresher Plan. This was an attempt to make it possible for psychologists working in hospitals and clinics to share their own expertnesses and check their own biases as part of their regular procedures. Listening to each other in staff sessions, even consulting on protocols, is a most inadequate exchange. The plan was very simple: just that every so often the staff paired off, and each of the pair observed the other in his usual procedures, with such discussion afterwards as seemed appropriate and with the firm provision that such discussion was privileged. On the next round different pairs would form, and so it would continue. I urged this in many institutions with all the eloquence at my command. It was listened to very politely, if uneasily; but it was, so far as I know, never implemented. How many of us who teach invite consultation from our colleagues on the efficacy of our teaching? Certainly the research worker invites his colleagues to look at his work, or rather at his report of his work, but we have already discussed the possibility of the entrance of bias into the work itself. If we cannot trust ourselves to our colleagues, how can we expect others to trust us?

We need to extend this sharing beyond our limited specialties. Stuart Cook (1958) has urged even more far-reaching and more important collaboration among psychologists. He was concerned primarily with the problem of the disruptive possibilities in the increasing professionalization of psychology, and he emphasized the great need for regular and frequent communication between the research worker and the psychologist in practice, pointing out that we need very much to keep accessible to the whole body of psychological theory the insights, the hunches, the observations which those who work with individuals can most effectively provide for us.

"They [such observations] insure the introduction into theory of variables or complexes of variables which, though they may be difficult to deal with, are of known import for behavior. They serve to balance the effect of the analytical processes of research and theory which lead us to simplify and condense. Carried out with links established to behavior as observed around us, such analytical processes are fruitful; based only upon phenomena germinated in a laboratory hothouse, they may well come to nothing. Concern with such laboratory phenomena, although obviously instructive, is kept in better perspective if we confront periodically the behavioral regularities of the natural environment. . . . Nothing requires greater effort than a disciplined analysis of one's experience for whatever reason it be carried out. Only a rare will and intellect are adequate to the task unaided. For most of us, the presence of colleagues would be necessary to keep us going and to help sort out the occasional useful thought from the expected abundance of duds. In order to provide for such mutual assistance among psychologists in professional service, we would need a new institution: a tradition of participating in small groups of collaborating associates who would meet regularly to discuss relevant experiences and mutual problems" (pp. 640, 641).

Others have been similarly concerned. Halpern, in her Presidential Address to the New York State Psychological Association (May 3, 1958), reported a survey which showed that an overwhelming number of our young psychologists were interested only in the practice of therapy, and, I would add, in a disturbingly limited way. Halpern went on to say:

"I am a little appalled by the fact that in all this clamor about treatment, about training for therapy, about improvement in treatment techniques, one hears only a very few weak, small voices talking about prevention. . . . What I am concerned about and what I am opposed to is our concept of ourselves as primarily, almost exclusively a service group, dedicated to the curing of emotional ills. Practically nothing is ever said about using the knowledge we gain from our experiences with treatment and from other sources to validate the personality concepts with which we are operating and find ways to relieve the present extreme need for treatment. It seems to me there is

something a bit amiss with a group of scientists who are so overwhelmingly service oriented and who, recognizing that life adjustment has been increasingly complex and difficult, offer to cure the ills resulting from the present state of affairs, but do little or nothing to help society learn how best to meet their interpersonal, emotional and social problems so that the present seemingly all-pervasive disturbances may be avoided."

It seems quite possible that in our concern with status, with the right to do what we feel we can do, we have seriously limited our exploration of what we could be doing. We have rallied to a finger-in-the-dike approach. This is no doubt admirable, but it is not adequate. My proposal essentially is not that we build new dikes, but that we drain the ocean.

We have, for example, been remarkably reluctant to proceed in the general field of education. I am not now talking about educational techniques, or progressive or unprogressive schools, but about public education in psychological knowledge. I do not know how many high schools there are now in which psychology is an elective subject, but I think there are not many. I know of none in which psychology is required, and I have run across only one discussion of the possibility of introducing it into elementary school.

I suspect that such a suggestion will horrify many people. Psychology, dealing with emotions, as some at least of it does, is highly dangerous, and you have to attain a certain age before it is safe for you to hear of it. I submit that this is ridiculous. Children's acquaintance with emotions is much more profound than their acquaintance with other aspects of the world. If we are ever to raise a generation of aware and confident people, we must deliberately start in infancy to help them become freely aware of themselves, and of what it is to be a human; to be able to accept and control and enjoy their emotions, their thoughts, and their bodies; to be able to tolerate their own and other people's problems.

We have made some stabs at parent education, but this can only be too little and too late. We know much about the crippling effect of repressions, but what do we know of techniques for avoiding these? Our mental health activities have concentrated much more on early diagnosis than they have on prevention, and more on prevention than on positive actions which would render "prevention" unnecessary. Very few of us are even honest with our own children, and teachers who have tried to be have often been fired. We rationalize much of this in terms of keeping the children in harmony with society, but what it generally comes down to is that the unlearnings we have come by painfully (in religion, in social behaviors, and so on) we hide from them, leaving them to struggle through the same unlearning, and hide it in their turn from their children. Brock Chisholm has put it:

"Millions of children in the world are now being tied to the certainties of ten and twenty and thirty generations ago by this mechanism wherein each generation refuses to let its children continue from the point it itself reached. By advocating that we should free our children of the 'certainties' of their ancestors, I do not mean that we should abolish religion or religious teaching. ... It is the teaching of unchangeable attitudes that makes trouble. The problem is not created nearly so much by the content of an orthodoxy as by the fact of an orthodoxy. It is not the teaching of an attitude—however it is taught—that is damaging, nearly so much as the teaching that it is fixed and final and that one is forbidden to think about it. This is damaging because children very early in their lives get the idea they should stop their thinking every time they run into anything uncomfortable or dangerous or threatening."

Now it is clear that we cannot get into the schools any teaching that will be objectionable to the majority of the parents, hence the problem of increasing awareness among the general public is basic. In the present anxious situation a better beginning can be made than we could have made some years ago. We are not ready to do what could be

done, in view of the present concern with education in this country; we have no direct research, but we do have some knowledge that can be put to use, and we could, if we would, get more.

Let me make it clear that I am not suggesting the introduction into the kindergarten of a psychology hour every day, or a "course in" pyschology in each grade. What I am suggesting for a beginning is an examination of the ways in which developing self-awareness can be encouraged within the present framework. As a concrete example, what of the content of children's readers? Could these not include stories relating directly to problems common and important to them? The arrival of a younger sibling is a pretty general problem. Is there any story about this in any child's reader? Is there anything which would help him realize that he is not alone in this, anything to make possible any perception or discussion of it outside of the emotion-charged family circle? Do we not avoid the problems which are the most important to the child and strive to turn his attention altogether to the things that seem important to us? Certainly he must learn to cope with the world without; he can do this more effectively if he can cope with the world within. I suspect that there are some principles and practices of yoga that could reasonably be adapted to child training without developing a nation of hypochondriacs. Physical education is not now designed to promote *pleasure* in bodily control. There is little that promotes genuine sensory exploration and esthetic appreciation. To be fully aware, to know and to enjoy one's self and others, to tolerate problems in the certainty of an eventual solution, these essentials of a rich life are not taught in our educational system, but guarded against. I believe that even the "best-therapized" of us have not begun to approach the degree of awareness that will be possible for future generations if we do our work well. We have reached our present capacity for awareness as a result of biological forces over which we had no control. Having reached this stage, however, it is no longer possible for us to evade responsibility, whether we let things slide or take over.

Even when, as I believe we could, we do develop such a program of education, in or out of school, it will require much work to be sure that it is accepted, and acceptable. This means social studies of an even broader sort than have yet been contemplated, or at least undertaken. To make people aware of what is at stake, to increase their freedom to do what needs to be done, these seem almost insuperable problems; but they are problems that we must solve. When we consider how nearly impossible it has been to institute anywhere any beginning of population control, although it is clear that this is an absolute essential if even a modest standard of living is to be achieved and maintained in the world of the future, we realize how great the difficulties are. It is not only the flat opposition of theological and other groups with vested interests, it is also apathy. Only a sharp awareness of the total situation on the part of a significant number of people everywhere can overcome this opposition and this apathy.

There was an editorial (1958) in the *Nation* which noted with dismay that psychologists are involved in developing nuclear weapons. Some of the remarks were not well taken, but there was this point:

"What [was asked] are psychologists for, except to make people aware of reality as a first step to coping with it? . . . Possibly some [psychologists] will consider using their insights, skills and techniques to bring home to people that their own lives, the lives of future generations, and all the achievements of a billion years of human and pre-human striving are actually, this day, hanging in the balance."

I have urged that we must deliberately exploit that awareness which has evolved in man to the point that it has brought with it the inescapable necessity of choice. Certainly this is not simple, nor do I offer it as a guarantee of survival, but it is our only weapon against disaster. It is a two-edged weapon: it leaves us with no hiding place. If man is to survive, it can only be because enough men believe in their species enough to face the loss of other beliefs.

The lines are being drawn between those who will believe mankind is more important than any nation, any governmental system, any religion, any institution, any belief and those who insist that only one government or one religion or one belief is right and must continue unchallenged and unchanged. The lines are being drawn; and, when the time comes to stand up and be counted, count me on the side of man.

William Schofield

A MODEST PROPOSAL

We saw in the selection by Roe that the challenge of the good life entails, in part, the development of preventive programs and that such programs should include the promotion of self-awareness. Here, Schofield assesses the current supply and effectiveness of counselors and psychotherapists, our "teachers" of self-awareness and the good life. He concludes that there is both an agonizing shortage of such teachers and, as noted also by Rogers, a conspicuous absence of an adequate body of scientifically supported technical information and skills upon which to base their practices. To correct these faults, Schofield offers certain realistic and sensible proposals, the principal one being the development of a new profession with training in "therapeutic conversation." While the proposed training program is primarily professional, we might inquire whether it would not be appropriate to take into account as well the issue of values. If it is true, as the readings in this book suggest, that human values cannot be separated from abnormal psychology, should we try to educate our psychotherapists to be philosophers as well as professionals? If psychotherapists influence and modify values, ought we to search for training programs that will impart not only specialized techniques and knowledge but also the wisdom without which the art of "conversational therapy" may very well be lost?

...In 1955, the United States Congress passed the Mental Health Study Act which provided for the establishment of a Joint Commission on Mental Illness and Health. This commission was charged to make a thoroughgoing appraisal of the extent of mental illness, the availability of resources for treatment and research, and the needs for the future. The following statement appears in the commission's final report (1961, p. 256):

"Persons who are emotionally disturbed —that is to say, under psychological stress that they cannot tolerate—should have skilled attention and helpful counseling available to them in their community if the development of more serious mental breakdowns is to be prevented. This is known as secondary prevention, and is concerned with the detection of beginning signs and symptoms of mental illness and their relief; in other words, the earliest possible treatment. *In the absence of fully trained psychiatrists, clinical psychologists, psychiatric social workers, and psychiatric nurses, such counseling should be done by persons with some psychological orientation and mental health training and access to expert consultation as needed*" [italics ours].

The Joint Commission recognizes the vital preventive and treatment potential of persons other than the acknowledged "experts." The above statement seems to suggest that it is as an unfortunate artifact of the "absence" of the psychiatrist and his colleagues that the important task of secondary prevention "should" be done by others. It would be more positive and realistic to emphasize that preventive counseling *can be* and *is done* efficiently by the non-experts, that it *must* be done by persons with something other than a stereotyped "full training," and that it is the effectiveness of these invisible therapists that keeps the experts from being completely swamped. It is time to recruit actively the assistance of these people, to encourage positively their important contribution rather than to acknowledge it reluctantly as better than nothing, and to provide reasonable avenues whereby their skills and sophistication may be enhanced.

Exciting empirical support for the feasibility of the Joint Commission's proposal has been generated by an experimental project at the National Institute for Mental Health. Under the direction of an experienced clinical psychologist, a group of mature housewives without previous professional training but with serious interest in mental health work was selected for a two-year program of part-time study and practice of psychotherapy under close supervision. Careful evaluation by three experts of the recorded therapy sessions of these women led to the conclusion that their skills were equal to those of psychiatric residents, analytic institute candidates, and graduate students in clinical psychology. On an objective, written examination in psychiatry prepared by the American Board of Psychiatry and Neurology these women scored above the national average. Upon completion of their training, all were employed in local mental health agencies (Rioch *et al.*, 1963).

The explicit psychotherapy needs of our population are currently being served primarily by the members of three major professions [psychiatry, psychology, and social work]. No one of these professions trains primarily and emphatically for the practice of psychotherapy. The training of the members of each of these professions is lengthy, expensive, and provides them respectively with unique skills and knowledge which are either irrelevant or at best tangential to the practice of psychotherapy. While there are a variety of schools of psychotherapy, diverse techniques and approaches to therapy, and different theories as to how it works, there is no evidence that the differences in these academic properties are significantly related to differences in the actual effectiveness of the psychotherapies carried out within them. As a matter of fact, the sheer amount of experience in doing therapy appears to be a major determinant of how

William Schofield, *Psychotherapy: The Purchase of Friendship.* © 1964, by permission of Prentice-Hall, Inc., Englewood Cliffs, New Jersey.

the therapists think about or conduct therapy. Major differences are found among the least experienced therapists; experienced therapists are more alike in their conceptualizations and practices than they are different.

As yet a very limited amount of practical research has been conducted into this phenomenon. It has not yet been demonstrated to the general satisfaction of behavioral scientists that psychotherapy is in fact effective in relieving neurotic symptoms or achieving major and lasting reorientation of disturbed personalities. The need for research is great and, in terms of the numbers of persons participating in therapeutic conversations, the opportunities are equally great. But, the highly trained experts who should be devoting major portions of their time to collaborative research are prevented (or dissuaded) from investigation by virtue of the pressure they feel to render those services whose efficacy is as yet uncertain!

If we are going to do more and better research, we have to provide more therapy and at the same time permit our most highly skilled experts to do less direct therapy. Obviously, we need more therapists — and the only logical way we can hope to get them is to develop a more efficient program for training therapists.

In its final report, the Joint Commission makes a half-step toward the recognition of the ideal solution (1961, p. xii):

"A host of persons untrained or partially trained in mental health principles and practices — clergymen, family physicians, teachers, probation officers, public health nurses, sheriffs, judges, public welfare workers, scout masters, county farm agents, and others — are already trying to help and to treat the mentally ill in the absence of professional resources. . . . *With a moderate amount of training through short courses and consultation on the job, such persons can be fully equipped with an additional skill as mental health counselors. . .*" [italics ours].

This is a reasonable proposal but it does not make explicit whether it is believed that such "short course" training superimposed on a different basic vocation would make a *psychotherapist*. While the *mental health counselor* could undoubtedly make a valuable contribution in meeting our society's mental health needs, he would not represent an optimal answer to the pressing demand for psychotherapy. The only thoroughly logical answer to that demand, in view of the utter impossibility of its being supplied by the present professions, is to create *a new profession* — to train properly selected persons to function specifically and exclusively as *psychotherapists*.

What would constitute the ideal program of training for the psychotherapist? How should candidates for this training be selected? What personal characteristics should they manifest? No one can say with certainty (Holt & Luborsky, 1958; Dallis & Stone, 1960). And it would be a mistake to propose a highly restrictive set of specifications for this new profession, for this would constitute a premature attempt at authoritative rigidification of standards of a kind that is already proving embarrassing to the existing mental health professions. In thinking about selection and training of members for this new profession it would be well to hold clearly in mind what their ultimate function and setting would be: they would work in hospitals, in mental health centers, in child guidance clinics, and in various social agencies where they would be under the general direction of and have continuous consultation with the senior professional staff in psychiatry, psychology, and social work; their primary and exclusive responsibility (except for special work entailed in research collaboration) would be to provide therapeutic conversation.

It is perhaps easier to specify those properties which would *not* be pertinent to their recruitment and training than to list those which would with certainty be applicable. A high level of academic performance would be less critical than substantial evidence of sound general intelligence. Modest intellectual endowment would perhaps prove a more positive qualification than extremely high intelligence. A balanced record of good scholastic achievement coupled with extracurricular interests and a reasonable number of effective social pursuits, including group participations, would probably make for a better candidate than would an outstanding academic record in the absence of nonscholarly interests and pursuits. Evidence of measured social interests and welfare motivations rather than of strong scientific interests and material motives would be pertinent. The young person who had revealed both interests and aptitudes for working effectively with others in personal settings would probably be a good bet. Thus, the person with a record of leadership in school activities, in camping, scouting, boys' clubs or girls' clubs, settlement house or other volunteer service activities would reveal some promise for effective response to training toward a personal service career.

Ideally, in the interests of a total educational program that would prepare for early entry and effective functioning in a professional role, the recruitment process should begin in high school. Potential psychotherapists should be encouraged as junior and senior high school students to become familiar with the field of mental health, the problems of mental illness, and the nature of the resources used in combating emotional disorder. They should have opportunity for field trips to hospitals and mental health clinics. They should be able to hear at first hand about the work of the psychiatrist, psychologist, and social worker, and they should be given an overview of the problems and challenges of psychotherapy. Ideally, as seniors, they should be able to elect introductory courses in general human psychology and in sociology.

Their undergraduate college work (perhaps leading to a bachelor's degree in psychology, sociology, social work, educational psychology, or possibly anthropology) should provide them with an orientation to the range and variety of individual differences in mental ability, personality, and subcultural memberships. They should study developmental and child psychology.

They should be exposed to the general facts concerning the physiology and psychology of emotion. They should learn about attitudes, their determinants, and their effects. They should study the laws of habit forming and habit breaking. They should learn something about the forms of mental illness and the theories of etiology and psychopathology. They should be introduced to the principles and techniques of interviewing, and the problems of person-to-person communication. During their first two years they should be encouraged and assisted in finding opportunity to function as volunteer-workers in some community social agency; hopefully in this context, they would have opportunity to observe experienced workers in a variety of therapeutic conversations. Not later than their senior year they should have a formal course in psychotherapy which should include opportunity to hear taped interviews by skilled therapists.[1]

If their undergraduate record was sound and they showed general aptitude for the field, they could then be screened for admission to an intensive one-to-two year graduate course in psychotherapy. Not over half of this graduate curriculum should be didactic. Assigned readings in a tutorial context and seminars could be designed to broaden their knowledge of psychodynamic theory, current psychiatric nosology and therapeutics, and patterns of state and federal programs in the mental health area. Through these media they would become acquainted with the general professional practices and contributions of psychiatrist, psychologist, and social worker.

At least half of their graduate training should entail closely supervised field-work experiences in a variety of in-patient and out-patient settings. Much of this would be devoted to direct observation of the total

1. With this much concentration on psychological subjects there would naturally be reduced time for study in other liberal arts and sciences; specifically the undergraduate student preparing for a career as a psychotherapist would take fewer courses in mathematics, history, and foreign languages.

therapeutic program, including individual and group psychotherapy, as conducted by experienced professional staff. At the end of their formal training, they would receive degrees as graduate specialists in personal counseling and be ready for full-time employment in a fully staffed clinic or hospital.[2]

The Joint Commission has recommended that the mental health professions "launch a national manpower recruitment and training program" (1961). Such a recruitment endeavor would be more likely to meet with success if it were directed toward high school students, who could be encouraged to consider a service career in the field of mental health for which graduate preparation would not be excessively long. Many persons who entered upon professional work as psychotherapists might subsequently be attracted toward further study and preparation in one of the existing mental health professions. Thus, the specialty of psychotherapy, as a new profession, would provide an "entry" occupation for the established professions and contribute positively to the recruitment endeavor.

The successful planning and instrumentation of a new curriculum toward the specific training of psychotherapist-specialists would demand the wholehearted sympathies, energies, and integrated collaboration of medicine, education, and the community. Obviously psychiatry, psychology, and social work should contribute to the training program. The assistance of community agencies would be required in providing not only the critical field experiences of the graduate program but in offering suitable appointments to the graduates. With respect for the recent and continuing professional antagonisms, especially those between psychiatry and psychology, the proposal that they might see fit to join forces in the creation of a new (and potentially threatening?) profession may seem to be the kind of romantic nonsense that only an impractical, idealistic professor could dream up. But the course of history suggests that social needs are inexorable, in spite of the slowness with which they are met.

In the absence of certain knowledge of what may prove to be the best possible programs for selection and training of psychotherapists, it is fortunate that throughout the country there are a number of universities and medical schools so situated with respect to each other and to large metropolitan complexes of ideal field training resources that it is possible for a variety of professional curricula to be evolved. There is opportunity for imaginative exploration of a variety of training patterns. The results of such programs, measured in terms of the efficiency of recruitment of trainees and of their effectiveness as therapists, would have to be carefully evaluated. Such evaluation might lead to an eventual relative standardization of training for psychotherapists (as it has for the present mental health professions); it might also lead to the finding of a real social need for a variety of therapists having different emphases in their preparation.

The thesis [here] has been that there is a great and growing social need which is presently being inadequately and inefficiently met by the limited resources of three quite different professions. As psychiatry, psychology, and social work have tried to contribute directly to the demand for psychotherapy they have suffered serious dilution of their basic and unique contributions. When prolonged individual psychotherapy is involved, the psychiatrist is perjuring medicine, the psychologist is failing what should be his basic commitment to research, and the social worker is being asocial (Schofield, 1963).

If these disciplines will take joint initiative toward the creation of a new, socially efficient and socially responsive profession

2. Again, it is pertinent to ask what the psychotherapist will not have studied. He is likely to have dispensed with courses in statistics, research methodology, community organization, social pathology, psychoanalytic theory (per se), psychometric theory, anatomy, and comparable "core" courses in the curricula of the three professional therapists we now recognize.

they will maintain proper consultative authority for that profession, they will help to meet the social need, and they will create the means whereby they may be freed for intensified, specilized efforts in accordance with their respective, unique and interdependent skills—to the end that we may gain better understanding, better treatment, and better prevention of mental suffering.

Gardner Murphy

HUMAN NATURES OF THE FUTURE

In this exploration of the future of human nature, Murphy offers some stimulating views. The nature of man is a fundamental question for teachers, parents, counselors, psychotherapists, and others who help shape human behavior and the course of human evolution. One of the lessons to be learned from evolution is that, by and large, those organisms unable to meet the changing demands of the environment perished. Our environment has vastly changed in the last fifty years and seems likely to change as much in the next half century. For psychotherapy, the implication is that goals should be viewed in relation to the process of change — that even the attitudes and values that clients derive from psychotherapy may require alteration as time goes on. If human nature itself is changing and developing, can we hope to find a lasting criterion of what is normal? If the nature of the actor and the environment in which he acts are in flux, can we expect to work out an immutable set of values that will always stand as a guide to desirable action? Or should we begin to think of our values as provisional guides that must be continually examined and modified as circumstances change? Surely we must make some value judgments, however provisional, for we play a large part in shaping our own future; if we cannot be certain of our destination, we might agree on our manner of travel.

The nature of today's crisis

The bombs that fell on Hiroshima and Nagasaki were toys compared with those now ready to be dropped at a moment's notice on the great cities of the world. In addition to the use of satellites and guided missiles, underground airstrips and submarines will soon provide launching points from which devastation can be spread, against which no adequate defense can be contrived. The circumstances which might lead the responsible decision-makers of the Soviet Union or the United States to launch an attack can scarcely be known to the outsider. In particular, the consequence of diplomatic or military defeat in any of several parts of the world might lead one or the other chief of state (or their lieutenants) to decide that retaliation is necessary and that risks must be taken. Where the duel will start is unknowable. So appalling are the prospects in terms of human destruction, suffering, chaos, destitution, and degradation that we automatically turn away and hope somehow to keep a certain number of months or years ahead of our rival, as he hopes to keep ahead of us, each grimly aware of risks too awful to be uttered.

It is true that as we pen these lines there are, here and there, some furtive signs of hope in terms of agreement upon the reduction or elimination of certain types of nuclear fuel testing, and for every such sign of hope we may be deeply grateful. We cannot, however, with any reasonable safety pretend that an agreement on high strategy for peace will put an end to a very long period of precarious and desperate uncertainty. It is as necessary for the momentum of the revolutionary Soviet world to keep moving as it is for the United States and the nations of the West to defend themselves. It is equally clear that an aggressive momentum is far easier to maintain than a posture of continuous essentially static defense; equally plain that a large number of the neutrals of the world, whose power in Asia and Africa grows daily, are more impressed by movement than by defense, more ready to accept a counsel of risk-taking than of acquiescence in the essentially defensive pose recommended to them by the big brother of the West. It is more and more apparent that, over the ease and casualness of Western civilization as a whole, a growing shadow is thrown by the wings of a moving eagle whose magnificent vitality and power speaks both through peoples' movements on the one hand and through the terror of concentration camps and secret police on the other. Inspiring and terrifying, exalting and shocking as the various aspects of the peoples' movements of China and Russia are to the men of the West, they have, from another framework, a vitality with which we of the Western tradition must be capable of coping or we are undone. We cannot answer with postures of defense or promises of massive retaliation alone.

Yet, does it not look indeed as if we were hopelessly trapped between two equally awful alternatives? On the one hand is the gigantic struggle between two powers so tremendous that either one can lay waste and scorch beyond recognition the very body of the other. The second alternative would be a form of capitulation, however gracious or ungracious, by which we would gradually yield the world to the authoritarian system of a small oligarchy equipped with all the attendant machinery of the secret police, the concentration camp, the regulation of the press, the indoctrination of the minds of children in terms of a highly dogmatic and authoritarian creed. Aside from the easy escape through wishful thinking, is there in point of fact any possibility other than these? If this much is faced in its full realism, and the premises maintained that giants must either live as giants or die as giants, there appears to be no escape for any of us but to hide in the hills in the hope that radioactive fallout will somehow not drift into our caves.

But before we look to see whether there are other realistic possibilities regarding the crisis, it might be well to see whether the *whole* of the crisis has actually been faced.

Today's crisis is not only the crisis of the cold war. We can hardly maintain that with the cessation of the cold war all would be well with humanity. Lurking immediately around the corner where stands the threat of World War III stand other critical issues which we in this century and the next must be ready to face. It is a period of seething new nationalism over half the earth's surface; almost universal problems of poverty and disease; the inevitable new awareness of the have-nots that their lives are barren, as they cast a hungry look at those whose lives are lived in gentler circumstances. We face the struggle for power between economic and ethnic groups within and among nations, and with this a rapid re-alignment of forces; great instability in each momentary power aggregation; and through it all the continuous search for ways in which the mass, though always relatively slow and handicapped, can in some sense regulate or control the elite leadership which would so like to claim power over human destiny. All of these problems have their solemn messages and they must be heard for decades, yes if not for centuries. Instead of saying that if once we can be sure of avoiding World War III all will be easy, we must face the fact that the survival of the Western democratic and technological society that we know is fraught with a million uncertainties in the decades ahead.

Despite all this, we have a kind of strength to which we have given little heed: the fact that human nature is changing at an extraordinary pace; that a new kind of humanity is coming into existence, rooted in current historical trends, especially trends arising from science and the urge toward discovery. Discovery of our own identity, belief in ourselves and in the use of the intellectual weapons of a democratic society—a science-minded and technology-minded society—can strengthen those moral, intellectual, and social devices without which, in such a world as this, there is no strength at all. The moral of a study of the unequal battle now being waged in the cold war and of our loss of many advantages which we could claim over the Soviet Union a few years ago lies not alone in the creation of powerful weapons. Insofar as we understand what is happening to us, we can understand the strength that comes from that peculiar amalgam of science and democracy that is ours—and can be the property of all humanity.

This is equivalent to asking whether the basic human nature which carries the life blood of the giants can itself begin to change? Is there a possibility that rapid changes in our deeper probings into the structure of our nature as human beings may make possible not only some amelioration in the world crisis but a series of steps important in the handling of future crises? Is there a possibility that a closer look at human nature, its roots, its ways of development, its forms of control, and the directions in which it is now moving may enable thoughtful members of our species to conceive of outgrowing the present crisis, breaking out of the present strait jacket, and defining a mode of human living in which such struggles as the cold war will become anachronistic, stupid, self-defeating, and profitless? Such questions are questions relating to the origin of humankind, the nature of its first culture, the development of its many civilizations, the process by which human attitudes, values, standards, and norms get consolidated and rigid stereotypes of nationalistic, legalistic, and moralistic codes become entrenched. Hand in hand with these go questions regarding the devices by which something fresh, creative, hungry for discovery in human nature may break through the crystallized norms and codes, including the codes of culture and nationhood, to discover, especially through the ways of science and the intellectual children of science, a new kind of human living.

It is a chance to take. Perhaps the effort will be fruitless. In this era, however, with the threat so desperate and the ways of escape so hard to discern among the shadows, an effort at this more fundamental search for human nature and its ways of outgrowing its present tragedy must be made.

[We shall here make] an effort to describe the sources available within human nature for the outgrowing of human nature, the constitution of new varieties of human thought, value, and aspiration.

The choice among futures

This approach does not mean, however, that [we are] crisis-oriented, or. . .concerned primarily with spelling out the exact nature of the kinds of crises and the possible modes of their resolution. On the contrary, though . . .the reader will return to the crises as part of the background of the present task, his *primary* and central obligation is of a different order. It is to use the information about man which has become available in the period of science in which we live: information from the physical sciences, from the biological sciences, from history and the social sciences, and from psychology which indicates what sort of thing man is, what directions *current* biological and social evolution may give to his life in the years ahead, and the areas of freedom in which he may actually discern possibilities and intelligently select among them.

This task, though carried out in a sobering awareness of the hazards we face, may well give us courage and strength to view the possibilities that human nature will constantly take new forms. We have, indeed, new tools for gathering knowledge about men, ancient tools made new by much refinement and modern tools from chemistry and electronics. These last decades have, moreover, seen great strides in our understanding of the basic physical underpinning of life; the nature of the evolutionary process; the form of growth from fertilized ovum to adult; the nature of the organization of the living system, whether it be amoeba or man.

Amazing new light on human nature comes, for example, from the world revealed by the electron microscope. Within the threadlike chromosomes one can study the arrangement of the genes. Through the methods of the biochemist, we can study the profound effects upon the new life of nutrition and disease during the pregnancy period and the dependence of growth and stature upon nutrition, sunlight, and the environment. Through the methods of physiology and psychology we can understand the effect upon intelligence of early stimulation or deprivation of stimulation. We are beginning to understand the delicate interdependence of hereditary and environmental factors in sensitizing the individual to major mental disease; the role of parental standards and community supports in the development of intellectual skills, especially curiosity, fortitude, the drive to get the answers to life problems; the extraordinary range of cultural diversity and of individual diversity within each cultural group.

The rich data obtained from all over the globe in recent years on the structure of human culture indicate the dependence of adult character structure upon patterns of child rearing. We have become alerted to the modifiability of attitude and feeling through the interaction of a variety of biological and social agencies, including drugs, hypnosis, mass suggestion; withholding of information; the early molding of tastes and wants through "imprinting" or "channeling", the early sensitization of the mind to sources of conflict, planting the seeds for future unconscious struggle against oneself.

Psychoanalysis has gone on to probe into many corners of man's deeply unconscious nature and has laid bare the orderly meanings behind many a bizarre contradiction. Experimental psychology has defined more exactly the ways in which man sees, hears, learns, remembers, thinks, and imagines. Unrecognized new fields, such as parapsychology, point to unrealized potentials whose meaning is all too dim.

New perspectives on the past have come from the intimate fusion of the physical and the social sciences, as in the discovery of radioactive carbon, which can now date within a few years many remnants and relics of a life long forgotten and can confirm and support and give richer meaning to documentary materials throughout all the age of recorded history. Lynn White has shown how the combination of historical, archeological, and psychoanalytic concepts may, as it were, stretch out some potentate or chamberlain upon the analytic couch, giving sudden meaning where before all was chaos. Anatomy, physiology, genetics, pathology provide a living unity to the erstwhile confused evolutionary picture of man's development against the background of his animal ancestry. Psychology, sociology, anthropology, economics, linguistics throw light deep into the shadows of the supposed irrationalities of his collective behavior. Ours is an era of such enormous gains in these sciences that we may be justified in asking what glimpses and guesses can be drawn from it all regarding some of the directions in which man may move.

The creation of new human natures

. . .That conception of science which represents man as genuinely capable of grasping certain aspects of the reality and moving slowly toward grasping ever more and more allows for a sort of deep-staining of the mind of the observer, selectively bringing out that which was hidden before the stain was used. Man's interaction with the things of this world through the methods of the arts and through the methods of science will produce more and more that is new in man as the centuries pass. The very process of interaction with that which was previously unknown produces new content, new stuff, new realities, new things to understand and to love, as well as new instruments of observation, new ways of knowing, new modes of esthetic apprehension. These, too, will change the nature of man, not simply by enriching that which lies under the threshold of his immediate nature but by broadening the doorway through which he passes, so that he may see more of the vista he approaches and may as he does so become always a larger man. It is because of man's capacity for intimate union with the stuff of this world through the methods of the arts and through the methods of science that he may hope to do more than to transcend himself, may hope to become in each new emergent phase of his life a new kind of man.

Lest our thesis should seem to have become obscure, let us say flatly here that we often look for human nature in the wrong place; we merely look inside the living system. We are trying, as it were, to get the golden eggs by killing the goose; or indeed by studying the pedigree of the goose we have hoped to find specifically where those eggs come from. Actually, they are not in the goose; they are not even in the life history of the goose or in the life history of geese on this planet. The golden eggs, or any products whatever which life yields, are in a sense the products of a system of events displayed and deployed through a vast system of forces. Indeed, life can be destroyed and any given avenue can be blocked, but to find the wellsprings of human nature by looking inside the capsule is to miss the field character of the event.

It may seem more effective to look for human nature in the existing societies, or in the present and past societies yielded by man's genius for social organization. This is, indeed, somewhat more effective, but not much. What has been realized at a given time has depended upon a wealth of specific time-determined and culture-determined events of which we know relatively few, and the plan or system of which we hardly understand at all. Even if "system theory" enables us to understand the potentialities within a given set of cultural organizations — such as determining what can and cannot be done by a Stone-Age culture as compared with a pre-Stone Age culture, or determining what can and cannot be done by a process of banking or a process of utilization of nonanimal power — we cannot extrapolate to the kinds of human nature which can and must exist when the present human nature interacting with the present and future forces in the universe have yielded a new human nature.

Regarding the field forces, we make a few discoveries every decade and still go on acting as if we thought there were no discoveries to make. The amazing range of chemical and bioelectric phenomena yielded in the last hundred years, the amazing new information about atomic structure which comes pouring in year by year certainly gives us a new system of environmental forces with which humankind must come to terms. Many of them, as we have already seen, certainly have direct effects upon genes; many others have limiting effects upon both genes and growth; many have an effect upon the extension and the variability of the genepool; and many of them, in interaction with cultural factors, specifically the organization of science and of medicine, are bound to determine in a major way within a few decades the evolutionary character, the direction, and the various kinds of subdirections which human evolution can display. At a less tangible level, the types of social organization and particularly the types of value systems which are bound to respond to this new multidimensional flow of forces will yield kinds of human nature which it is not within the power of even the most prophetic to glimpse today. Our task, rather, is an attempt at a systematic and sober panoramic survey of the *kinds of directions which might be taken within the very large areas marked as unknown on the map.*

From such a way of thinking, the future seems to become even more difficult to divine than from a purely cultural viewpoint. It seems virtually certain that mankind, having created for itself a new environment and having undergone various transformations in the process, will not recognize itself in the mirror of a few thousand years hence. Against this, profound resistances will inevitably be mobilized, because we shall, insofar as we do effective planning, plan ourselves out of existence. It is doubtful, however, whether we shall plan ourselves out of existence any more rapidly than the Commercial and Industrial Revolutions have thrown out of existence the kinds of humanity which existed a few centuries ago or which industrial and technological developments are bound to produce with or without planning. There is no solution for the problem of our insecurities here. We must face them and make the alternatives as clear as we can, taking our chances with those forces in ourselves and in the cosmos about which we shall always remain insufficiently informed. We can only say that the more research we have and the more carefully we sift the evidence from present and future research, the less likely the creation of an internal contradiction, a self-defeating humanity, a humanity cultivating those attributes which we already know to be nonviable or productive of more distress than joy.

We have already asked what can be done about the huge blind spots which man has always created for himself. The problem is especially pressing when we ask what will happen when the "other side of the organism," the side which no culture has ever played upon, begins to be drawn into active play. We try to imagine events which involve the operation of natural laws which we cannot at present glimpse. Each era creates its own system of ideas, and new events which cannot be fitted into the scheme, such as the three-dimensional activities unintelligible to the Flatlanders, require either to be cast aside or to be reduced or forced into the existing scheme. Before the isolation of oxygen, for example, the phlogiston theory held sway, even though decade by decade it became more and more obvious that the theory was unsound. The point was that no radically new way of conceiving the whole issue had been clearly formulated, and chemists would rather go on with a makeshift that was known to be wrong than work without some sort of conception.

We face the increasing probability that the system of science developed from the time of Galileo to that of Einstein will prove more and more inadequate as a fit for human nature, and in particular that the ideas of Darwin and Freud, magnificent and liberating as they are, will have their own hour in court and have to be replaced by radically different conceptions. We shall fight frantically against this, of course. But the entire world system — and man system, so to speak — will have to be refurbished. In our search for "science talent" we are not likely to search for those who look for the unusual or the impossible. In our Utopiologies we have small place for those who can go off at right angles from the known. It is not difficult to extrapolate the present changes in culture and to dream up a world of "man and superman"; and it will not be too difficult, on the basis of present biological data, to dream up a new picture of the biology of humankind. What will be difficult, however, will be the imagining of that kind of reciprocity between the new man and the new social order which will certainly be realized within a few centuries.

Is there any reason to end upon an optimistic note, despite the mess which humanity has been making of the world in the last few decades? There are two such reasons which lie in present attitudes toward science. First, we have somehow become less afraid of studying ourselves, looking straight at, through, and into ourselves; and without a great deal more knowledge of ourselves, and of the nature of our dependence upon one another, we can do but little in the realization of human potentialities. Secondly, if curiosity be the soul of science, curiosity is not only a tool in the discovery of needed truths; it is in itself one of those satisfiers that lead on and on to ever fresh delights. The hunger for discovery rather than practical gain was the mother of both science and philosophy, and though science today is often deflected from the satisfactions of curiosity into the production of competitive tools of many sorts, the flame of curiosity, once kindled, cannot be put out. One may feel that out of this era of political interference with science, and frequently of intimidation of scientists, no good can come, but there is another approach. Socrates had to drink the hemlock, and Giordano Bruno to die at the stake, but the stifling of the quest for understanding is a trick that no despot has ever fully mastered. If there is in mankind a potential love of his neighbor that can be nourished through centuries and become more and more a norm, which, however imperfectly, we strive to realize, there is also a potential craving to understand the world which, as fast as it is satisfied, broadens into a greater craving, works into new material, works in a richer and broadening fashion.

Such an approach would mean not simply the fulfillment of the known biological nature of man or the elaboration of the known potentialities of culture but a constant probing of new emergent qualities and realities given by a system of relationships that can today hardly be glimpsed; a leaping into existence of new realms of experience; *not an extrapolation of the present, but new in kind.*

The realization of human potentialities lies in studying the directions in which human needs may be guided, with equal attention to the learning powers of the individual and the feasible directions of cultural evolution. The last thousand years have created a level of scientific and esthetic satisfaction which has already made human nature different today from what it was in the middle ages; yet this is merely a beginning. Even this much of an evolution has hardly commenced in the area of interpersonal relations, where modern psychology, including psychoanalysis, has shown us more about the roots of conflict and destructiveness among people than about the development of positive social feeling. If we cannot make rapid gains in the control of conflict, there will be no human future. But if we can, the future extension of scientific and esthetic interest, together with the evolution of greater capacity for satisfaction in relations between people, will not constitute a goal or a Utopia, but will define a widening theater for the development of new potentialities.

C. MARSHALL LOWE
Value orientations—an ethical dilemma

Allport, G. W. *The individual and his religion.* New York: Macmillan, 1950.

American Psychological Association. *Ethical standards of psychologists.* Washington, D. C.: APA, 1953.

Fromm, E. *Man for himself.* New York: Rinehart, 1947.

Fromm, E. *The sane society.* New York: Rinehart, 1955.

Fromm, E. *The art of loving.* New York: Harpers, 1956.

Green, A. Social values and psychotherapy. *J. Personality,* 1946, *14,* 199-228.

Jung, C. G. *Modern man in search of a soul.* New York: Harcourt Brace, 1933.

Krutch, J. W. *The measure of man.* New York: Bobbs-Merrill, 1954.

Lindner, R. *Prescription for rebellion.* New York: Rinehart, 1952.

May, R. *Man's search for himself.* New York: Norton, 1953.

Niebuhr, R. *The nature of man.* New York: Scribners, 1941.

Rogers, C. R. Divergent trends in methods of improving adjustment. *Harvard educ. Rev.,* 1947, *18,* 209-219.

Rogers, C. R. Some issues concerning the control of human behavior. *Science,* 1956, *124,* 1060-1064.

Rogers, C. R. Necessary conditions of therapeutic change. *J. consult. Psychol.,* 1957, *21,* 95-103. (a)

Rogers, C. R. A therapist's view of the good life. *Humanist,* 1957, *17,* 291-300. (b)

Rogers, C. R. A process conception of psychotherapy. *Amer. Psychologist,* 1958, *13,* 142-149.

Rosenthal, D. Changes in some moral values following psychotherapy. *J. consult. Psychol.,* 1955, *19,* 431-436.

Shaffer, L. F., & Shoben, E. J. *The psychology of adjustment.* Cambridge: Riverside, 1956.

Shoben, E. J. Work, love, and maturity. *Personnel guid. J.,* 1956, *34,* 326-332.

Shoben, E. J. Toward a concept of the normal personality. *Amer. Psychologist,* 1957, *12,* 183-189.

Skinner, B. F. *Walden two.* New York: Macmillan, 1948.

Skinner, B. F. Some issues concerning the control of human behavior. *Science,* 1956, *124,* 1057-1065.

Smith, M. B. Toward scientific and professional responsibilities. *Amer. Psychologist,* 1954, *9,* 513-516.

Walker, D. E., & Peiffer, H. C. The goals of counseling. *J. counsel. Psychol.,* 1957, *4,* 204-209.

Williamson, E. G. Value orientation in counseling. *Personnel guid. J.,* 1958, *36,* 520-528.

Wrenn, C. G. The ethics of counseling. *Educ. psychol. Meas.,* 1952, *12,* 161-177.

O. H. MOWRER
What is normal behavior?

Adler, A. *Problems of neurosis.* New York: Cosmopolitan, 1930.

Adler, A. *Social interest: a challenge to mankind.* London: Faber & Faber, 1938.

Allport, F. H. Psychology in relation to social and political problems. In P. S. Achilles (Ed.), *Psychology at work.* New York: Whittlesey House, McGraw-Hill, 1932.

Bentham, J. *Principles of morals and legislation.* Oxford, Clarendon, 1879.

Cannon, W. B. *The wisdom of the body.* New York: Norton, 1939.

Cobb, S. *Borderlands of psychiatry.* Cambridge, Mass.: Harvard Univ. Press, 1943.

Darrah, L. W. The difficulty of being normal. *J. nerv. ment. Dis.,* 1939, *90,* 730-739.

Dearborn, W. F. *Intelligence tests.* Boston: Houghton Mifflin, 1928.

Freud, S. The defence neuro-psychoses (1894). *Collected papers.* Vol 1. London: Hogarth, 1924. (a)

Freud, S. The justification for detaching from neurasthenia a particular syndrome: the anxiety-neurosis (1895). *Collected papers.* Vol. 1. London: Hogarth, 1924. (b)

Freud, S. Further remarks on the defence neuro-psychoses (1896). *Collected papers.* Vol. 1. London: Hogarth, 1924. (c)

Freud, S. *Civilization and its discontents.* London: Hogarth, 1930.

Freud, S. *New introductory lectures on psychoanalysis.* New York: Norton, 1933.

Freud, S. Formulations regarding the two principles in mental functioning (1911). *Collected papers.* Vol. 4. London: Hogarth, 1934. (a)

Freud, S. A neurosis of demoniacal possession in the seventeenth century (1923). *Collected papers.* Vol. 4. London: Hogarth, 1934. (b)

Freud, S. *The problem of anxiety.* New York: Norton, 1936.

Fromm, E. *Escape from freedom.* New York: Farrar & Rinehart, 1941.

Hacker, F. H. The concept of normality and its practical significance. *Amer. J. Orthopsychiat.,* 1945, *15,* 47-64.

Hull, C. L. *Principles of behavior.* New York: Appleton-Century-Crofts, 1943.

Jones, E. The concept of a normal mind. *Int. J. Psycho-anal.,* 1942, *23,* 1-8.

King, C. D. The meaning of normal. *Yale J. Biol. Med.,* 1945, *17,* 493-501.

Kluckhohn, C., & Kelly, W. H. The concept of culture. In R. Linton (Ed.), *The science of man in the world crisis.* New York: Columbia Univer. Press, 1945.

Kroeber, A. L. The superorganic. *Amer. Anthrop.,* 1917, *19,* 163-213.

Maller, J. B. Personality tests. In J. McV. Hunt (Ed.), *Personality and the behavior disorders.* New York: Ronald, 1944.

Mowrer, O. H. The law of effect and ego psychology. *Psychol. Rev.,* 1946, *53,* 321-334.

Mowrer, O. H. On the dual nature of learning — a reinterpretation of conditioning and problem-solving. *Harvard educ. Rev.,* 1947, *17,* 102-148.

Mowrer, O. H., & Kluckhohn, C. Dynamic theory of personality. In J. McV. Hunt (Ed.), *Personality and the behavior disorders.* New York: Ronald, 1944.

Mowrer, O. H., & Ullman, A. D. Time as a determinant in integrative learning. *Psychol. Rev.,* 1945, *52,* 61-90.

Murdock, G. P. The science of culture. *Amer. Anthrop.,* 1932, *34,* 200-215.

Olson, W. C. *The measurement of nervous habits in normal children.* Minneapolis: Univer. Minnesota Press, 1929.

Opler, M. E. Cultural and organic conceptions in contemporary world history. *Amer. Anthrop.,* 1944, *46,* 448-460.

Opler, M. E. Biosocial basis of thought in the Third Reich. *Amer. sociol. Rev.,* 1945, *10,* 776-786.

Pavlov, I. P. *Conditioned reflexes.* London: Oxford Univer. Press, 1927.

Perry, R. B. *General theory of value.* New York: Longmans, Green, 1926.

Raup, R. B. *Complacency: the foundation of human behavior.* New York: Macmillan, 1925.

Roback, A. A. *The psychology of character with a survey of temperament.* New York: Harcourt, Brace, 1928.

Stewart, G. R. *Man—an autobiography.* New York: Random House, 1946.

Thorndike, E. L. *Human learning.* New York: Appleton-Century-Crofts, 1931.

Tiegs, E. W., & Katz, B. *Mental hygiene in education.* New York: Ronald, 1941.

Vernon, P. E. *The measurement of abilities.* London: Univer. London Press, 1940.

Viteles, M. S. *Industrial psychology.* New York: Norton, 1932.

THOMAS S. SZASZ
The myth of mental illness

Hollingshead, A. B., & Redlich, F. C. *Social class and mental illness.* New York: Wiley, 1958.

Jones, E. *The life and work of Sigmund Freud.* Vol. III. New York: Basic Books, 1957.

Langer, S. K. *Philosophy in a new key.* New York: Mentor, 1953.

Peters, R. S. *The concept of motivation.* London: Routledge & Kegan Paul, 1958.

Szasz, T. S. Malingering: "diagnosis" or social condemnation? *AMA Arch. Neurol. Psychiat.,* 1956, *76,* 432-443.

Szasz, T. S. *Pain and pleasure: a study of bodily feelings.* New York: Basic Books, 1957. (a)

Szasz, T. S. The problem of psychiatric nosology: a contribution to a situational analysis of psychiatric operations. *Amer. J. Psychiat.,* 1957, *114,* 405-413. (b)

Szasz T. S. On the theory of psychoanalytic treatment. *Int. J. Psycho-Anal.,* 1957, *38,* 166-182. (c)

Szasz, T. S. Psychiatry, ethics, and the criminal law. *Columbia law Rev.,* 1958, *58,* 183-198.

Szasz, T. S. Moral conflict and psychiatry. *Yale Rev.,* 1960, *49,* 555-566.

M. BREWSTER SMITH
"Mental health" reconsidered: a special case of the problem of values in psychotherapy

Adorno, T. W., Frenkel-Brunswik, Else, Levinson, D., & Sanford, N. *The authoritarian personality.* New York: Harper, 1950.

Allport, G. W. Personality: Normal and abnormal. In *Personality and social encounter.* Boston: Beacon, 1960.

American Psychological Association, Ad Hoc Planning Group on the Role of the APA in Mental Health Programs and Research. Mental health and the American Psychological Association. *Amer. Psychologist,* 1959, *14,* 820-825.

Clausen, J. A. *Sociology and the field of mental health.* New York: Russell Sage Foundation, 1956.

DuBois, Cora. *The people of Alor.* Minneapolis: Univer. Minnesota Press, 1944.

Foote, N. N., & Cottrell, L. S., Jr. *Identity and interpersonal competence.* Chicago: Univer. Chicago Press, 1955.

Ginsburg, S. W. The mental health movement: Its theoretical assumptions. In Ruth Kotinsky & Helen Witmer (Eds.), *Community programs for mental health.* Cambridge: Harvard Univer. Press, 1955.

Jahoda, Marie. Toward a social psychology of mental health. In Ruth Kotinsky & Helen

Witmer (Eds.), *Community programs for mental health*. Cambridge: Harvard Univer. Press, 1955.

Jahoda, Marie. *Current conceptions of positive mental health*. New York: Basic Books, 1958.

Joint Commission on Mental Illness and Health. *Action for mental health: Final report of the joint commission*. New York: Basic Books, 1961.

Klein, D. C. Some concepts concerning the mental health of the individual. *J. consult. Psychol.*, 1960, *24*, 288-293.

Levine, L. S., & Kantor, R. E. Psychological effectiveness and imposed social position: A descriptive framework. Paper presented at the symposium, Positive conceptions of mental health: Implications for research and service, American Psychological Association, Chicago, September 5, 1960.

MacGregor, G. *Warriors without weapons*. Chicago: Univer. Chicago Press, 1946.

Maslow, A. H. *Motivation and personality*. New York: Harper, 1954.

Myrdal, G. *An American dilemma*. New York: Harper, 1944.

National Assembly on Mental Health Education. *Mental health education: A critique*. Philadelphia: Pennsylvania Mental Health, Inc., 1960.

Peters, R. S. Private wants and public tradition. *Listener*, 1960, July 14, 46-47.

Riesman, D. *The lonely crowd*. New Haven: Yale Univer. Press, 1950.

Shoben, E.J., Jr. Toward a concept of the normal personality. *Amer. Psychologist*, 1957, *12*, 183-189.

Smith, M. B. Research strategies toward a conception of positive mental health. *Amer. Psychologist*, 1959, *14*, 673-681.

Snow, C. P. *The two cultures and the scientific revolution*. New York: Cambridge Univer. Press, 1959.

Szasz, T. S. The myth of mental illness. *Amer. Psychologist*, 1960, *15*, 113-118.

White, R. W. Motivation reconsidered: The concept of competence. *Psychol. Rev.*, 1959, *66*, 297-333.

RUTH BENEDICT
Anthropology and the abnormal

Boas, F. The social organization and the secret societies of the Kwakiutl Indians. *Rep. U. S. Nat. Mus. for 1895*, 1897, 311-738.

Boas, F. Ethnology of the Kwakiutl based on data collected by George Hunt. *Bur. Amer. Ethnol., 35th Ann. Rep. to the Secretary of the Smithsonian Instit.* (2 vols.) Washington, D.C.: Govt. Print. Office, 1921.

Boas, F. Contributions to the ethnology of the Kwakiutl. *Columbia Univer. Contrib. Anthrop., Vol. 3.* New York: Columbia Univer. Press, 1925.

Boas, F. Religion of the Kwakiutl. Vol. II. *Columbia Univer. Contrib. Anthrop., Vol. 10.* New York: Columbia Univer. Press, 1930.

Boas, F., & Hunt, G. Kwakiutl texts. *Mem. Amer. Mus. Natur. Hist.: Jesup North Pacific Expedition, Vol. 3.* New York: Stechert, 1905.

Callaway, C. H. Religious system of the Amazulu. *Publ. Folklore Soc.*, London, 1884, *15*.

Coriat, I. H. Psychoneuroses among primitive tribes. In *Studies in abnormal psychology*, ser. 6. Boston: Gorham, n.d.

Czaplicka, M. A. *Aboriginal Siberia: a study in social anthropology*. Oxford: Clarendon, 1914.

Dewey, J. *Human nature and conduct: an introduction to social psychology*. New York: Holt, 1922.

Dixon, R. B. The Shasta. *Bull. Amer. Mus. Natur. Hist.,* 1907, *17,* 381-498.

Fortune, R. F. *Sorcerers of Dobu.* New York: Dutton, 1932.

Grinnell, G. B. *The Cheyenne Indians.* New Haven, Conn.: Yale Univer. Press, 1923.

Hecker, J. F. C. *The black death and the dancing mania.* Tr. by B. G. Babbington. New York: Humboldt, 1885.

Novakovsky, S. Arctic or Siberian hysteria as a reflex of the geographic environment. *Ecology,* 1924, *5,* 113-127.

Parsons, E. C. The Zuni La'mana. *Amer. Anthrop.,* 1916, *18,* 521-528.

Sapir, E. A girl's puberty ceremony among the Noofka. *Trans. Roy. Soc. Canada,* 1913, *7* (3rd ser.), 67-80.

ROLLO MAY
Historical and philosophical presuppositions for understanding therapy

Cassirer, E. *An essay on man.* New Haven, Conn.: Yale University Press, 1944.

Fromm, E. *Escape from freedom.* New York, Rinehart, 1941.

Fromm, E. *Man for himself, an inquiry into the psychology of ethics.* New York: Rinehart, 1947.

Hoch, P. H., & Zubin, J. (Eds.). *Anxiety.* New York: Grune & Stratton, 1950.

Hunt, J. McV. The problem of measuring the results of psychotherapy. *Psychological Service Center Journal,* 1949, *1,* 122-135.

Kardiner, A. *The individual and his society — the psychodynamics of primitive social organization.* New York: Columbia University Press, 1945.

Kierkegaard, S. *Philosophical fragments, or a fragment of philosophy* (1844). Tr. by D. F.

Swenson. Princeton: Princeton University Press, 1946.

May, R. Historical roots of modern anxiety theories. In P. H. Hoch & J. Zubin, *Anxiety.* New York: Grune & Stratton, 1950. (a)

May, R. *The meaning of anxiety.* New York: Ronald, 1950. (b)

Mowrer, O. H. *Learning theory and personality dynamics.* New York: Ronald, 1950.

CARL R. ROGERS
Psychotherapy today, or where do we go from here?

Alexander, F., & French, T. M. *Psychoanalytic therapy.* New York: Ronald, 1946.

Bergin, A. Teachers College, Columbia University, personal communication.

Ellis, A. *Reason and emotion in psychotherapy.* New York: Lyle Stuart, 1962.

Eysenck, H. J. *Dynamics of anxiety and hysteria.* New York: Praeger, 1957.

Festinger, L. *A theory of cognitive dissonance.* Evanston, Ill.: Row, Peterson, 1957.

Harper, R. A. *Psychoanalysis and psychotherapy: 36 systems.* New York: Prentice-Hall, 1959.

Kelly, G. A. *The psychology of personal constructs* (2 vols.). New York: Norton, 1955.

Levinson, B. M. The dog as co-therapist. Paper given at convention of the American Psychological Association, Sept. 1961.

Lewis, M. K., Rogers, C. R., & Schlien, J. M. Time-limited, client-centered psychotherapy: two cases. In A. Burton (Ed.), *Case studies in counseling and psychotherapy.* New York: Prentice-Hall, 1959.

Lindsley, O. R. Operant conditioning methods applied to research in chronic schizophrenia. *Psychiatric Research Reports,* 1956, No. 118-153.

Sato, K. Implications of Zen Buddhism for psychotherapy. *Psychologia, 1,* Dec. 1958.

Snyder, W. U. In S. W. Standal & R. J. Corsini (Eds.), *Critical incidents in psychotherapy.* New York: Prentice-Hall, 1959.

Standal, S. W., & Corsini, R. J. (Eds.). *Critical incidents in psychotherapy.* New York: Prentice-Hall, 1959.

Time magazine, May 19, 1961.

Whitaker, C. A., Warkentin, J., & Malone, T. P. The involvement of the professional therapist. In A. Burton (Ed.), *Case studies in counseling and psychotherapy.* New York: Prentice-Hall, 1959.

Wolpe, J. *Psychotherapy of reciprocal inhibition.* Stanford: Stanford Univer. Press, 1958.

C. H. PATTERSON
The place of values in counseling and psychotherapy

American Psychological Association. *Ethical standards of psychologists.* Washington, D.C.: Author, 1953.

Biestek, F. P. The non-judgmental attitude. *Soc. Casework,* 1953, *34,* 235-239.

Bixler, R. H., & Seeman, J. Suggestions for a code of ethics for consulting psychologists. *J. abnorm. soc. Psychol.,* 1946, *41,* 486-490.

De Grazia, S. *Errors of psychotherapy.* Garden City, New York: Doubleday, 1952.

Deutsch, F., & Murphy, W. F. *The clinical interview.* New York: International Universities Press, 1955.

Ginsburg, S. W. Values of the psychiatrist. *Amer. J. Orthopsychiat.,* 1950, *20,* 466-478.

Ginsburg, S. W., & Herma, J. L. Values and their relationship to psychiatric principles and practice. *Amer. J. Psychother.,* 1953, *7,* 546-573.

Green, A. W. Social values and psychotherapy. *J. Personality,* 1946, *14,* 199-228.

Greenspoon, J. The effect of two non-verbal stimuli on the frequency of two verbal response classes. *Amer. Psychologist,* 1954, *9,* 384. (Abstract)

Hand, H. C. America must have generally democratic high schools. In *General education in the American high school.* Chicago: Scott, Foresman, 1942. Chapter 1.

Ingham, H. V., & Love, Leonore R. *The process of psychotherapy.* New York: McGraw-Hill, 1954.

Jahoda, Marie. Toward a social psychology of mental health. In M. J. E. Senn (Ed.), *Symposium on the healthy personality. Supplement II: Problems of infancy and childhood.* New York: Josiah Macy Foundation, 1950.

Jahoda, Marie. The meaning of psychological health. *Soc. Casework,* 1953, *34,* 349-354.

Maslow, A. H. *Motivation and personality.* New York: Harper, 1954.

Meehl, P. E., & McClosky, H. Ethical and political aspects of applied psychology. *J. abnorm. soc. Psychol.,* 1947, *42,* 91-98.

Mowrer, O. H. Motivation and neurosis. In J. S. Brown, et al., *Current theory and research in motivation.* Lincoln, Nebraska: Univ. of Nebraska Press, 1953. (a)

Mowrer, O. H. Some philosophical problems in mental disorder and its treatment. *Harvard educ. Rev.,* 1953, *23,* 117-127. (b)

Murphy, G. The cultural context of guidance. *Personnel guid. J.,* 1955, *34,* 4-9.

Parloff, M. B. Communication of values and therapeutic change. Paper read at symposium on "Evaluation of Process and Results of Therapies: I. General Problems of Methods and Theory." American Psychological

Association, New York, N.Y., August 31, 1957.

Parloff, M. B., Iflund, B., & Goldstein, N. Communication of "therapy values" between therapist and schizophrenic patients. Paper read at American Psychiatric Association annual meeting, Chicago, Ill., May 13-17, 1957.

Rogers, C. R. Client-centered therapy. Boston: Houghton Mifflin, 1951.

Rogers, C. R. A theory of therapy, personality, and interpersonal relationships, as developed in the client-centered framework. Chicago: Author, 1956. Mimeo.

Rosenthal, D. Changes in some moral values following psychotherapy. J. consult. Psychol., 1955, 19, 431-436.

Seeley, J. R. Guidance: A plea for abandonment. Personnel guid. J., 1956, 34, 528-535.

Shoben, E. J. New frontiers in theory. Personnel guid. J., 1953, 32, 80-83.

Smith, M. B. Optima of mental health; a general frame of reference. Psychiatry, 1950, 13, 503-510.

Sullivan, H. S. Conceptions of modern psychiatry. Washington: William Allanson White Psychiatric Foundation, 1947.

Sutich, A. Toward a professional code of ethics for counseling psychologists. J. abnorm. soc. Psychol., 1944, 39, 329-350.

Taylor, Charlotte P. Social and moral aspects of counseling. (Letter to the Editor.) Personnel guid. J., 1956, 35, 180.

Verplanck, W. S. The control of the content of conversation: reinforcement of statements of opinion. J. abnorm. soc. Psychol., 1955, 51, 668-676.

Verplanck, W. S. The operant conditioning of human motor behavior. Psychol. Bull., 1956, 53, 70-83.

Walker, D. E., & Peiffer, H. C. The goals of counseling. J. couns. Psychol., 1957, 4, 204-209.

Weiss, F. Psychoanalysis and moral values. Amer. J. Psychoanal., 1952, 12, 39-49.

Weisskopf-Joelson, Edith. Some suggestions concerning Weltanschauung and psychotherapy. J. abnorm. soc. Psychol., 1953, 48, 601-604.

Zilboorg, G. Clinical variants of moral values. Amer. J. Psychiat., 1950, 106, 744-747.

CARL R. ROGERS AND B. F. SKINNER
Some issues concerning the control of human behavior: a symposium

Coleman, C. Bull. Amer. Assoc. Univ. Professors, 1953, 39, 457.

Freund, P. A., et al. Constitutional law: cases and other problems. Vol. 1. Boston: Little, Brown, 1954.

Hacker, A. Antioch Rev., 1954, 14, 195.

Hacker, A. J. Politics, 1955, 17, 590.

Krutch, J. W. The measure of man. Indianapolis: Bobbs-Merrill, 1953.

Meerloo, J. A. M. J. nerv. ment. Dis., 1955, 122, 353.

Negley, G., & Patrick, J. M. The quest for Utopia. New York: Schuman, 1952.

Niebuhr, R. The self and the dramas of history. New York: Scribners, 1955.

Oppenheimer, R. Amer. Psychologist, 1956, 11, 127. (a)

Oppenheimer, R. Roosevelt University Occasional Papers No. 2, 1956. (b)

Popper, K. R. The open society and its enemies. London: Rutledge and Kegan Paul, 1945.

Ratner, J. (Ed.). Intelligence in the modern world: John Dewey's philosophy. New York: Modern Library, 1939.

Rogers, C. R. Client-centered therapy. Boston: Houghton Mifflin, 1951.

Rogers, C. R. Teachers Coll. Rec., 1956, 57, 316.

Rogers, C. R., & Dymond, R. (Eds.). *Psychotherapy and personality change.* Chicago: Univer. Chicago Press, 1954.

Skinner, B. F. *Walden Two.* New York: Macmillan, 1948.

Skinner, B. F. *Science and human behavior.* New York: Macmillan, 1953.

Skinner, B. F. *Trans. N.Y. Acad. Sci.,* 1955, *17,* 547.

Skinner, B. F. *Amer. Scholar,* 1955-56, *25,* 47.

Skinner, B. F. *Amer. Psychologist,* 1956, *11,* 221.

Vandenberg, S. G. *Amer. Psychologist,* 1956, *11,* 339.

Viteles, M. *Science,* 1955, *122,* 1167.

ANNE ROE
Man's forgotten weapon

Chisholm, B. *Prescription for survival.* New York: Columbia Univer. Press, 1957.

Cook, S. W. The psychologist of the future: scientist, professional, or both. *Amer. Psychologist,* 1958, *13,* 635-644.

Editorial. *Nation,* 1958, *186,* 402-403.

Huxley, J. *New bottles for new wine.* New York: Harper, 1957.

Kubie, L. S. Social forces and the neurotic process. In A. H. Leighton, J. A. Clausen, & R. N. Wilson (Eds.), *Explorations in social psychology.* New York: Basic Books, 1957.

Naylor, J. C., & Lawshe, C. H. An analytical review of the experimental basis of subception. *J. Psychol.,* 1958, *46,* 75-96.

Rogers, C., & Skinner, B. F. Some issues concerning the control of human behavior. *Science,* 1956, *124,* 1057-1066.

Simpson, G. G. *The meaning of evolution.* New Haven: Yale Univer. Press, 1949.

WILLIAM SCHOFIELD
A modest proposal

Dallis, N. P., & Stone, H. K. (Eds.). *The training of psychotherapists—a multidisciplinary approach.* Baton Rouge: Louisiana State Univer. Press, 1960.

Holt, R. R., & Luborsky, L. *Personality patterns of psychiatrists.* Vol. I. Menninger Clinic Monograph Series No. 13. New York: Basic Books, 1958.

Joint Commission on Mental Illness and Health. *Action for Mental Health.* New York: Basic Books, 1961.

Rioch, Margaret J., Elkes, Charmian, Flint, Arden A., Udansky, Blanche S., Newman, Ruth G., & Silber, Earle. National Institute of Mental Health pilot study in training mental health counselors. *Amer. J. Orthopsychiat.,* 1963, *33,* 678-689.

Schofield, William. Logistics in professional psychology. In *Manpower and psychology: proceedings of a workshop.* U.S. Dept. of Health, Education, and Welfare, August, 1963.